Beliefs and Human Values
A Minimalist Philosophy of Values

Richard Sheriff Jones

Order this book online at www.trafford.com
or email orders@trafford.com

Most Trafford titles are also available at major online book retailers.

Note for Librarians: A cataloguing record for this book is available from Library
and Archives Canada at www.collectionscanada.ca/amicus/index-e.html

Printed in Victoria, BC, Canada.

ISBN: 978-1-4251-7313-5 (sc)
ISBN: 978-1-4251-7314-2 (e)

*We at Trafford believe that it is the responsibility of us all, as both individuals and corporations,
to make choices that are environmentally and socially sound. You, in turn, are supporting this
responsible conduct each time you purchase a Trafford book, or make use of our publishing services.
To find out how you are helping, please visit www.trafford.com/responsiblepublishing.html*

*Our mission is to efficiently provide the world's finest, most comprehensive book publishing
service, enabling every author to experience success. To find out how to publish your book, your
way, and have it available worldwide, visit us online at www.trafford.com*

Trafford rev. 7/2/2009

 www.trafford.com

North America & international
toll-free: 1 888 232 4444 (USA & Canada)
phone: 250 383 6864 ♦ fax: 250 383 6804 ♦ email: info@trafford.com

"Anyone who has ever tried to present a rather abstract scientific subject in a popular manner knows the great difficulties of such an attempt. Either he succeeds in being intelligible by concealing the core of the problem and by offering the reader only superficial aspects or vague allusions, thus deceiving the reader by arousing in him the deceptive illusion of comprehension; or else he gives an expert account of the problem, but in such a fashion that the untrained reader is unable to follow the exposition and becomes discouraged from reading any further. It is not sufficient that each result be taken up, elaborated, and applied by a few specialists in the field. Restricting the body of knowledge to a small group deadens the philosophical spirit of a people and leads to spiritual poverty."

Albert Einstein[1]

---

[1] Part of the foreword by Dr Einstein to *"The Universe and Dr Einstein"* by Lincoln Barnett. Published by Victor Gollancz Ltd 1955

4

To Ruth, Wendy and Ann

Acknowledgements

I am most grateful to Allen Holland, Professor emeritus of Philosophy at Lancaster University. He gave me invaluable advice and drew my attention to many important highways and byways in philosophy. But of course, I remain responsible for the opinions expressed.

Professor Sir David Weatherall, FRS has been my guide, philosopher and friend, especially when traversing much of the uncharted waters between science and philosophy. Again, I remain responsible for all the opinions expressed.

Foreword

In a world in which over half the population of its richest and most scientifically advanced countries refuse to accept the overwhelming evidence in support of Darwinian evolution, and in which many of its inhabitants are killed every day in the name of religion, humankind's fundamental beliefs are, quite rightly, coming under increasing scrutiny. How are the remarkable advances in cosmology, other branches of physics, and biology to be reconciled with ancient religious beliefs which, despite the inhumanity and suffering that they have spawned, have also been vital sources of cohesion for societies and comfort to those who require an explanation for their transient existence on a lonely planet?

When the Greeks invented science and this method of understanding sensory experience was immeasurably extended after the Renaissance, it appeared to have created an unbridgeable gap between beliefs about the physical world and beliefs about human values. This has not been satisfactorily resolved despite great effort over 500 years. But the author suggests that progress is possible. There are erroneous conceptions of the relations between mind and matter, and between beliefs and human values that merit exploration.

Progress reflects the abandonment of old beliefs and their replacement by new ones. As scientific knowledge advances, elements of ancient beliefs inevitably must be modified if conflict is to be avoided, for the world today is simply not what it was thought to be like when those beliefs were formed centuries or millennia ago. This applies to scientific theories, concepts that define democracy, and beliefs that may or may not flow from religious origins. While science advances at a remarkable pace, sceptics and the libertarian West ignore or destroy beliefs, or invent their own, while the rest of the world clings to old ones. In short, humankind has not yet learned how to manage their beliefs, a fact that threatens their welfare, and even their existence.

These questions are of fundamental importance for all our futures. Unfortunately, so far answers are not forthcoming, particularly from the recent polemics that have addressed them. As in the case of scientific research, they will not be answered unless they are more clearly defined. This is the object of Richard Sheriff Jones' book, and I wish it all the success it deserves.

Professor Sir David Weatherall, FRS.

Oxford.

April 2008.

The Dialogues

Note: The figures in brackets in the text indicate the number of the Discussion to which reference is made.

Introduction

Understanding Human Values

When young and confronted with the problems of what to do in life and how to earn a living, we have no experience and little time to reflect. Later, we have the time and experience to ask further questions, such as: what can we know and what does it all mean? The birth of a grandchild brings these questions into sharper relief. In the conversations that follow, I discuss with a young person the questions with which humans are confronted on the road to a mysterious future. This work does not assume specialist knowledge on the part of the reader. It begins with questions that a teenager might ask.

I have used the dialogue form to bring together knowledge from formal education and experience with knowledge from science and history. The cut and thrust of discussion aims to preserve the presentation of historical episodes and the wisdom of the sage. My young interlocutor is encouraged to ask awkward and challenging questions and to think the unthinkable. Dialogue permits the discussion of many difficult problems within a relatively small compass.

Humans find many ways to travel through life. Each moves from a past that has been experienced into an unknown future that is about to be revealed. It is the anticipation of this transition from the past to the future that provokes for each individual, in ways to be examined, the ideas that embrace hopes, fears, convictions and the motivations to find objectives.

The ideas and beliefs in all ages have taken many forms, each being a unique response to the human situation. But since each individual lives in a community, its members tend to hold ideas in common and similar ideas are often held with little change for many centuries. J M Keynes put it like this: 'Belief in the material progress of mankind is not old. During the greater part of history such a belief was neither compatible with experience nor encouraged by religion', and, 'A great transition in human history will have begun when civilised man endeavours to take control into his own hands as opposed to the predominant blind instinct of mere survival'[2]. Yet

---

[2] From the Preface to *Population,* by Harold Wright, Camb. University press 1923.

each, as a free agent, could have responded to new experiences in different and unique ways. This possibility, after a long intellectual struggle that will be described in outline, eventually motivated the formation of the democratic societies of today.

In the earliest times, life was hazardous and brief. Humans found themselves in the grip of immense natural powers that ruled their lives; there was also the enemy over the hill and the ever-present certainty of death. The only protection, which was universally adopted, was belief in supernatural powers and gods that could protect them in this and a possible future existence in return for prescribed rituals, ceremonies and sacrifices.

How did change come about? The Greeks took the Phoenician alphabet and out of it constructed the ancient Greek language. This language crucially made it possible to store and transmit knowledge easily and accurately from person to person. Then some Greeks stopped believing, observed details of the world about them and invented science. But it was soon realised that science does not answer many questions that were perplexing humans: questions about good and evil, right and wrong, life and death. And also such questions as, what is justice? What are beauty, happiness and their opposites? The response of the Greeks to such questions was to invent philosophy.

It is noteworthy that Athenian society was sufficiently liberal for these intellectual advances to appear in the 5th century BC, when the Olympian Gods were still powerful and Pericles had the Parthenon built to house a statue of the goddess Athene. And so it was that at the very time when the Greeks were fighting for survival against the Persian Empire and then Sparta, they were also waging the much more significant intellectual battle for the future of civilisation. But the power of ancient beliefs and the political elite in Athens were such that they brought about the death of Socrates.

History shows that from mythological times, imposed beliefs and the authority of tribal leaders invariably restrict the thoughts and actions of humans to within narrow limits. If one assumes that antiquity was not a golden age, as Rousseau thought it was, then the immeasurable improvements in the human situation since those times are likely to have been due to the reduction or removal of those restrictions on human capabilities.

Since humans are seemingly unable to exist except in communities, the problem became, how could restrictions on individual freedom due to beliefs and the power of the state be minimized? The Greeks were the first to make inroads into these problems yet, although they invented democracy, they failed to make it work. But the Enlightenment and the Romantic Age that followed the Renaissance decisively broke through these barriers. The torrent of new ideas in the 16-18th centuries and the evolution of the democratic ideal in the 18th and 19th centuries were enormous contributions to problems that are, as yet, without final solutions, as the 21st century is revealing. Humans are inventive at finding new ways of restricting their own thoughts and behaviour, as for example the attractiveness of belief in such ideas as 'political correctness' is currently showing.

This result is hardly surprising, for there has been no agreed description of what is producing such ideas and beliefs. Terms such as the 'subjective', the 'self', 'mind', and 'soul', or the denial that some or all of these exist, contribute to descriptions that are in consequence, distorted, inaccurate and incomplete. They contain the residues of ideas long past their usefulness. There does not appear to be any satisfactory overall description of the intellectual functions that produce the ideas and beliefs of today and many academics think that solutions will never be found.

In order to investigate these questions and provide accurate descriptions, it is essential to begin by being clear about the distinction between philosophy and psychology. In brief, philosophy investigates those elements of the subjective (to be defined) that are *common* to all people and defines the limits of what can be known. Psychology describes the *differences* between individuals and the significance of these for their welfare. These differences are measurable and hence psychology is a science, or capable of becoming a science, whereas philosophy is not. Psychology has a therapeutic dimension in respect of individuals and their welfare that philosophy does not have. Philosophy describes all that it is possible to know about individuals and their responses to sensory experience. But if philosophy were purely descriptive and hence 'neutral' as some philosophers have contended, it would be a pointless exercise. The position adopted here is that it has influential relations with social, political and religious affairs and therefore that philosophy does have relevance in an age of rapid scientific and technological advances.

Recent American literature reviewed here suggests that, since the Platonic aims of philosophy have not been fulfilled, philosophy has no future. But the conclusions reached in this work show that this is false. Philosophy is the response to the lay and scientific exploration of the universe and this would only cease if that exploration were to come to an end, which does not appear remotely likely in the foreseeable future.

The structures and functions of the human body and brain have been fashioned over millions of years by the evolving genome. Brain structures and functions are accompanied by 'mind functions'. The latter have now evolved to the point at which they determine much, but not all, of what the body does in response to motivations from mind.

How should this situation be described? The genes that together comprise the *genome* have determined the specific structures and functions of body and brain and thereby set the limits to what can be thought and physically achieved by mind. Currently, brain/mind relations are under investigation by scientists and are described here in outline. But when one considers mind, it is immediately obvious that discrete 'nodes' of ability exist, such for example: to do mathematics; to appreciate logical thinking; to learn and speak a language; to be aware of specific feelings; aesthetic experiences and human values such as the appreciation of good and evil. A complete description of all these abilities and their inter-relations is required and is conveniently called here the *minome* and its nodes of activity, *minodes* (13). Unlike the genome, only the human minome exists, for it is not possible to be aware of the minds of other species. A formal description of the minome, its development and its activities today is one of the main aims of this work. Since it is important to know how it evolved, and is still evolving, it was essential to consider the historical experiences that brought it about.

Important also is the fact that there is considerable variation in the minome, and hence in the minodes, from person to person and culture to culture. Individuals possessing outstanding, or greater than average abilities are easily recognised as scientists, mathematicians, or composers, for example. But equally important and more difficult to recognise are those with anomalous or poorly developed minodes because these individuals may create problems in society.

The minome has reached a critical level of development for it has put humans virtually in charge of their own destiny. Back in the mists of time, when the minome as we know it must have barely existed, humans were manifestly not in charge of their destiny. But now that the minome is in charge, those forces that ruled their lives have diminished and been replaced by others. But some of these have proved to be no less threatening. For example, although humans have gained control over disease and natural resources, the result has been a growth in population that is rapidly outstripping the resources of the planet to meet their essential needs. Also, although humans have discovered the democratic method of living peacefully in society, they are still at the mercy of forces due to conflicting religious beliefs, racial differences and nationalism. The significance of these has been immeasurably enhanced by the fact that advances in technology have made it possible for humans virtually to annihilate themselves. The historical background to these seismic events is surveyed and the results are described.

In theory, the invention of democracy has diminished the power of the state, but we have not yet learned how to manage the power of beliefs to disrupt democratic communities, or impair and distort their functions. Also, the concept of democracy is not an end-point; it is merely a staging post leading to some other version more appropriate to a different age.

PART 1
What is Consciousness?
(Discussions 1-4)

Discussion 1

"I begin by being provocative: every idea one has during waking hours that is expressed in words and sentences takes the form of a belief of one kind or another, believe it or not!"

"That sounds like one of those radical statements about the way things work to which you introduced me when I was growing up."

"Certain aspects of life are unknowable, but these have not been well defined. Much tribulation has been caused by the belief that it is possible to explain things unknowable in human terms. Mistaken beliefs about how the universe works arose in the distant past, yet confusions and errors still abound, but will diminish as humans learn how to manage beliefs. I propose to explore a philosophy of minimalist beliefs, one that is evolving fitfully today. In order to arrive at conclusions we shall need to consider what beliefs are and survey how they have evolved to produce the current unsatisfactory situation.

Up to the time when you left university I was concerned to introduce you to the main ideas in science, religion and philosophy, and to look at these in a critical, historical light. I did this because these have a crucial influence on the ethical views of individuals and of society as a whole."

"But now that I have been out in the wide world for a few years, things already begin to look different. You taught me to approach ideas with some scepticism – to reject beliefs unless unavoidable or based upon firm evidence.

Now you are suggesting that we cannot get away from beliefs, which seems confusing. It is certainly true that most of the people I meet express an extraordinary variety of beliefs in most fields of life, political, social, ethical and the meaning of life as expressed by a wide variety of religions and 'spiritual' sects. Also, at the slightest hint of the failure of science-based medicine for example, people willingly 'believe' in one or more of the vast array of 'remedies' and 'cures', just as they did in the days before science had taught us to be more critical.

So I think you may be right that modern humans still live in a world of beliefs, as they always have done. Where are they going? I should have thought that, faced with the ever more explosive pace in the search for knowledge, humans would have found by now more certain foundations for civilisation. Yet it seems to be the case that disagreement in most fields is not only evident at the edges; but penetrates to the heart of most topics, including the sciences. Why should that be so? Where is the solid ground? I had thought that if one was sufficiently sceptical, one became aware of an unknowable dimension to life, but at the same time, one was left with a core set of ideas, which were pretty firmly established in that they were free from the necessity for beliefs.

Now that does not seem to be the case, not only for the generality of the population, but also for the intellectuals, those who 'know', or think they know, and it is they and the media, after all, who point the way for the less discerning masses. I think you will agree, this is not a very satisfactory state of affairs!"

"Many pages of discussion could be devoted to the state of western civilisation today, but to embark on such topics would obscure our objectives. These are to reach conclusions, which hopefully will eliminate some of the confusing beliefs that still permeate societies today like a blanket of fog, or we may even try to get beyond belief and find out what is there! Our main objective will be to focus on the frequency with which beliefs participate in the thoughts and actions of everyday life and thereby contribute to confusions. We need to discover which beliefs are inevitable and which are a matter of choice. Also, whether there are differences in the 'security rating' of beliefs: the probability of a belief being true. Then, there is the question of which beliefs can be discarded because there is no evidence for their truth or falsity, especially if they are doing harm rather than good. Crucially, there is the problem of what happens when one tries to move beyond belief in respect of important questions in life. We shall find that human kind has always lived within a cocoon of beliefs serving a variety of purposes.

The question that arises is the extent to which that is inevitable."

"The fog of dubious ideas which shrouds us appears to have increased despite the freedoms and libertarian ideas of society today. I used to think that it was the discipline of religious doctrines that were necessary to sustain belief, but these do not always seem to be necessary."

"They were necessary in order to ensure the *specific* beliefs of a religion, but relax or remove these and the result was not the absence of belief, for all kinds of others rapidly appeared. These ideas have replaced the fading and now virtual disappearance of the theocratic straight jacket of the Middle Ages. It took centuries of strife and schism for it to fade, but only towards the end of the 20th century was it realised, to the surprise of many, that there were deleterious consequences for society caused by withdrawal of the stability that those medieval beliefs had provided. But this, of course, had to be set against the new freedoms and libertarian advantages for society that followed during the Romantic Age and beyond. The apogee of often-confused ideas appeared during the 20th century when that clear Medieval view of the world based on belief had lost nearly all of its force. If you had lived, say in the 13th century, you would have been a serf, or have entered one of the professions, all of which were related in some way to the Church. You may have entered the Church as a priest. Life would then have been mapped out for you from the cradle to the grave and its length, if you were lucky, would have been no more than 30-40 years.

What Is Consciousness?
Discussion 2

In view of that discussion I had better define what I mean by 'belief'. I take a belief to be a set of ideas (which I define later) that is stated to be 'true'. If you assert that X is true, meaning by 'true', absolute certainty, the sceptic might claim that you cannot prove it. But the riposte of course is that, equally, the critic cannot prove that it is false. Yet, it remains the case that whenever we make an assertion of any kind, we have to accept that in some sense we believe it to be true, otherwise if you think about it, life would be impossible. Therefore we will be forced to the view as a result of what follows that beliefs are no more than *tentative* assertions of what may or may not be true.

Many of the problems of present day societies appear to be due to the fact that its members have not yet learned to *manage* belief systems in a rational and objective manner. We must return to that later.

Two landmarks in the History of Ideas

Up to the time of the Greeks, humans responded to everything they did not understand with beliefs, the truths of which they did not question. The *first landmark* occurred when the Greeks discovered that when the temptation to believe is rejected, it becomes possible to observe and describe the world in a way that had a new meaning. This approach they developed to invent science. And to investigate what science could not explain, they invented philosophy. Science emerged when accurate observation and description were applied to sensory experiences. Philosophy emerged when the same methods were applied to the study of those questions about life and the unknowable that could not be answered by science."

"But how can one say anything about something unknowable?"

"Much of Greek philosophy is based on just such ideas. After 'physics', Aristotle described 'metaphysics'. This was a system of ideas about an aspect of the meaning of life. It was formed from a premise, followed by logical deduction leading to a conclusion. Perhaps most of the confusions in philosophy down the centuries have centred on metaphysics. In physics the premises are elements of sensory experience, but the conclusions must be shown to be true by experiment and the deductions that follow, before they become a part of the tentative knowledge of science.

These new ideas seemed, at least in some degree, to be independent of beliefs and certainly cut across many established ancient belief systems. This advance in the use of ideas was of extreme importance, for it revealed that ideas could open up new vistas of knowledge previously unsuspected. Progress in these directions was then held up at the end of the Hellenistic period by the resurgence of older beliefs from the east and then the appearance of Christianity and Islam. These monopolised ideas about the world until after the Renaissance in Western Europe.

It was then that the *second major advance* occurred, again in science and philosophy (and also in many other areas with which we are not directly concerned), but with a difference. It did not take long for the scientists to establish a methodology that worked and to which the crucial technique of experimentation was added. The scientists also further refined the methodology to meet new practical needs, which was the beginning of the technology that has transformed the modern world.

It was during this period of the Enlightenment that philosophers also made significant progress. However, there was also confusion and conflict. Kant produced a new metaphysical system that he claimed was logically secure. But no convincing 'final solutions' came into view, as we shall find.

Another consequence of the second major advance in the evolution of civilisation was the modification of Christian beliefs by schism so that their grip on societies diminished. But the beliefs of religion and the evils that arise from tribalism and nationalism still persisted. These additional problems in society arose from non-religious beliefs. They are important because they are problems which have not yet been resolved, progress has been slow and humanity suffers as a consequence."

"Although beliefs appear to have formed a fundamental aspect of human thought since homo sapiens came into existence, that no longer seems to be the case. Beliefs are obviously grounded in ideas, but what are ideas?"

"We will need to consider ideas and their part in consciousness further. But I had better start at the beginning!

Discussion 3

A starting point

Consider life at a unicellular level. The essence of life is that the organism has to communicate with its immediate surroundings for nutrient in order to exist. It became dependent on its environment because it had to ingest nutrient and excrete the waste products of metabolism.

Multicellular organisms later started to develop cells sensitive to the environment and later, cells within the organism evolved into a sensory system that was crucial to the whole process of evolution. But the organism could not 'know' this and so, as at all stages of evolution, it is difficult for many to avoid the temptation to *believe* that some guiding hand is at work. This may be true, but the truth or falsity of such metaphysical beliefs can never be proven.

Later, specific sensory organs gave awareness of nutrient in the immediate environment and various reflex motor responses became possible to retrieve it. I am omitting a huge amount of detail that evolved over a vast time scale because, at each stage, there developed numerous different ways of achieving the same end. Hence the endless sequence of species that appeared and then finally disappeared. Whether this was due to the operation of the Darwinian principle of survival of the fittest, we do not know, but like all scientific theories, this may be accepted as true until shown to be false.

This *reflex mechanism* required conducting cells that triggered the motor response to sensory stimulation. These cells developed into a spinal cord with sensory nerves entering and motor nerves leaving it. But this still only provided a reflex response.

A further crucial phase was the development of a brain. Now extensions of sensory nerves entered this mass of nerve cells and extensions of motor cells left it. The sensory nerves were now not only from the skin, but also from specialised parts of the skin that had developed into eyes and ears.

I have been leading up to the question: when did consciousness appear? Sensory experience from the skin could give only very limited information about the environment, and the assumption must be that up to this stage the mechanism was reflex rather than by means of consciousness. But once seeing and/or hearing had also developed, information from the environment became greatly enhanced. In order to take advantage of this sensory experience, a wide variety of sophisticated motor systems developed, such as are found in countless species. At this stage, we can be sure that a state of consciousness existed. An essential part of this was the development of memory, for without this nothing could function. Although fascinating, we do not need to speculate on when consciousness first appeared and in which species.

We now have a primitive *sensory-motor axis*. This dual archetypal mechanism allows the animal to sense food in a particularly favourable situation and to retrieve it. Consciousness enables, for example, the insect to link the input and output sides of the axis in a way that allows choice: when to respond; which object to respond to and how to retrieve it. At this level, consciousness is limited to the need to receive and respond to these essential requirements. That is all it is there for.

But, this sensory-motor mechanism became more sophisticated as evolutionary changes occurred. When one considers the degree and variety of motor abilities and the sensory requirements to match these, which developed in a vast variety of fish, bird and animal species over millennia, one appreciates the power of this dual archetypal mechanism to bring about and sustain vast numbers of new species. And it is all based on the simple principles of survival that animal eats plant, and animal eats animal. Obviously, there was no question of ethical values at this stage! We will have to discover where these came from.

Much later in evolution, after the abilities to hear and vocalise had developed, it became possible to communicate with other beings in the environment by making sounds. And later still, when the ability to produce specific noises had become more precise, communication by spoken language was possible. Still later, even greater precision and a semi-permanent record were achieved by the hugely important step of extending memory by inventing script to make possible a written record. Although the brain and consciousness had been evolving over millions of years, these more recent developments occurred in more recent times. But before all this could happen, the existence and handling of ideas must have already become well developed.

It has to be remembered, however, that many functions still depend upon reflex mechanisms operating through the spinal cord and independently of the brain and consciousness. Also, in higher animals, an independent and complex *autonomic nervous system* developed to control the functions of all the internal organs. Although 'autonomic' in the sense that it functions independently of the brain and consciousness, certain relationships do exist. Thus, breathing and alimentary functions are independent, yet some voluntary control is possible; genito-urinary functions are autonomic, yet elements of voluntary control also exist."

"Why are these details of interest for our project?"

"Because this sensory information, particularly about sexuality, is of crucial importance for the minomic functions of reason and the Sensibilities, summarised in (6). Also, we will find that when we speak of 'meaning' and 'understanding', it is to these functions that we are referring (7).

I should explain that I use upper case to describe the three main Sensibilities of Feeling, Aesthetics and Values. But each contains a multiplicity of sensibilities to which I refer in lower case."

"So, the axis mechanism originally had the function of supporting the survival of the species. But throughout recorded history its scope extended beyond the immediate environment to all aspects of life and death. It is also true, is it not, that since the advent of science it has been used to investigate how the world works and has even been regarded as the tool that may unlock the secrets of the universe?"

"That is so, and it is a profound change. The original functions of the axis mechanism had been confined to providing nutrition and defending against predators. Then humans adapted the mechanism to try and answer more ultimate questions about life and death. It is as though humans had placed themselves in charge of the evolutionary mechanism of survival of the fittest. In order to understand this remarkable change, we need to examine the whole process in more detail."

"I suppose it is this change that has driven the progress of western civilisation since Greek times?"

"Yes and humans are still trying to exploit to the full and understand these relatively new possibilities.

<u>Units of sensory experience</u>

Our endeavour is to contribute to that understanding. The first question that arises is, what is it that is experienced? At the heart of consciousness, and perhaps the essence of it, is an active process. The reception of sensory experiences (whatever that may mean) has characteristics determined by one or more sensory receptors, e.g. a flash of lightening, or a conversation between two people. These you will notice have space-time dimensions and have motion that is directional. They are immediately stored as the memory of the events.

Although this binary process of reception and storage is continuous, memory recall produces static images of discreet duration. For these *units of experience* to acquire *meaning,* they must be repeated on future occasions so that the subject comes to recognize what has already been experienced. Additional meaning is acquired when these units of experience are shared with other humans.

A degree of some kind of meaning must have existed prior to the invention of spoken and written language in order to explain how humans and perhaps the higher animals could have developed within communities. But when spoken and written language appeared, the units of experience and their meaning were greatly enhanced in number, accuracy and increased the capacity for survival.

The word 'idea' is commonly used to encompass this process of experience/memory/meaning, initially without the constraints and formal additions of words and sentences. I use it as follows: to have an idea, is to capture in the memory experiences that subsequently acquire well-defined meanings through language, mathematical symbols, musical notation and logic. Thus, the notion of 'idea' enters consciousness prior to its conversion into the form of language. Philosophers have analysed language and debated how it acquires meaning and I return to this question in later discussions (27, 28). But note that I have been using the word 'idea' loosely as in everyday life, but later I define it more precisely as something *of unknowable origin* that comes into consciousness representing elements of objective and subjective experience."

"I can see now that what I regarded as the simple notion of 'having an idea' presents the philosopher with the very difficult problems of what idea is, and how it acquires meaning."

<u>Systems of Ideas</u>

"All human thought takes the form of ideas that come to have defined meanings when expressed in the form of language. We cannot get beyond that to some superior view of an ultimate reality. Wittgenstein expressed this by saying something to the effect that we cannot get outside of language, or to put it more specifically, outside of a system of ideas that describe what we *believe* to be true. Philosophy, he said, is a battle against the bewitchment of our intelligence by language (17).

We live within endless systems of ideas that flow continuously through consciousness. The adult is never indifferent, as the young child is, and is always judgemental because new ideas are immediately compared and contrasted with the pre-existing normative, ethical profile (15) from the Sensibilities (6-9).

At any one moment, the ideas of which we are aware, including ideas from the memory, define the limits of consciousness. Although memory is an unsatisfactory term, it will do to define those limits together with the variety, quantity and quality of the ideas retained. The memory extends during childhood in ways determined by the innate abilities and the environment to which these are exposed. But with advancing age, memory diminishes and may be lost in a variety of ways.

And so, although we use language to describe sensory experiences, we have no idea what these experiences really are and what they mean. This has been the stimulus for much philosophical investigation since Greek times (7). Although it has caused a lot of controversy, as we shall find, the scientists were able to ignore these problems and carry on regardless."

"That sounds a pathetic situation to be in! Obviously, there is no certainty there, just belief!"

"Although you can appreciate now the philosophical uncertainty about language, nevertheless, it can be used to define specific categories of ideas. Fictional ideas are characterised by the fact that they describe events that have never formed a part of sensory experiences. Also, they do not constitute belief systems because the things described are not believed to exist, by definition. Apart from these fictional ideas, we are aware of the following different kinds of knowledge,

Forms of Knowledge

1. *Religious ideas* that describe things that cannot be shown to exist with certainty, but are derived indirectly from sensory experiences. They are beliefs that are systems of ideas validated by faith, the conviction that they are true.

2. Ideas formed from common sensory experiences, such as finding one's way about in the world, are belief systems that are accepted as true because each experience is confirmed by repetition.

3. The products of logical and mathematical procedures that utilise ideas or symbols to express relations that are self-evidently true, that is, are not dependent on external evidence.

4. Scientific ideas that utilise forms of reasoning in 3 to give the belief systems of 2 a much greater probability of being true. As already mentioned, the Greeks discovered that careful observations and accurate measurements of the relationships between objects of sensory experience reveals a certainty about these relationships that had not previously been recognised as a result of the casual experiences of daily life. These are *verifiable beliefs, or hypotheses,* and if proved to be true they comprise scientific knowledge. But we shall find that this knowledge is still a belief in the sense that all scientific knowledge is only tentatively true, for it is always open to revision in the light of new evidence.

5. Ideas from the normative beliefs derived from the Sensibilities (5-13).

All these exist as forms of knowledge with variable degrees of certainty. Religious knowledge is distinctive in that although it is about things that do not exist, they do have a reference point in the sensory world. For example, even the ideas of heaven and hell have their origins in the sensory experiences of everyday life. Belief implies the presence of an element of uncertainty expressed in a system of ideas so that its content may be true or false. 'Knowledge' implies beliefs that have a degree of certainty based on evidence supplied.

I need to make an important distinction here between knowledge of whatever degree of certainty and the *hidden* events in consciousness that give rise to it. These I describe in discussions (6) and (9-13). They comprise what I call the *minome* and the curious thing about them is that they are unknowable. By that I mean that we cannot be aware of them directly, but only by their effects, that is the various kinds of knowledge just outlined."

"You cause me to wonder what *is* knowable. Does the outer world, of which we are so clearly aware, actually exist? What is the origin of sensory experience?"

"This is one of many fundamental problems that confront humans who wish to discover more about the world in which they live. I will mention some of them here and refer to them again later in the contexts in which they occur. We will find that sensory experience includes a dimension that is unknowable. But these ideas from the objective dimension of experience are mirrored by subjective ideas that form in *response* to these, (6). The subjective and objective origins of ideas together give rise to the impression that 'I' as a subject, often called the 'agent', (to be discussed later 16), am regarding a completely separate objective environment. We cannot be sure that this duality exists, so that belief as opposed to certainty arising out of this problem cannot be avoided. What is the relation, for example, between things perceived in consciousness and whatever it is that gives rise to sensory experience? Western philosophers have wrestled with these problems and Kant was particularly concerned with *perception*, as we shall find later. Doubtless much will be revealed by further scientific investigation.

Integral to all these questions are the problems of time and space. We think of space as a sensory dimension having properties that are easily measurable, but soon discover that it extends from the infinitely small to the infinitely large, neither of which is measurable. Time marks the measurable movement of objects in space, yet this also is indefinable as we shall find. So, immediately we try to find out more about time and space, problems arise! In order to solve them, Kant claimed that space and time are properties of the mind, not the objective dimension. This will be discussed later (23)."

"That seems to make matters worse!"

"It does. I have spoken of space and time as though they exist, but we have no direct awareness of either. All we *are* aware of are objects in motion. Even the word 'object' creates scientific and philosophical problems. A simple and seemingly solid object in space for example, which we call matter, seems to melt on investigation into something unknowable at the sub-atomic level. The quantum scientist discovered that an object is made up of an infinite number and variety of atoms and sub-atomic particles in ceaseless motion."

"And what causes that motion, in fact all motion in the universe?"

"Scientists call it '*energy*' and that is also something of which we have no sensory perception. The term was invented to explain all movement in the universe. The belief that it exists is necessary to satisfy the equations of the scientist, which describe the movement of objects at the sub-atomic level and in stellar space. The philosopher stops to ask whether these things are in any sense real and exist 'out there', or are they again functions of the perceiving mind?

Despite future revelations of science and the endeavours of philosophers, we shall find that at times we do have to grapple with the unknowable. However far the physicist chases the origin of matter and the sense data that stimulate the sensory organs and provide all knowledge, he won't reach final conclusions – that is, ones that explain everything. These are positions where we have to suspend beliefs and not seek to explain by indulging in more beliefs. All these are problems that we shall refer to again during our discussions."

"So, when we are dealing with something unknowable, ideally one suspends belief. When one endeavours to move 'beyond belief', I take it that is you mean, and since this may not be possible, the most we can really achieve is the removal of false belief systems?"

"Yes, or at least reduce to a minimum the wealth of beliefs that cause the confusions which characterize societies today. But we will review some of the ideas that have been produced down the centuries before we reach our conclusions. An important aspect of all these problems is to separate off things thought to be knowable from the unknowable."

"And that has not been done?"

"Not with sufficient clarity to prevent unnecessary confusions. In order to appreciate the significance of this and other issues, we must briefly consider these questions historically in our next discussion."

"Why have we not discussed **Charles Darwin** (1809-1882) and natural selection?"

"That may seem surprising, but the focus of our discussion has been on what is knowable and what is unknowable. Darwin's theory has generated an enormous amount of interest and research. Doubtless a great deal will be discovered about evolution and it is impossible at present to know where this will lead."

What Is Consciousness?

Discussion 4

History of Ideas

The mind is never empty and never at rest except when asleep. It is full of systems of ideas, which succeed each other in rapid succession. Humans seem to live two lives: the immediate world of work and pleasure, or very often misery. Then there is a world of ideas, a more obscure and hazy, inner world expressing a variety of feelings; of beauty and ugliness; of good and evil, right and wrong. And here, the transience of life, the spectres of illness and death are never far away. This duality has been there throughout historic times and probably long before.

In the distant past, the life of the individual was thought to be ruled by hidden powers that controlled everything. These became gods; even ancestors were often regarded as gods that could be placated by worship and by ceremonies and sacrifices. Over many millennia, the gods diminished in number, but not in power. The power to control good and evil, like many other mysterious things in life was invested in the gods. Such beliefs made the lives of primitive humans more tolerable, and often more fearful.

But the power of reason to make sense of the world increased with time, including the capacity to be logical and numerate: to be aware of contradiction and falsity, to examine beliefs in order to appraise their validity. These are the intellectual capacities that came to the fore in Greece and did so again in the Middle Ages and more penetratingly, during the European Enlightenment and the Romantic Age. The ideas that influence the people of today did not appear de novo. They contain elements from past history, including extensions back to mythological times. Therefore, the history of ideas is important in understanding the problems of today. I want to pick out certain ideas from various historic periods, which appear to have importance today.

An amalgam of these residues and the ideas of contemporary society I take to be what constitutes our culture. There was a well-developed culture during the Babylonian civilisation about 2000 years BC in lower Mesopotamia, and it continued during the succeeding Chaldean period. These relatively well-developed civilisations came to an end when Babylon was captured and absorbed into the Persian Empire in 539 BC.

The Babylonian, the Phoenician and Egyptian civilisations influenced the development of Greek culture. There had been much turmoil among the civilisations of the eastern Mediterranean between 2000 and 1000 BC. The Minoan culture was centred on Crete and the Mycenaean culture in the Peloponnese, but these were brought to an end by the ravages of the mysterious Sea Peoples and then by the Dorians from the north. There followed a dark age between the 12th and 9th centuries, which preceded the appearance of Greek culture. During this period, the Greeks managed to develop a powerful language and written script that greatly facilitated the development, preservation and communication of ideas.

Here we have the possibly unique experience of being able to observe a community in its formative stage. Humans living together take on characteristics, which come to distinguish them as a community, that is, something distinctive and different from other groups of humans, and these differences are due to what they believe and what they do. 'Doing' includes the fact that some of the more aggressive members come to exert influence over the rest in terms of what they persuade the rest to believe and do. History shows that the power exerted by most leaders inhibited the potential for individuals to develop and express their personalities and abilities to the full. That is why centuries of intellectual sterility passed while the powerful elite spent their time building and losing empires.

The uniqueness of Greece was that from its early, formative stage, there was relative freedom of thought within what soon became the Greek Empire. This environment produced an intellectual elite who explored many new fields of ideas. They applied their capacity for accurate observation of sensory experiences to the full and applied their abilities and sensibilities in innumerable ways never attempted before. The vigour with which ideas were pursued to the limit was matched by the physical energy and competitiveness expressed, for example, in the Olympic games.

The crucial factor that allowed these intellectual voyages of discovery to happen was their willingness to discard old beliefs in order to allow new ideas to form. The Greeks were intellectually adventurous to a degree not achieved before and possibly not since. The sceptics distinguished between things knowable from sensory experience and things unknowable, usually thought to be matters of belief in the power of gods or spirits. Uncertainty about the latter led **Protagoras** (b 500 BC) to say, '*With regard to the gods, I cannot feel sure that they are or are not, nor what they are like in figure; for there are many things that hinder sure knowledge, the obscurity of the subject and the shortness of human life.*'[3] The beliefs of a rich mythology, culminating in the Olympian pantheon of gods, soon became outmoded as the torrent of new ideas led to the foundations of science, philosophy, art, drama and literature, all of which are the foundations of the culture of today.

While the intellectual elite bestrode the civilised world as never before, the Delphic Oracle and the mystery religions bubbled away at the edges. The Eleusinian mystery religion promised renewal, re-birth and immortality. The Orphic religion drew a distinction between the body that came from the earth below, and the soul that came from the heavens. These and many other beliefs influenced **Pythagoras** (c 530 BC), **Socrates** (469-399 BC) and **Plato** (427-347 BC). These philosophers taught that behind the world of everyday life there was the real world, a hidden reality which only philosophy could reveal. It was as though the blind beliefs of primitive societies had not disappeared, but had become transformed by observation and reason into other beliefs.

There was plenty of metaphysics: the philosophers utilised beliefs, but these were not the uncritical beliefs of the mystery religions; rather an attempt to describe the universe as it is in a rational manner. More accurate observation and critical appraisal produced the sufficiently sceptical minds of the early scientists and philosophers.

The Greeks changed the human vision of the universe dramatically. This vision has since been extended and is more detailed and accurate. But it remains uncertain as to whether the abilities and sensibilities, which made this possible, can be exploited further to open new dimensions of original thought. Perhaps the main achievement of the Greeks was to describe the world as they

---

[3] *History of Western Philosophy*, p97   Bertrand Russell   George Allen and Unwin Ltd 1947

thought it was as a consequence of observation, not simply as determined by beliefs in supernatural powers.

Since Greek times, the history of ideas has taken the form of a struggle to explain everything on the one hand, and on the other to achieve the more limited objective of the attempt to explain only what can be observed. Philosophy arose out of a thirst for knowledge without beliefs. But rationality proved not to be a sufficient safeguard against falsity. The reasoning could be faultless, yet the conclusion wrong. There was that little problem of secure premises upon which validity depends, a problem which still produces philosophical problems that are often insuperable.

Virtually all philosophers and theologians since the Greeks have relied on belief and reason. And, to anticipate, we shall find that these are not alternative ways of regarding the universe, but to a degree, are complimentary. The problem has become a matter of understanding the nature of thought and the realisation that *belief establishes premises that are inevitably insecure, yet are an inherent part of all understanding.*

The lights began to go out on the Greek achievement when the Empire, under **Pericles** (495-429 BC) lost the Peloponnesian war with Sparta (431-404) BC. Democracy, which had been of a limited kind, had failed, but philosophy flourished during the 4th century. Plato and **Aristotle** (384-322 BC) lived at this time, but the tide had turned and Greece came under the rule of the Macedonians in 338 BC. The *Hellenistic Age* commenced with the death of Alexander the Great in 323 BC and ended with the Battle of Actium in 31 BC, an event that completed the Roman hegemony over the eastern Mediterranean.

The Hellenistic Age was characterised by the resurgence of primitive religious ideas, such as Orphism, Dionysian Rites, the Cults of Isis and Osiris. Waves of mystery religious and cult beliefs flooded Greece from the east, including the old Indo-Iranian Mithras cult, Star worship, the Gnostic sects, who claimed knowledge of god, and Astrology from Babylonia[4]. As a consequence of this inward flow of beliefs, the freedom to explore new ideas lost

---

[4] *In Search Of Ideas* Richard Sheriff Jones. Unpublished

impetus.

But the Greek spirit was not yet dead. **Gilbert Murray** (1866-1957) gives an excellent account of this period of Greek culture.[5] Two philosophers appeared during the Hellenistic period when fears and superstitions had engulfed the world again. **Zeno** (334-262 BC) founded the Stoic school of philosophy at Athens in 317 BC, where he taught. He accepted the findings of the scientists that the world is not a chaotic place and claimed that observation reveals an understandable natural order. He taught that this order is maintained by *phusis*, the life force. Man must live in harmony with this in order to achieve *Arête,* or Goodness. Only this gives contentment, whatever misfortune strikes. There is no god, only a universal movement, *pronoia,* towards perfection, (see Gilbert Murray below).

The Greek scholar, **Epicurus** (342-270 BC) moved to Athens in 310 BC and there taught philosophy. He claimed that people tortured themselves unnecessarily with fears due to superstitions, or false beliefs, and the fears go when these are abandoned. He avoided the transcendental optimism of the Stoics as well as mysticism and the need for the existence of the gods. People should be free to believe whatever they wish about the gods. Wisdom, he claimed, is the knowledge of how to avoid trouble and conflict whether from the beliefs of religion, nationalism or other causes.

Epicurus disagreed with the sceptics who denied the possibility of knowledge. He developed an atomic theory in which the atoms are in ceaseless motion. These account for all movement including the actions of living things and for free will, which is almost as far as we have got today! The major work of Epicurus, *On Nature*, described the physical universe, the limitations of possible knowledge, the minimal role of the gods and religion. In some respects, his views on physics and epistemology were remarkably modern and there are aspects of his philosophy that accord with the views presented here. He came at the end of the classical period of

---

[5] *Five Stages of Greek Religion* Gilbert Murray Watts and co London 1935

Greek philosophy. His objective was to deny the belief that life is ruled by the gods of mythology. He replaced this with the science-based belief that all life is determined by natural forces and that if there are gods, they live in another realm. He thought that if the gods exist, they must be essentially peaceful; for how could the evils of the natural world come from such powers? The Roman poet, **Lucretius** (94-55 BC) brought *On Nature* to the attention of the Roman world in a poem, *On the Nature of Things,* which is modelled closely on Epicurus. It is translated into prose by R. E. Latham[6] and analysed in a book by David Sedley[7].

Sedley points to the problem that although Lucretius was a great admirer of Epicurus, his poem begins with a prayer to Venus to intercede with Mars, the god of war, to bring peace to the Roman Republic. Sedley asks how could this be reconciled with the views of Epicurus who was totally opposed to such ideas? He had sought to replace the old Olympian order with one based on science. Sedley believes that the Greek poet and philosopher, **Empedocles** (495-435 BC), must have influenced Lucretius and illustrates the extent to which the old beliefs of mythology had been through the philosophical 'mill' during classical times and such beliefs had diminished by the time of Lucretius.

Murray gives a brilliant survey of this transition of Greek religion from primitive times through what he calls the 'Olympian reformation' and the influence on it of science and philosophy. The Olympians had replaced the primitive order of superstitions, monsters, barbarous practises and eternal torture. The Olympians, who were superhuman, represented a new and civilised order of humane values that became enshrined in Greek literature.

One objective of the Stoics and Epicureans, living in an age when the classical Greek miracle was fading, was to counter the tide of polytheism coming from the east. They were desperately defending Greek ideals in the Hellenistic age, but Murray criticises

---

[6] Penguin Books Ltd, 1951

[7] *Lucretius and the Transformation of Greek Wisdom* David Sedley. Published by Cambridge University Press, 1998

their followers: *'When they are almost free from the popular superstitions, when they have constructed complete systems which, if not completely logic-proof are calculated at least to keep out the weather for a century or so, open up curious side doors at the last moment and let in all the gods of mythology'.*

Archimedes of Syracuse (287-212 BC) was one of the last of the Greek scientists. His method of combining mathematics and experimental enquiry foreshadowed the Renaissance of science in the 15th century.

Under the Empire, the elite of Greek society moved west to become the educationalists of the Roman Empire. Murray comments on this period: *The great thing to remember is that the mind of man cannot be enlightened permanently by teaching him to reject some particular set of superstitions. There is an infinite supply of other superstitions always at hand; and the mind that desires such things, that is, the mind that has not trained itself to the hard discipline of reasonableness and honesty, will, as soon as its devils are cast out proceed to fill itself with their relations."* He quotes a message left by an old Epicurean on a fragment of stone in Cappadocia about 200 AD in which the writer tries to cut away the harmful accretions of superstition and fear so rife among the populace at that time[8]."

"Would you not agree that these comments are valid throughout most of the world today?"

"Certainly. And in the West, there are still differences and arguments regarding beliefs about allowable details of dress and diet derived from such beliefs that upset some societies at times.

The Transition from Greece to Rome

The Roman Empire was a multi-faith community until 337

---

[8] 'Being brought by age to the sunset of my life, and expecting at any moment to take my departure from the world with a glad song for the fullness of my happiness, I have resolved lest I be taken too soon to give help to those of good temperament…the most of men lie sick, as it were of a pestilence, in their false beliefs about the world, and the tale of them increases, for by imitation they take the disease from one another, like sheep'. He summed up his message: 'Nothing to fear in God; Nothing to feel in death; Good can be attained; Evil can be endured'.

AD when the Emperor Constantine made Christianity the religion of the state. The early Fathers had fashioned its theology during the first few hundred years AD. St Augustine welded the doctrines of the church with other elements, including Neoplatonism. This philosophical system was founded by **Plotinus** (204-269 AD) of Alexandria who later taught in Rome. Neoplatonism was based closely on the teachings of Plato and Aristotle. However, both Plotinus and his follower Porphyry rejected Christianity on account of its personalised supernaturalism and the idea of salvation through grace and faith. But **St Augustine** (354-430) amalgamated the teaching of the early Fathers and the philosophy of Plotinus to form what became known as *Augustinian Neoplatonism.* This was the accepted theology in the Middle Ages (1000-1500). Another distinctive element that St Augustine introduced was *Divine Illumination,* a belief that true knowledge is not from the senses but from an inner experience that gives immediate certainty. In the terminology developed here, this is the Value Sensibility plus associated belief."

"Christianity must have appeared to be firmly established at this time, yet during the lifetime of St Augustine the northern boundaries of the Empire were crumbling due to pressure from barbarian tribes migrating from the east to form states in Western Europe. And they were, after all, our ancestors!"

"That is so. St Augustine became bishop of Hippo in N. Africa in 395 AD. By that time the now enfeebled Roman Empire was being invaded along its northern border by these barbarian tribes and Rome fell to Alaric, king of the Visigoths in 410 AD. At this point St Augustine wrote *Civitas Dei* in which he outlined a Christian view of history. He was convinced that the earthly cities of man were about to perish at the hands of the barbarians and that only the enduring City of God, inhabited by the elect, would prevail. He died when the Goths were besieging Hippo in 430 AD.

When Rome fell, the worst fears of St Augustine appeared to have been realised. But history is full of surprises. The invaders must have been astonished by what they found: the scale and profusion of architectural and artistic achievement; the complexity of social, political and legal attainments. Yet, instead of destroying, they adopted many of the laws and customs, and duly converted to

Christianity. These events ensured that the belief systems of Christianity endured until the present day. But it was clearly a period of huge social and political upheaval. By the later Middle Ages, they had set up monastic seats of learning and universities. But it took 500 years, the Dark Ages, for these tribes to become the new leaders of civilisation."

The Dark Ages (500-1000) and Islam

"What were the historical events that brought this about because in the early Middle Ages (500-1000) a new belief system, Islam; appeared in 631 AD and came to dominate the Mediterranean basin and even parts of Europe, Spain and the Balkans?"

"The Dark Ages tend to be ignored as simply a period of turmoil, or one during which the Church in Rome established its foundations. But there were a few major figures during this bleak period. **Boethius** (c 480-c 526) helped to transmit Greek culture to the West and may be said to have begun the tradition of Latin philosophy that continued until Kant. He was Master of the Offices under King Theodoric, but was later accused of treachery, imprisoned and executed. He wrote on Plato, Aristotle and the Trinity and in the 'Consolations', written when in prison, he wrote on philosophy and gave a famous definition of time and eternity: *'Eternity therefore is a perfect possession altogether of an endless life, which is more manifest by the comparison of temporal things, for whatsoever lies in time, that being present proceeds from times past to times to come, and there is nothing placed in time which can embrace all the space of its life at once. But it has not yet attained to-morrow and has lost yesterday'*[9]. He wrote educational works that were in use throughout the medieval period: the Trivium (grammar, dialectic or logic and rhetoric) and the Quadrivium (arithmetic, geometry, music and astronomy). **Cassiodorus** (d 510) of Italy and **Isodore,** (d 536) bishop of Seville were also major figures with encyclopaedic knowledge.

These early foundations of Western culture were greatly extended to include science and philosophy following the

---

[9] *Consolation of Philosophy* Boethius, H F Stewart, Published William Heinemann Ltd 1918 sect v, vi, p401

Renaissance. And as we shall find, from the 19ᵗʰ century onwards its scope was broadened to include not only the elite, but all members of society."

"Why was it that Islam separated itself off and did not participate in these cultural developments?

"Let me explain. **Mohammad** (570-632) united the desert Arabs of Arabia under the banner of a new religion. Soon after his death the tribes issued forth from Mecca to 'protect their interests' and by 635 had captured Damascus. Islam emphasised peace but it was spread by the sword, by jihad. The Arab Empire finally extended from the cities of the Silk Road in the east, across the southern border of Byzantium and along the southern shores of the Mediterranean. In effect it created an iron curtain along the length of the Mediterranean. It captured the North African states and entered Spain in 710. The invasion of Europe extended temporarily to Poitiers about 70 miles south of Paris. Christian Europe at this point was cut off from the centres of civilisation at Baghdad and cities south of the Oxus River, such as Bukhara, Samarkand and Tashkent, together with the silk route to China[10].

Despite the exclusion of Europe from the old traditional, cultural centres, Greek, Arab and Persian in the East, there were many exchanges of ideas between these old cities and the west. Baghdad became an important repository for Greek texts and their translation into Arabic. Many were subsequently transmitted to the West via Spain, especially at the time of the 'golden age' of **Haroon al Rashid** (786-709), the period when the Arabian, 1001 Nights was written.

There is a vast literature of this period. A few general descriptions refer to Islam and Arab culture[11]. After 1000 AD, the

---

[10] *The Silk Road* Frances Wood Published by the Folio Society 2002

[11] *In Search of Ideas, chapter 7 The Rise of Islam* Richard Sheriff Jones, 1995 (to be published) *The Road to Mecca,* Mohammad Asad, Published by the Muslim Academic Press. ISBN 1-90235000-6

Faith and Power, The Politics of Islam Edward Mortimer Pub Faber and Faber 1982 ISBN 0 571-11944-1

Arab Empire broke up into Principalities and ceased to be a threat to Europe, after which the Crusades commenced. But later, during the Ottoman Empire, under the leadership of the Turks, the Balkans were again invaded by Muslim armies. The Western European states left it to the Serbs, Hungarians, Bulgarians and Bosnians to defend Europe during the 14th and 15th centuries.

What was left of Christianity in the east disappeared when Constantinople fell in 1453[12]. Although the Ottoman Empire in turn became weak, it did not finally come to an end until the twentieth century."

"Europe appears to have been under threat then from about seven hundred AD onwards."

"Although the threat was real at times, that is not why I mention these historical facts, for there is a much more important reason relevant to 21st century democracies in the West. When the iron curtain isolated Christian Europe, although it prolonged feudalism and caused hardship, it did not impede intellectual progress that soon developed an unprecedented momentum that has continued until the present day.

My point is that when the Arabs cut Europe off, they also cut themselves off from these cultural riches, which soon created a wide gulf between east and west. They and the other Islamic autocracies in the east confined education and cultural achievements mainly to teaching the Koran and Hadith (law by tradition) in Madrassas and Mosques. There were scholars of note[13], but culture in the East did not evolve as it did in the West. They developed their own highly distinctive culture[14]

The Arabs, Peter Mansfield Published by Pelican Books 1979

[12] *A History of Europe, chapter 34 The Ottoman Turks* H A L Fisher Published 1936, Edward Arnold and Co

[13] See *Islamic Philosophy and Theology* and also *A History of Islamic Spain by* Montgomery Watt 1992 Published by Edinburgh University Press

[14] *The Spirit Of The East* An anthology edited by Gaury and Winstone Published by Quartet Books Ltd 1979 ISBN o 7043 22307

It was not until the discovery of oil in the 20th century that the Islamic countries became rich and, as a consequence, sought power and improved standards of living by importing the benefits of science and technology, together with the technical and educational requirements to support their use. But they were indifferent to most forms of Western Art and they positively rejected Western ethics."

"What was the reason for that divergence?"

"*Eastern culture* developed by exploring the sensory world in the context of Koranic beliefs and the Hadith. It was controlled by Shari'a law (or Gods law as interpreted by learned men). In particular, Western attitudes to sex, drink and drugs are abhorred and atheism is unacceptable – all these are rejected as evidence of Western decadence. It follows that the problem for Muslims today is how to import the products of Western culture, yet keep out Western decadence, which is somewhat difficult for them to achieve. They are correct in that there is plenty of Western decadence, and in some measure our project is to understand its origins.

Western culture, in contrast, developed by exploring the sensory world in the context of the tentative beliefs of science as distinct from the faith based beliefs of religion. But when Muslims come to live in the West, the huge cultural differences become apparent. Their ethical beliefs and practices are so different that it is proving difficult for east and west to find common ground and the consequence is the clash of cultures that we are experiencing today.

The beliefs in themselves do not matter, providing there is tolerance, but the practices do matter, for they may result in physical violence. Many Muslims feel threatened by an alien way of life against which some think they have to defend themselves, if necessary violently. This is a problem with which democratic governments are wrestling and is a question we will consider later (Parts 5 and 6). It is an example of one of the driving forces that bring about continuous change in democratic countries.

The Scholastic Period

The ascendancy of beliefs reached a climax during the scholastic period of the later Middle Ages. Augustinian Neoplatonism had welded the doctrines of the early Fathers of the church with elements of Platonic philosophy and these ideas dominated the 10th and 11th centuries of scholastic endeavour.

Neoplatonism and Divine Illumination provided the links between earthly and heavenly existence. It is not surprising that the application of reason was remarkably uncritical during this period, as exemplified by **Anselm's** (1033-1109) dictum: *'Credo ut intelligam',* I believe in order to understand.

During the 12th and 13th centuries, thought moved from Augustinian to the much more critical Thomist theology. **St Thomas Aquinas** (1226–1274) attempted to tackle the perennial problem of the relationship between the natural world of sensory experience and belief in a supernatural world. Aristotle's works were beginning to reach the west and become available in translation. Although Aristotelian science was by that time over 1500 years old, it seemed a new and a scientific, or rational way of approaching the problem of belief in the supernatural.

Beginning with sensory experience, St Thomas attempted to establish a verifiable link between the earthly phenomena with which science deals and the supernatural beliefs of the Church. Sensory experience now became crucial to understanding. By the standards of today, this attempt to provide a rational basis for belief failed, but it must be said that a further 500 years of intense philosophical debate has proved to be not entirely fruitful. The main result has been to establish more clearly what reason can and cannot do.

By the 13th century, scholasticism had reached its zenith and already individuals were appearing who were to lay the foundations for the unprecedented intellectual progress to follow in the form of the Renaissance and the Enlightenment. **Roger Bacon** (1214–1294), a Franciscan, was in some respects a scholastic in that he accepted that ultimate truth lies in a supernatural realm, accessed by scripture, revelation and Divine Illumination. But he emphasised the role of mathematics and experimental science as the only method of gaining knowledge of the natural world, both of which had been ignored by the scholastics and indeed since Greek times. But he took the scholastic view that all knowledge served the object of adorning theology, the Queen of the sciences.

Duns Scotus (c1266/70-1308) emphasised more strongly than St Thomas the inevitable separation between reason and faith. One transcendent Being exists and is manifest in two modes, one revealing God and the other revealing all that exists in the natural world. As a Platonist, he rejected Thomist-Aristotelian metaphysics. Thus he produced a discontinuity between the natural world and the supernatural.

The last word in the scholastic debate was supplied by the rather neglected but powerful mind of **William of Occam** (1285-1349). St Thomas had thought that in the observable world he could establish premises that would enable him, by his method of 'analogy' from experience of the natural world, to establish partial knowledge of religious truths. But he accepted that revelation and faith in the doctrines of the church were also necessary. Half a century later, Occam arrived at the position that it is not possible to build bridges between the natural and a supernatural world; only faith could secure the latter. He distinguished between 'intuitive knowledge' which may be true or false, (faith based beliefs), and 'demonstrative knowledge', (verifiable beliefs). Thus he pointed the way directly to the methods of empirical science and philosophy, which dominated thought until the present day.

Before we leave the medieval period I must mention Islamic culture in Spain. There had been some interchange of ideas between Christian and Islamic scholars until the recapture of Spain was completed in 1492[15]. After the Arab Empire disintegrated towards the end of the first millennium in the east, education in the Muslim world became confined to the study of the Koran. The two cultures then went their separate ways. In the west, enormous changes occurred due to scientific, philosophical and technological progress. These naturally had repercussions on all aspects of culture, beliefs and ethical principles, as we shall see. But the migration of Muslims westwards in recent years has produced, not unnaturally, a profound clash of cultures that will take decades to resolve."

"I now have an introduction to the ideas that have come

---

[15] *A History of Islamic Spain*   W Montgomery Watt Published by At the University Press Edinburgh 1965

Islamic Philosophy and Theology W Montgomery Watt At the University Press Edinburgh 1962 down to the modern period from remote times. There can be no doubt that these ideas have immensely contributed to the world of today.

Now I would like to know what those former 'barbarians', our ancestors, who settled in Western Europe have been able to achieve. History since the Middle Ages seems to have been remarkable for both its complexity and productiveness. How do I find my way without spending five years reading large textbooks?"

"I can only reply, follow me!"

Part 2
Consciousness, Beliefs And Values
Description and Analysis
(Discussions – 5-13)

Discussion 5

"Central to our discussions is the description of mind, or consciousness. Our next objective is to describe this in the light of modern knowledge. Then I want to examine these conclusions in the light of what scientists and philosophers are saying (14-16).

After that, I return to the historical description from the Enlightenment up to the early 20th century (17-28).

Then, in the next part of our discussions (29), we discuss the social and political implications of our investigations. This will begin to bring out conclusions from our philosophical investigations that we arrive at in the final discussions (Part 6).

Perception and Sensory Knowledge

All sensory experiences in the human are from special sensory organs and from the internal organs to give taste, hunger, pain and all the manifestations of sexuality. Sensory awareness during waking hours is continuous, unavoidable and ever changing.

The acquisition of knowledge from sensory experience may seem simple at first sight, but it has proved to be extremely complex. Data arriving at sensory nerve endings is perceived in consciousness as all the sights, sounds, tastes and smells etc of which we are familiar. Philosophers, and especially Kant, have been particularly interested in the problem of perception because all the mysteries mentioned earlier arise out of the process of acquiring sensory experience. A vast amount of recent work has been done on this subject but I don't want to consider this in any detail. Dennett has summarized recent literature[16] and I will discuss his findings later (7)."

"Don't we know where sensory experiences come from or what they are?"

"No, and it could be said that most of the problems of philosophy arise from this simple fact."

"That's amazing! What is the difficulty? When I see a red rose, surely that is what is out there?"

"The problem is, what exactly *is* out there? And when the scientist investigates, as we shall find, he ends by describing molecules and atoms that we cannot even see, we can only describe what we think is there."

"And if I say it is beautiful, I can only describe that in words, which I suppose is even more unsatisfactory, for how do they relate to whatever is out there? I can appreciate your point! We had better move on to something easier."

"So far we have been describing some events in consciousnesses that are made possible by exposure to sensory experience. It is appropriate now to collect together the main subjective elements of consciousness, the minome, which are the hidden drivers that produce knowledge. Sensory objective experience is crucial, for without it the subjective, the 'mind' could not exist and perhaps no state of consciousness at all could exist. Sensory experience gives,

1. Lay and scientific knowledge of what is directly experienced via the senses. And additional to this,
2. Countless other systems of knowledge, including all varieties of religious, ethical and social knowledge.

In logical terms these are quite different, a fact that causes much confusion.

---

[16] *Consciousness explained* Daniel C Dennett 1991

Published by Little Brown and Co, and the Penguin Press

Discussion 6

The Components of Consciousness

A distinction must be made between the functions described below, the minome (see also 13), and the *products* of these, which are all forms of knowledge and skills (see 3, Forms of Knowledge). Together, these comprise the extent of consciousness. The functions below make possible the appearance during childhood of the growth of ideas and accompanying actions that evolve to produce language, drama, art, science, philosophy, religion, music and so on. The following components of these activities are discernable.

1. Rationality, the process whereby the perception of meaningless sensory information becomes transformed into meaningful ideas.
2. Logic, mathematics, and statistics make possible the application of greatly increased accuracy and the greater understanding, which that brings when applied to the analysis of rationalised sensory phenomena.
3. The Sensibilities, (of Feeling, Aesthetics and Values) that describe the range of possible responses to sensory experiences (9-12) and these include the ethical dimension (15).
4. The Abilities comprise the active ways in which the subject responds to the environment of sensory experience that includes other beings. These form the executive side of the primitive sensory-motor axis (3 and 13). They make possible the acquisition of all forms of knowledge.
5. The Dynamics of consciousness, the active process of thinking (13).
6. Memory, without which none of the other functions is possible.
7. The Ethical dimension (15).

All are aware of these phenomena in consciousness and although they differ from individual to individual, they are often referred to as 'subjective', as distinct from 'objective' sensory experiences from the sensory organs. This created the dualism described by Descartes that philosophers have tried to find ways of abolishing, or explaining ever since.

Subjective experiences are found to be reasonably uniform, between individuals and therefore may be shared with others. The subjective is often called 'mind' as a purely descriptive label. It is important to appreciate that when I describe the processes of reasoning (Rationality and Logic), motivation (the Sensibilities, including the ethical, and the Abilities), the Dynamics of consciousness, ideas and Memory, I *do not* mean that these things *exist* in some sense. I simply imply that these are things of which we are aware."

"You mean that although they are things of which we can be aware, they have no sensory components."

"Yes. We can only be aware of them because they handle ideas. They comprise what I call the minome and although it has the basic structure outlined and presumably formed during the evolution of the genome, it develops and changes with age and with environmental experiences. Hence, the manifestations of the minome (Introduction and 13) are not static, but evolve during the lifetime of each individual to reveal the unique characteristics of each person. I emphasise that accurate details of these phenomena are crucial in order to avoid errors and false beliefs. Errors occur when factual details are omitted or are inaccurately described, which leads to illogicalities and false beliefs. I will be drawing a distinction later between consciousness and the minome because they must not be thought of as equivalent terms (28).

There is another important point of clarification I must make. The list above describes subjective functions but this is not 'subjective knowledge'. These functions enable the subject to *obtain knowledge* when they respond to sensory experience. Hence, in this sense all knowledge is '*responsive knowledge*' and is from sensory experience of the inanimate and living universe."

"Why do you say that *all* knowledge is responsive and from sensory experience? Surely, it should be from the subjective aspects of brain function?"

"No, because these in isolation are again not forms of knowledge about anything. They are the means whereby knowledge is acquired. Further, we only accumulate knowledge about all things human, for example, as a consequence of interactive relations with other beings. If sensory experience of these did not exist, we would appear to ourselves very different beings – in fact we would not be human! These points will become clearer as we proceed.

"How did all these subjective functions arise? They are not there in the animal, or at least presumably only the rudiments of some of them."

"It appears probable that consciousness grew from nothing in early evolutionary development, as described earlier. Consciousness was not needed at this stage. The development of a tactile sense, vision and hearing greatly increased the capacity to search and direct the motor activity required for retrieval. These made possible the acquisition of primitive knowledge. Consciousness then must have existed, since it was necessary for the animal to link the input and output sides of the axis. This linkage then brought the possibility of choice: when to respond and to which objects and how to retrieve. That was crucial to progress.

Even at the animal level, and probably whenever conscious life in evolutionary terms had developed to the point of it being necessary in order to link sensory and motor activities for nutritional purposes, it operates in terms of motivation to form 'objectives'. The lion hunting its prey forms an objective. But the objective includes, on the basis of past experience, the calculation of how far away and under what conditions it has a hope of making a kill - a relatively sophisticated objective at this level of evolutionary development. Although humans live in the present, all action necessitates the formulation of objectives about the future. But, unlike the animal, man's horizon extends to long-term objectives and questions of life and death. This is an important extension beyond the original purposes of the axis and must be considered further.

The success of the sensory-motor mechanism brought into being ever more complex forms of life. The human organism represents the current stage of development of this mechanism. Ideas derived from sensory information bring about motor activity and one consequence is science and technology. That in turn reveals new sensory information about the environment, which then directs further exploration. These new views of the world reveal ways in which our ideas about the universe have extended and there appears to be no limit to these extensions.

But that has not always been the case: In the high Middle Ages, the 12th-13th centuries, men thought *through beliefs about the supernatural,* that they were putting the finishing touches to a theocracy that explained everything and that soon the task would be complete. Then came a pause as Europe suffered the horrors of the Black Death and the 100 years war, and after these came the Renaissance. By the 16th and 17th centuries, men thought that this time, *through science and reason,* they were revealing a materialistic universe and again it would not be long before the task could be completed. History is rife with beliefs of these kinds. Future progress will depend on learning not to believe more than it is possible to know. The essence of the human problem is that we have yet to learn how to manage beliefs, and that is a theme we must pursue.

The original axis mechanism, you will recall, had ensured the physical means of survival. But primitive humans had already evolved to think of the evils of this life on two levels. There was the original physical objective of survival by human effort. Then there were essential beliefs in hidden powers to supplement these efforts and to give support and comfort in the face of failure and the inevitability of death. The history of philosophy is the attempt to replace ideas about this second level of beliefs in mysterious hidden powers with something else."

"So beliefs in supernatural powers were beginning to reveal serious cracks, and controversies arose. And today?"

"Vastly more knowledge and still plenty of confusion and beliefs!"

"At least I now have an idea of what is meant by consciousness and the minome. But it seems to be incomplete – it is like a house that resembles a museum. It is not full of the very *active* events of everyday life, which is the normal state of affairs. But I expect this is because all the subjective engines of brain function have not yet been described."

"I now want to explain how the model works. In all the descriptions to follow, it should be noted that I do not aim to provide any logical explanations, or 'proofs' for what there is, but simply give accurate descriptions of what we are aware.

Discussion 7

Rationality And New Ideas (component 1, Discussion 6)

'Meaning' or 'understanding' is a difficult concept to define. Relationships between events or objects can be defined and in this sense given meaning. But we have seen already that frequently an ultimate, or final explanation is not possible on account of awareness of some aspect that is unknowable. But at the simplest level, although sensory experiences on arrival in consciousness are in themselves completely meaningless, yet the mere repetition of the same sensory images does produce familiarity, which is the beginning of 'meaning'. I reserve the term 'rationality' for the process of replacing chaos with 'sense', or meaning. It describes the process of marshalling ideas and the ability to recognise that they 'make sense'. This implies no more than that the ideas accord with past experience and common usage. Then the process of repetition and learning plus the collection of systems of ideas produces greater understanding. It is then that the abilities, described later (13), are utilised to achieve objectives.

I distinguish between this use of ideas and the appearance of *new ideas* that characterize all progress in science, art and ethics. This flow of new ideas is powerful, purposeful and motivated by the sensibilities and I will discuss this later (8).

Rationality is a distinct property of conscious life. It describes the flow of ideas through consciousness and entails learning the appropriate ways of utilising sensory experiences in order to achieve desired objectives. It is a part of the process of learning how the world works. The child learns how to speak, to read and write, to appreciate time and motion. The effectiveness of the rationalising sensory experience is greatly enhanced as a consequence of the acquisition of language skills. Words and symbols are used to record a state of constant relations and it is this that gives the language meaning. But there is nothing logically necessary about the words and symbols used, for they can be translated into other languages. This contrasts with things that have relations with logical content where there is only one correct solution, as in mathematics.

We live partly in the past, a world of memories, and partly in the future, a world about to be. Hence at each moment of consciousness we have to decide what to do next. And if we don't decide, then events will follow by default. To live rationally involves making decisions about what is to happen next. The development of reasoning is observable from early childhood onwards. It must be assumed that sensory information received in early infancy means nothing and shapes, colours and movement appear chaotic. Perhaps the only sense of time is in terms of intervals between sensations of hunger. Then, through repetition there comes the recognition of a pattern of familiar objects, especially parents, and the immediate environment. Later, dimensions, shapes, colours and time become more precisely defined. Alongside this process, motor skills develop and contribute immensely to the exploration of the objective dimension. Only in the 'teens do reason and logic enter fully into ideas and actions. And there are conditions such as autism in which the individual fails to establish a conceptual relation with the environment."

"You say that sense data arrive in the brain, that is, in consciousness, but what is consciousness? I tend to think of it as a receptacle into and out of which ideas flow."

"There is no evidence that it is like that. It is as large or as small as the systems of ideas, or knowledge accumulated by each individual. Consciousness *is* the ideas that appear as a consequence of the various functions listed above. An integral part of consciousness is memory, which tends to be thought of as something separate, but that cannot be the case. If events experienced could not be re-called into consciousness, which is the memory of them, there would be no state of consciousness. Loss of memory limits what we can be aware of; it sets a limit to the totality of what can be called consciousness. A person, who learns to speak five languages, or to know a thousand years of history, has increased his range, or extent of consciousness by virtue of memory. The same principle applies in the case of other disciplines: mathematics, the sciences and literature. Consciousness is tenuous. I mentioned that ideas are continuously formed, rejected or stored in the memory where they tend to fade. But when the agency that keeps the process active becomes less so, we feel sleepy and when it is inactive, we fall asleep. So the continuous flow of ideas is crucial to sustaining consciousness.

Apperception

One must distinguish between *'perception'*, the receipt of sensory information in consciousness, and *'apperception'*, which is 'the mind regarding itself'. This phenomenon of self-consciousness was drawn attention to by Leibnitz. Kant described the 'transcendental unity of apperception', which he said explains the interconnectedness of ideas. Apperception certainly describes an important component of all conscious activities: the ability to review, compare and contrast rapidly sequences of ideas. It has been a neglected phenomenon, but I propose that it is a central feature of all thinking. It is an integral part of making choices, philosophising and scientific investigation.

It is important to note that apperception is not something we are aware of directly; we are only able to observe how ideas change in relation to one another. It is a property of the minome and I will return to it again later when describing the minome (13).

Logic, Mathematics and the solution of Problems (component 2)

By the 'teens, the individual becomes aware of the nuances of language, the fallacies and contradictions that may arise. The use of language in order to distinguish between truth and falsity has evolved since Greek times into formal logic. The use of elements of logic is the end point of a long process during childhood and afterwards of the further development of language skills, so that sensory experiences become more meaningful. The Greeks were able to make these advances only after they had adapted and incorporated the Phoenician alphabet into the Greek language[17].

Another advance was the use of number. In its developed form, this aspect of reasoning is mathematics. Rationality makes possible a world that is not meaningless, but logic at its simplest adds the possibility of distinguishing between truth and falsity. If we could not make this distinction, we would still not be able to make head or tail of sensory experience. Logic and mathematics have become of increasing importance for the extension of scientific

---

[17] *The Phoenicians* G E Markoe   The British Museum Press 2002 Folio ed. 2005

knowledge.

The detailed analysis of sensory experience, as in the detective work required to solve a murder mystery, or a scientific problem, entails the application of logic or deductive reasoning. This power of reasoning enabled humans to learn much more about the behaviour of things at rest and in motion. It became possible to give precision to the description of objects large and small in the universe.

The work of **Euclid**, (300 BC), **Pythagoras** (c530 BC) and others introduced the concepts of measurement and the laws of geometry and mathematics. When one considers that human history extends to many millennia, it is remarkable that a description of these powers of human understanding only appeared less than three or four millennia ago. It led to huge changes in the extent of knowledge and the ways in which it is possible to manage the environment. The logic of language and number comprise these relatively newer aspects of the understanding to give what is commonly called 'knowledge'."

"The use of mathematics is surely only a way of saying that X=X, made elaborate by the use of symbols, so why use it?"

"Because when applied to the sensory experience of things in motion, and everything *is* in motion, it yields far greater accuracy than is otherwise possible. Newton invented the calculus because he wished to apply this mathematical device to give additional accuracy to his description of bodies in space under the action of gravity, especially in the solar system, that would not otherwise have been achievable. Mathematics and logic have been the keys to acquiring much of our knowledge. But, all of this is a simplification and I will return to these questions later.

Aristotle (384-322 BC) investigated the scope of deductive logic: the ability to deduce or infer valid conclusions from given premises. He described the logic of the relations between propositions expressing classes of things in the form of syllogisms, e.g.: if all As are Bs and some Bs are Cs, (the premises) then the conclusion must be that some As are Cs. Up to the time of Kant this form of logic was accepted as final. But in the 20th century a new, symbolic logic was developed.

We will find that logic makes it possible to formulate the tentative beliefs from sensory experience that comprise scientific knowledge (8). When we have discussed the Sensibilities (9-13) it will become evident that logic is also the means whereby the normative beliefs of ethics and religion are established. This reached its climax during the scholastic period in the later Middle Ages."

"Why did it take until the Renaissance before science as we know it appeared?"

"Because Greek initiatives were stifled by the twin forces of religious beliefs and the powers of nation states – the Macedonian and then the Roman Empires. It was over 1500 years before these restraints had declined sufficiently to allow the initiatives and enterprise of individuals to become active again.

Description And Analysis
Discussion 8

<u>Logic, Scientific knowledge and Inductive logic (component 2, continued)</u>

Following perception, sensory experience is rationalised to give meaning. This is a slow process of learning during childhood as brain functions develop. But the Greeks found that the extent of knowledge of the natural world could be greatly extended by accurate observation, logic and mathematics. The Greeks also began to develop the technique of experimentation, which of course has been vastly extended over the last 500 years, which brings us to this discussion.

The initial step in the acquisition of scientific knowledge is accurate observation of sensory phenomena. In everyday life it may be noticed that one event regularly follows another: for example, a ball thrown into the air always comes back to earth again; or a skin rash always follows eating eggs. When such regularities of occurrence are observed, the scientist may form the belief, or 'hypothesis' that this relationship is true and then designs a protocol to find out by experiment whether the relationship is true or has occurred by chance. The hypothesis differs from the beliefs of religion in two respects: (1) it is possible *to test for truth or falsity* and (2) on further investigation, *it is possible to discard if false.* If true, the belief then takes on the status of scientific knowledge. But this, in turn is discarded, or modified, if further observations reveal evidence of inaccuracy or falsity. The categories of knowledge were referred to earlier (3). Improved methods of validation have been developed and refined, particularly during the 20th century and include more refined mathematical and statistical procedures.

The essence of the scientific method is the use of inductive logic. When the scientist sets out to prove that a series of regular occurrences exists, he obviously cannot test every example of it in the universe. Therefore he relies on a test sample, which he hopes will represent all possible occurrences. The scientist infers the existence of a general law from the examination of a relatively minute representative sample out of an unknown and potentially infinite number of occurrences. This is the method of induction. But it follows, as David Hume pointed out (20), that such knowledge can never be certain and this limitation applies to all scientific knowledge."

"It is surprising that the method works at all."

"Einstein would agree and said something to the effect that it always surprised him how much human understanding could discover about nature."

"The process of converting beliefs into knowledge of some kind is all that is implied when we use the term *'meaning'*. And this statement applies whether the phenomena are about events in the next village, in heaven, or in the latest scientific theory describing sub-atomic events completely inaccessible to direct observation.

The existence of the *regular occurrence of some events* is the only evidence we have that there is order in the universe. And *because* there is order, rationality and logic are able to create understanding and knowledge. But if order were universal, the world would be mechanistic and a life of consciousness would not be possible.

Equally, it is crucially important also that *random events do occur* (and are usually ignored). If it were not for these, it would not be possible to discover regularities. Only on account of these are options and choices possible. These could not exist in a strictly mechanistic universe, or in a chaotic universe. Hence, knowledge is only possible *because* randomness and regularity both exist.

Life and the evolution of living organisms depend upon these components: Both have now been demonstrated at the sub-atomic level and both are experienced in everyday life, a result that one might have expected. You will now appreciate that both are essential for a rational description of life, as we experience it. Forming an objective depends upon making a choice and this applies to the human as well as the animal hunting for food. Life as we know it has developed in such a way as to require these two dimensions of existence. The advancement of quantum science in the 20th century demonstrated why this had to be the case. I will come back to progress in science later (16).

Science as understood today is quite different from what Kant thought it to be in the 17th and 18th centuries. It appeared then to be revealing a final picture of the world as it really is, which was not in accordance with the beliefs men had held in the Middle Ages. We know now that neither Medieval, nor Enlightenment views about the way the world works were correct. The inductive method tests the truth or falsity of an hypothesis Even if true, it is always liable to be replaced by a more accurate or correct hypothesis. Hence Newton's description of gravity has been replaced with Einstein's more accurate description. There is no end to this process of knowledge acquisition. So each step in scientific investigation must be regarded as no more than a staging post on a journey that will probably never end."

"The word 'intuition' is often used in relation to the formation of hypotheses in science and in other contexts. Is this some special ability?"

"The term is applied to a set of new ideas which seem to appear 'out of the blue' and has the effect of appearing to explain something formally inexplicable. But the interesting point is that often the intuition, concerning some scientific problem, or the composition of a piece of music, when it first comes to mind is in the form of ideas and has then to be expressed in linguistic, mathematical or musical notation before it acquires meaning and can be communicated to others. And then sometimes there is no adequate way in which to express the new idea and a new word, symbol, or other device has to be invented. These problems I will discuss later (28).

It should be noted that Kant gave a different meaning to 'intuition'. The 'forms of intuition' for him are how the mind imposes the ways in which we can have possible and meaningful sensory experiences, as explained later (23, 24).

Intuitive ideas all refer to the ways in which the subjective 'I' and the sensory world of animate and inanimate things inter-relate. It may be about the way in which people relate to each other, or to a new scientific hypothesis describing the subject's ideas of how things might relate to each other. But, however indirectly, one can trace in these relationships that at their root they have the primitive sensory-motor axis as the means whereby the subject interacts with the environment. Intuition is a special example of how the mind continuously forms ideas, as already described, and will be referred to again later."

"I am sure that many are concerned, as they have been since the age of materialism in the 17th century, that advances in science will leave no room for religion, or the 'spiritual'."

"That is false, for science is confined to discovering things that are potentially knowable, whereas these fears are usually about things that are inherently unknowable. But that in itself does not make them more tenuous, for all of science is also about things, inherently unknowable. I will also return to this question later."

Discussion 9

The Sensibilities and Abilities (components 3 and 4)

"Knowledge is like pictures of the universe. This is the universe in which I live, including my body and brain, and also other humans. But when I refer to myself, 'I', I am not talking about all that; I am referring to the variety of ways in which I *respond* to it all. The motivation to respond is the nitty-gritty of living. This response, philosophers seem to have found much more difficult to say anything coherent about. Why is that?"

"Because there has been much difference of opinion as to how humans *do* respond to sensory experiences. It has tended to be dismissed as 'psychology', or because it cannot be verified in the manner of science, or because it has been regarded by some philosophers as metaphysical or, simply nonsensical, as we shall see later. But, of course, it is useless to pick and choose when analysing what is going on in consciousness. Kant based his whole philosophy on a logical framework and as a result everything else became distorted. Carnap and others of the Vienna school would only accept sensory experience because this is verifiable by the method of science (27). Everything else, they claimed, is merely an expression of 'emotion' and is therefore false. But sensory experiences cannot be understood *without* describing accurately the responses to these experiences. Hence my next step in the description of consciousness is to examine these responses.

There is much confusion, even in books on philosophy and psychology, over the terminology used to describe some states of consciousness and how they relate to one another. Hence, care will be taken over definitions and classification of the ways in which the subject responds to sensory experiences, including encounters with other people."

"Is it not the case that the subjective, the mind, has been regarded as a dark and difficult subject? But since psychology is a science, it should be able to give a reasonably accurate description of it."

"That is true. But descriptions in psychology, as in philosophy, have been marred by the tendency to become entangled in metaphysics – explanations of how things are thought to work.

Kant (23) uses *categories of the understanding* to explain how the sensory world is linked to the subjective, whereas I only describe what can be observed, namely, sensory experience plus the Sensibilities that I am about to describe.

Instead of Kant's logical approach, psychologists make reference to a different metaphysical frame and describe the subconscious, the preconscious, archetypes and some aspects of dream analysis that are used in therapeutics. But these go beyond things of which we can be aware. In dreams, rational and logical functions are in abeyance, but the sensibilities do still function to some degree. Here, the psychotherapist takes advantage of the fact that the subject may become aware of sensibilities that are kept hidden when fully conscious. But psychology as a science can be used legitimately to compare and contrast aspects of the subjective as between *different subjects.*

My task is different; it is to describe in the first place, those aspects of the subjective *common* to most people. Sensory experience gives knowledge of the subject as a body, a thing in motion, and describes its relations to the objective dimension containing other bodies, animate and inanimate. The Sensibilities describe the *responses* of the subject to these sensory experiences. But responses must include acting in ways that are in accordance with the principles governing the functions of the sensory-motor axis. Hence, the responses must be about motivation and events in consciousness must include a description of this phenomenon."

"We have been discussing how sensory experience is acquired and converted into a usable form, which is knowledge. But this, as I understand, would be quite purposeless if it were not possible to make use of it?"

"I agree and therefore, onto this foundation of sensory experience is brought to bare the *Sensibilities*, which are the ways in which the subject is *able to respond to*, and therefore make use of, those experiences. These responses are essential, for otherwise knowledge, for example scientific knowledge, as described so far remains totally useless. It would be like a car with all the necessary parts but no driver to give the motivation to respond to events and achieve objectives. The three Sensibilities do this and these include the essence of human values.

But one can anticipate the description of values in the light of the discussion so far. The sensibilities are activated when the subject is exposed to sensory experiences. They are the various ways in which it is possible to respond to those experiences, as opposed to the possibility of responding through the manifolds of Kant's Categories (23). The sensibilities provide the *driver*: the motivation, direction and purpose; that is, the use to which the car is to be put. I do not think that this description of the relationships between sensory experience and the sensibilities has been accurately described in philosophy.

The subject responds simultaneously to each sensibility, (Feelings, Aesthetics and Values), and hence the action that follows is usually a composite response to these three in combination. This is a much more complex response than is found in the animal with its response primarily or entirely confined to feelings.

Another fundamental point is that each of the main Sensibilities, for Feeling, Aesthetic and Value, is made up of an indefinite number of specific sensibilities. These are generated by the beliefs of individuals in response to specific environmental circumstances, or specific beliefs, natural or supernatural that an individual may hold. It follows that the responses to sensory experiences are complex. We are embarking on a description of the minome and the structure being described *must be capable of responding to all the complexities that exist.*

<u>Motivation and Beliefs are from the Sensibilities</u>

Clearly there is motivation to hunt in the animal, but in the human when there is language and speech, beliefs accompany motivation. Thus, particular motives accompany the beliefs of religion, the tenets of a political party, the hope of a good holiday, or acts that will affect the welfare of other persons for good or ill. The permanency or otherwise of beliefs varies from the transient to life long. The intensity of beliefs varies greatly from the fanatical extreme to the benign and benevolent of a minimalist philosophy or of some religion."

"Can you expand on your rather dramatic suggestion that whenever there is motivation, there is a belief that something is true or that some event will occur? When I am day dreaming, or night dreaming, ideas flow but there is no awareness of motivation or belief."

"That is true, but when exposed to sensory experience, the position is different. You are frequently confronted with making decisions such as, 'is that right?' The directing agent interrupts the flow and the subject's ideas expand on this to produce a fully developed case that so and so is good and certain actions would be right. I call these conclusions beliefs because they take the form of verdicts on the past and postulates or hypotheses about the future. You hope that such and such will turn out to be true but cannot be certain. These are the starting points for systems of ideas on all subjects, as mentioned above.

In general, the sensibilities give a sense of direction and purpose as well as providing the motivation to achieve objectives. They draw on sensory information and apply the relevant motor activity – in accordance, for example, with the ways in which the sensory-motor axis operates in the human. We are able to do this because the sensibilities bring into the light of consciousness unique dimensions of awareness that sensory experience alone does not provide, and without the sensibilities there would be no point or purpose in having the highly developed and sophisticated abilities that produce knowledge, for it would not be possible to use it.

Each of the sensibilities is accompanied by commotions in consciousness that are unique to the function and purpose of the particular sensibility evoked, and these commotions are accompanied by the motivating ability to respond to the sensibility aroused."

"Why do you link the sensibility and motivation?"

"Because that is what is actually observed. These points will become clearer when the sensibilities have been described. I will be maintaining that the source of all motivation is from the sensibilities and mediated by the abilities. This is how the axis mechanism operates and must be regarded as an intrinsic property of human understanding. Note that I do not imply that something called 'motivation' exists any more than causation or energy exists (20). It simply describes the relations between responsive ideas and sensory experience.

The fact that motives are determined by the sensibilities has led some to the view that human actions are not 'free', so that choice does not exist: the brain is a clockwork mechanism. The assertion that there is no choice because the mind is mechanistic cannot be proven. And to assert the opposite also cannot be proven.

What *can* be validated scientifically is that choices made are influenced by things such as specific genes and, for example, by strong sensibility responses and by belief systems as in religion. But we do not know how many and to what degree other factors influence choice. It is obvious that when choosing a, b, or c, we do not start with a blank sheet: we are hedged about by the environment on the one hand, and on the other, our sensibilities and abilities, that is, our physical and mental capacities to respond, that vary from person to person. Although these impose limitations on what at first sight appears to be 'free choice,' that is how the understanding works. To argue that these environmental and subjective limitations remove *all* freedom is a metaphysical belief for which there is no conclusive evidence (see the discussion page 57).

The order of appearance of the Sensibilities following birth seems likely to correspond to the order of their appearance in evolutionary history. Feelings are probably present from birth and increase strongly to their full development by the beginning of adolescence. The Aesthetic Sensibility appears approximately between three and six years and develops fully during adolescence. The Value Sensibility is not there significantly below about ten years, which is why indoctrination with a belief system before that age is possible through the implantation of a pre-formed ethical profile, (see ethics, 16). But I will contend that awareness of values could not form without pre-existing *feeling* sensibilities. It will become evident also that a person could not develop their own ethical profile without the simultaneous awareness of the presence of the other sensibilities."

"In describing the sensibilities, are you not inventing things, and attributing to them the idea of motivation – indulging in the luxury of metaphysics in order to explain things otherwise inexplicable? When does a description become metaphysical? I take it that all understanding, that is, making sense of things, involves rationality/logic/number. These are involved in the acquisition of scientific knowledge, yet this is not metaphysical. So why does the understanding   of   responsive   knowledge   tend   to   become metaphysical?"

"It does not become metaphysical! The responses may be regarded as the imprints on sensory experience that the subjective, the minome, makes possible. I want to make the position very clear here, for this is where descriptions go wrong. Rationality, logic and number are subjective functions that are legitimately applicable *only to the analysis of sensory experience.* It is wholly inappropriate to apply these in an attempt to analyse other subjective functions. The reason for this is that these functions are not analysable, for there is nothing to analyse. GE Moore put this very clearly in his book, *Principia Ethica*[18] and I will return to it later (15).

The mistake has been to apply logical methods to minome functions. I think it has at last been appreciated that this does not work. If you *do* apply logic, you end with metaphysics. Understanding the sensibilities is simply a matter of following the descriptions in the discussions to follow carefully. Everyone has similar although not identical awareness of the various sensibilities.

The evolutionary development of the sensibilities is important. The animal, operating under the control of the primitive sensory-motor mechanism, responds to sensations of hunger, sex, pain etc, with various feeling sensibilities and these are accompanied by the motivation to achieve appropriate objectives. There is always a choice of goals. The basic model is: sensory information > feeling response, > choice of objective > motor action.

But during the course of evolution, the objectives sought have gone well beyond the animal requirements of searching for food, avoidance of pain, self-preservation and reproduction. Preservation for the human becomes a search for self-preservation in response to fears and then, much later in evolution, the preservation of other beings, for without them, present day human societies would not function. These objectives have become possible on account of the other Sensibilities.

By this further extension, there is the objective of preservation in the broadest sense that will maximize human welfare and minimize the fears of disease and mortality. This is achieved by

---

[18] *Principia Ethica* GE Moore Cambridge University Press 1903

extension of the primitive self-preservation responses motivated by the Feeling Sensibility to include an accompanying Value Sensibility response with variable beliefs attached.

The development during the course of evolution of the three Sensibilities has made it possible to tackle a variety of social problems and find new solutions. We will see towards the end of this story that philosophers are somewhat at a loss to know what the future role of philosophy is to be. But I think it has a great deal to contribute towards solving current problems. We must remember John Locke, whose work is now sometimes disparaged, wrote in the 17th century: 'it is ambition enough to be employed as an under-labourer in clearing the ground a little and removing some of the rubbish that lies in the way of knowledge'. I maintain that there is still plenty of rubbish lying in the way of knowledge

Discussion 10

The Feeling Sensibility

The Feeling Sensibility is a spectrum of sensibilities operating in a similar fashion. It is the only Sensibility that is present in animals, but in man it has many distinctive, additional features. It is the most primitive and basic of the three Sensibilities. All feeling sensibilities are associated with desires, or instincts, that is, motivation directed towards particular, selected targets. This implies the desire of the subject to change in some way the bodily status in relation to the environment, including other humans, in order to achieve different feelings that accord with the subject's desired needs or objectives.

As we have seen (5), sensations give rise to distinct sensory experiences in consciousness from within the body and from without via the sensory organs. The *feeling sensibilities are quite separate from these sensations* and are distinct commotions in consciousness that are *provoked* by and are responses to specific sensory experiences. They are expressed by the use of such terms as satisfaction, comfort, contentment, relief, pleasure, happiness, anger, fear, frustration, misery, sorrow and all the various feelings associated with love and hate. It will be apparent from this list that these sensibilities arise in response to internal bodily sensations, but mainly to sensations from without, including inanimate and animate objects, especially other humans. The list does not include such responses as remorse, guilt and righteousness for example, for these are responses from the Value Sensibility.

Primitive life, without consciousness, or perhaps at the very earliest stage of the development of conscious life, responds to the sensory experience of feeling pain and hunger with a feeling sensibility response of unpleasantness, which is motivating. On the other hand, if there were no state of consciousness such sensory experiences would evoke reflex responses, requiring only a nervous system without a brain and consciousness. This would limit the possibilities of the response. When there *is* consciousness, however, such responses must be recognised as feeling sensibilities of the simplest kind.

In order for a sensibility to operate, at this primitive level of consciousness there must be sensory information from within the body and from the environment outside, which includes other bodies. At some point in evolution skin sensations +/- visual and +/- auditory sensations appear. Thus, hunger pains produce unpleasant feelings within and an integral accompaniment of these feelings is the motivation to remove them. Feeling motivation activates the motor response side of the primitive axis and results in actions that are inevitably on a trial and error basis. And here one sees the origin of choices, for these, as a result of experience, lead to ever more efficient and effective responses. And as a consequence of the operation of evolutionary factors it is not difficult to appreciate how primitive consciousness becomes ever more sophisticated. The feeling responses and actions increase in number and complexity. And in modern times, science and technology have vastly increased the power and range of possible responses by extending exposure to new environmental situations.

The chief drives, or kinds of motivation that accompany feelings have to do with the avoidance of pain and fear, the search for pleasure, sex and therefore survival, and the power to achieve these ends by various means, including aggression. The feelings that appear in consciousness, like the sensations to which they are responses, form a continuous background throughout waking hours, which modify the behaviour of the subject in the direction of promoting the subject's own welfare and happiness, *irrespective* of the welfare of others. Clearly, these sensibilities have nothing to do with ethical motivation and are 'animal-like'. They are instinctive, meaning that there is a strong tendency in the case of some feelings to appear and cause the subject to respond in certain ways. This is seen most clearly in the cases of the responses to the sensation of hunger and to sensations from the sexual organs.

From the moment of waking in the morning, ideas and feelings flow through consciousness that may include events from the memory, but also possible events of the day yet to come and how they are to be managed, arousing hopes, anxieties, conviction, confidence, or possible failure. One knows that the future is never a clear blue sky and may be dark and stormy. We speak of moods, which may vary from elation to depression. It is these subtleties of feeling and the ideas that accompany them that form a continuous background to all other events in consciousness arising from the other Sensibilities.

Apart from this, the main function of the feeling sensibilities is to *motivate the subject to use Abilities* in the form of motor skills in order to achieve desired objectives. Feelings have strong outward expressions, so that others know clearly what the subject's feelings are. They take the form of facial expressions and often bodily actions, as in anger. These outward expressions of feeling are often said to re-enforce *'emotions'*. But emotion is an unsatisfactory term because it is used in various ill-defined ways. I use *'emotion' solely to describe facial and other bodily expressions of feeling*. It follows from these characteristics that feelings come from the part of consciousness that often communicates with other beings most strongly and directly. Facial and other outward expressions of feeling are seen most strikingly in higher animals as well as humans.

That may appear to be false when we come to consider the strength of the Value Sensibilities: for example, the opinion that 'the action of X is extremely evil'. But one has to remember that the formation and expression of values could not happen *without prior* feelings, a point that I will be stressing later. The point is that without prior feelings (and for that matter prior aesthetic responses), *there would be nothing for the Value Sensibility to respond to*. That is why I maintain that the three Sensibilities always operate in unison.

Also, feelings are of relatively short duration, but can be repeatedly evoked and in this they differ from the Aesthetic and Value Sensibilities. But some feelings may be prolonged and then we speak of a mood of elation, for example, when we are happy and the world seems an enjoyable place. This mood is strongly, but not entirely due to feelings. We are only able to experience this mood because, occasionally, we may experience black depression. Feeling sensibilities are therefore a powerful means whereby individuals interact with each other in a given environment. Feelings are possibly the most powerful force governing human relations. Extremes of feelings produce sadistic and masochistic individuals, for example. But, it will be evident that if feelings were the totality of human conscious activity we would not be human, but remain as animals."

"It could be argued that the behaviour of some humans

demonstrates that they operate primarily at that level of maturity. And this often seems to have a sexual basis."

"Much work has been done, such as that of **Panksepp,** and vastly more will follow to compare animal with human feelings and behaviour[19]. It emphasises how basic human feelings are, for similarities can be found between normal and also some abnormal patterns of behaviour in the human and behaviour in rats, mice as well as higher animals.

Sexuality dominates the feeling relationships between humans and expresses itself in a multiplicity of ways. It begins to express itself within a year or two of birth in that children at this early age may show the beginnings of gender differences. These increase during early childhood and show marked differences during adolescence; but as you know, there are many variations and these cause great ethical problems in the current, still relatively primitive phase of social development. But the actual description of these is quite straightforward. Some males are attracted to males who are adults, but others are attracted to children, male or female. The same variations from the norm apply to females. These are biological variations for which there are no explanations at present and simply have to be accepted. But as we shall find, it is ethical beliefs about what is right and wrong in this context that create endless problems.

Sexuality is the feeling sensibility that binds individuals into tribes and modern societies. This is also true for all the variants of sexuality. The homosexual feels a part of society just as the heterosexual does.

But social problems arise when there is any deviation from whatever is regarded as the norm, whether in sexual preferences, colour of skin, physical strength or other departures from an indefinable norm. These quickly arouse hatred, aggression and bullying at young ages and lead to categorising on a moral basis among adults. Hence, as I have just said, societies are still relatively primitive."

"How are these to be overcome?"

---

[19] *Affective Neuroscience: The Foundations of Human and Animal Emotions* Jaak Panksepp. Oxford University Press 2004 (paperback)

"Only by accepting biological facts for what they are and not attempting to impose ethical beliefs as though 'some humans know best' and by implication, the rest must obey.

Deviations from the norm of all feelings are relatively easy to recognize. This illustrates the power of feelings and the fact that they persist without change throughout life, except for some mellowing with age.

Discussion 11

We have to continue our description to find out what it is that makes us human. And the answer is that we possess two additional Sensibilities not found in animals. The first of these is the Aesthetic Sensibility.

<u>The Aesthetic Sensibility</u>

This Sensibility, like Feeling, is a spectrum of sensibilities exhibiting a unique commotion in consciousness associated with motivation that attracts or repels animate and inanimate objects. Unlike the dictionary definition of the aesthetic, it is in reality a spectrum of sensibilities extending from the attractive and beautiful to the repulsive and ugly. We cannot be indifferent but can suspend judgement. The slightest change in the appearance of a face, for example, may make the difference between attraction and repulsion.

There is no perfect beauty or extreme of ugliness. Therefore there can be no question of measurement, and this applies to all the Sensibilities."

"Can you make that distinction clearer?"

"Take areas of yellow and green of particular shapes. These can be given linguistic and mathematical expression in various precise and measurable ways, which thus become sensory knowledge. Bur that is not what the Sensibilities are! Those who have tried to 'verify' a sensibility, as in scientific work, inevitably fail. They confuse the use of abilities to obtain knowledge of the sensory world with the *responses* to this experience, which we are now discussing.

The aesthetic response to this experience of colour would be to attract or repel and the appropriate linguistic expression of this would become an item of responsive knowledge somewhere in the beautiful/ugly spectrum.

The *motivation* to attract or repel is present, as with feelings, but the Aesthetic Sensibility is unique in that it is directed outwards towards animate and inanimate objects including other humans and includes the subject's own bodily appearances. If it were not for the self-consciousness awareness of the latter, we would be oblivious of how we appear and act in all social contexts: thus we distinguish a cultured and civilised appearance and behaviour from behaviour judged to be uncouth or objectionable. This response, as we shall see, has important repercussions when taken together with the feeling and value responses."

"I remember you making that point in our earlier conversations when I was younger and said something to the effect that, 'I think my hair style seen in a mirror is super', which is a subjective response about myself. But your reply was that the exterior of my body exposed to sensory impressions is a part of the environment."

"Yes it is. The Aesthetic Sensibility does not only appear transiently at appropriate moments to supply judgements about a hairstyle, or the beauty or ugliness of a picture, for example. Most, and perhaps all, sensory experiences become invested with responsive aesthetic awareness. And since sensory input is continuous during waking life, there is a virtually continuous background of feeling, aesthetic and, as we shall find, value responses to all activities. This is essential for the way humans live and exploit their capacities to the full, including the pursuit of technical skills. Artistry, for example, permeates religion, war, architecture, furnishing and fine art.

Aesthetics are a feature of all responses and even the mathematician takes cognisance of the aesthetic[20]. **Paul Dirac** (1902-1984) commenting on a result said, 'If one is working from the point of view of getting beauty into one's equation, one is on a sure line of progress'[21]. The scientist sees beauty through the microscope and the astronomer likewise through the telescope. The soldier adorns his weapons and music adds to the pomp and circumstance of war. Fashion plays an enormous part in social life. It can be appreciated that this Sensibility has a spectrum that spans all human activity at all times. Probably most of the desires of humans today spring from the aesthetic: one has only to mention the appeal of, and desire for the car!

It has already been emphasised that this Sensibility operates

---

[20] The Road to Reality - Roger Penrose. BCA publications 2004

[21] Scientific American 208 (5) (1963) - Paul Dirac

only in the presence of prior feelings. The aesthetic sensibilities modulate the subject's responses to the feeling sensibilities, and together these determine the responses to the totality of relevant sensory experience. They participate in helping to give direction and purpose to all activities. I say 'helping' because the Value Sensibility has an even more powerful influence on our overall behaviour.

We shall find that the value sensibilities could not function effectively, and probably not at all, without concurrent responses to feeling and aesthetic experiences. They also are always in play and act to motivate. Value responses oversee feeling and aesthetic responses and have a modulating function, as we shall find. The Aesthetic and Value Sensibilities are crucial to all human relationships. We do not have options, and respond to sensory experiences necessarily using all three Sensibilities.

Later I shall discuss the significance and manifestations of all three Sensibilities through what I later call the 'riches of the universe' and in the context of the lives of specific individuals (33, 34, 35 and 36).

For some, a garden is a constant requirement because it gives access to those riches. For others, access is via the sound of, or the composition of music, or by playing an instrument. And for still others, experience of the world of sensory experience is in nature, or its portrayal through a brush on canvas

Discussion 12

The Value Sensibility

This Sensibility is also unique to humans. It is a commotion in consciousness that finds expression in highly distinctive ideas. But before the appearance of Greek science and philosophy, these ideas were focussed on beliefs, which obscured the essence of the Sensibility. When, after the Renaissance, the beliefs that had made man the central point and purpose of the universe had faded, the idea of *human,* or more accurately, *noetic values* then became more apparent, as I will explain in a moment. Their main characteristics are the awareness that there is something about a human that is intrinsically valuable."

"I think you maintain that every sensibility carries with it a belief."

"Let me explain. We only become aware of Value and the other Sensibilities when expressed in terms of the belief that X is beautiful or Y is good. But the attachment of specific beliefs over time may change or disappear, so I conclude that there is something there that is independent of belief and enables us to respond in these ways. In other words, it seems that we can be aware of values without the necessity of specific beliefs. But, I have to add that the hidden something is only *revealed* by belief. This is entirely in keeping with minomic functions that are only revealed when put to use. How do we do that wisely?

This awareness of values begins when the subject attaches intrinsic value to his/her life and this has doubtless existed among humans for many millennia. But more recently there has been an increasing realisation of the significance of the *value status* of other humans. This has been written about by many, but **Shaftesbury** (1631-1713),[22] [23] who collaborated with Locke, clarified this

---

[22] *Inquiry Concerning Virtue and Merit* Shaftesbury 1699

[23] *Characteristics of Men, Manners, Opinions* Shaftesbury 1711. See Shaftsbury's *Philosophy of Religion and Ethics* by S. Green, Athens, Ohio, 1967

distinction, as a principle of ethics that has gained wide acceptance today. He spoke of a 'moral sense' not necessarily accompanied by belief, which is the Value Sensibility"

"That presumably expresses an attitude of benevolence?"

"Yes, and the motivations that accompany these values include, for example, the idea of responsibility for others. But the value response that conveys value status varies from what you might consider good and benevolent to what another person night judge to be evil and malevolent. As a consequence, the sensory experiences portraying behaviour, plus the feeling and aesthetic responses of that other being are judged by the subject to be good or evil and the actions right or wrong. This event is the essence of ethics and clearly is an enormous leap forwards from the position in the animal, which does not have these reservations about the value status of other beings.

I distinguish between the conscious awareness of something valuable and the ideas used to express these values. It is the awareness of value that is primary; ideas then cluster around the specific sensibility and may be given vocal and linguistic expression. Beliefs then form and may change on reflection or may last indefinitely, even a lifetime. This contrasts with feelings, which tend to form rapidly, for example anger, and are usually of short duration. Aesthetic responses last longer but tend to change with new sensory experiences."

"We discussed earlier how beliefs form, but what are beliefs?"

"This is an important question. You will recall that the acquisition of scientific knowledge begins with an hypothesis, the belief that something is true. When proven to be true it becomes an item of scientific knowledge, but that is still regarded as a belief, which stands until a better result is obtained. Now responsive knowledge differs in important respects. A person regards X as good and that belief stands until that person is persuaded by new evidence that Y is a greater good."

"But how does one arrive at any belief: why is X regarded as better than Y?"

"Now we arrive at the fundamentals and limits of human understanding! As each person gains more experience, a system of beliefs about all manner of things is built up, (a process of ethical profiling that I will discuss later). These beliefs are modified and re-built in many respects in response to evolving external events, including advances in scientific knowledge – new advances in medical treatment, for example, but also in weapons of mass destruction.

You ask: how do we arrive at these beliefs? We have streams of ideas posing questions passing through consciousness and potentially, an endless stream of answers that together may create an infinite regress. Theoretically, what is believed to be good is replaced by something better, but in view of the flow of ideas, no final conclusion is possible. If this were the case, clearly no opinion could be formulated about anything. *It is the selection from this stream of what appears to be a good quality 'fish', or set of ideas that creates the opportunity to select and 'land' it.* It then must be 'processed', or converted into a belief. This essential step of conversion into linguistic form is necessary before the belief becomes of use; that is, communicable to others. Later I will explain why it is necessary to distinguish between a stream if *ideas* and specific *beliefs* that have been fished from the stream, converted into language and then expressed as a well-defined belief (28). Once that happens, the belief may be temporary or become life-long."

"How are the 'fish' made use of – we don't eat them!"

"The ideas may form your plan for the day, a chapter in a book you are writing, the solution to a scientific problem, etc.

It is worth noting that the streams of ideas are frequently interrupted by transient sensory experiences, which is why fruitful 'thinking' is best done in quiet places. But thought may become seriously impaired for some people by frequent sensory interference and amounts to an illness.

Belief in an ethical value motivates the individual and thereby affects others in the community for good or ill. When the sensibilities convey the idea of *benevolence*, the cohesiveness of the community is increased, but contrary values may cause violence and disruption. The idea of benevolence leads to acts carrying *responsibility*.

Twenty first century democracy, however, exhibits an additional important phenomenon because government has taken increasing responsibility for the welfare of individuals who exhibit, for example, poverty, malnutrition, lack of education, or ill health. The consequences have been that many individuals opt out of responsibility for their own welfare and blame society for all their failings. The abandonment of individual responsibilities has become a new problem awaiting solution.

One has to remember that all the sensibilities are open-ended: there are no absolutes so that any judgement inevitably takes the form of selecting a point where belief forms somewhere on a scale. Nevertheless, as in science, the objective is to arrive at ever greater accuracy."

"To what end? Accuracy of what?"

"Judgements can only refer to the natural world and the welfare of subjects in society, or welfare in a non-natural, or supernatural world.

The Value Sensibility takes on a unique and heightened significance on account of the ever-present awareness in the human of *mortality*. It has become enhanced as philosophy and science have more clearly defined a dimension of the Sensibilities that is inherently unknowable. And for the Sensibilities, that is another way of stating that an inherent property is open-endedness."

"And I suppose knowledge from the sensibilities becomes enhanced when one considers the position in the animal kingdom: one species perforce depends upon the destruction of another for food and therefore existence. Bearing in mind these ugly biological facts, plus disease in all living things, it does not seem surprising that humans have to climb a steep ethical mountain to an unknown destination in order to try and escape from their inherited predicament."

"I would emphasise that it is through belief systems of infinite variety that humans have learned to accommodate to this predicament that includes the unknowable dimensions that encompass them on all sides.

I call all values that belong to, or are associated with ideas about the subject, or self, *'noetic values*[24]*'*. The expression 'human

---

[24] *Noetic Values* Richard Matthew 1999 (unpublished)

values' often carries connotations such as religious beliefs, that for the moment I wish to avoid, although beliefs of some kind inevitably form. But when specific beliefs are identified and rigorously set aside, the awareness of values remains undimmed. There remains awareness of good, or evil; right, or wrong, together with the awareness of awe, dread, or mystery accompanied by the awareness of something unknowable. These are the responses to sensory experiences; they are about conditions in this world and these responses are the foundation of the ethical dimension (15). They are the basis for the formation of the *ethical profile*, an inevitable and unavoidable composite of ideas and values, unique to each individual, as we shall see.

The view I am developing, especially with respect to all three Sensibilities, I believe to be an accurate description. It offers a unified description of brain functions and their relations to sensory experience in such a way as to make explicit the relations between the so-called subjective and objective dimensions of consciousness. It avoids the confused anthropomorphic fallacy of attributing human characteristics to non-human entities, such as gods or planets.

The Value Sensibilities are not exteriorised in the same direct and immediate fashion as the Feeling and Aesthetic Sensibilities. As I have emphasised, they are a response to these other two Sensibilities. Value sensibilities are at the heart of the inner, subjective and largely hidden aspects of the personality. They are therefore the most difficult for others to know, accommodate to and understand. But what is within, what gives rise to *the idea of meaning,* in so far as this is possible, is from all three Sensibilities.

Conscious life is in one sense a dual existence because the inner life can never be fully exteriorised. What is revealed as the 'self' is what appears to other people as a consequence of responses to environmental experiences. The subject keeps hidden what is judged to be harmful to the 'self' and reveals only what is thought to be advantageous.

Although we control to some degree what remains subjective and what is exteriorised, it will be evident that it is not possible to exteriorise everything, nor is it possible to keep everything subjective. Human nature is such that we are forced to communicate with the environment in order to survive, or we die.

But the private, subjective dimension is indispensable because that is where all thought takes place and choices are made. It is where all scientific and responsive knowledge is formed. All three Sensibilities *motivate* the abilities to give outward expression to ideas and actions."

"Is the Value Sensibility more important, or more powerful than the others?"

"In an important sense it is. It is involved in all thought because it is always active in combination with the other Sensibilities. We have seen that feelings dominate all motivation in the animal world. And there, the Ability-Feeling mechanism obviously functions well without values for survival purposes. But in humans, feelings have a strong effect on all ethical values held: it would not be possible to arrive at ethical evaluations without prior feelings because values appraise and modulate feelings; that is how values work. The value sensibilities could not function in the absence of pre-existing commotions in consciousness due to feelings, aesthetics and their potentials for promoting motivation. Values felt by the subject must be derived from *something* in order to arrive at a moral decision. That 'something' is the feeling and aesthetic responses to other individuals. All such decisions are the subject's verdict on his/her own feelings and the actions they may cause him/her to carry out in response to the ideas/actions of another person, or persons.

The Sensibility profile differs from subject to subject and this makes the dominant feelings of one person choleric, for example, and another subdued, or even tempered. Such innate differences are reflected in the ethical responses. Thus, one person may have strongly expressed moral values and another does not, at least outwardly. These differences have important consequences for individual behaviour. I do not want to go into details here, for that is a matter for psychologists, but one thing can be said: there is no evidence that the Sensibilities vary throughout life. Once they have become set before and during adolescence, the fundamentals remain unchanged, although the details of their outward expression may change dramatically in response to environmental events or belief systems acquired."

"So is it the modulating effect of Values on the other

Sensibilities that makes us human?"

"Yes it is. And it is the dynamic relationships between these that comprise the ethical dimension. When we relate to other beings in terms of moral values, again we have to relate to something, and that something is the observed thoughts and actions of that other person, which are the consequences of that person's own Feeling, Aesthetic and Value Sensibilities that make up his/her ethical profile."

"What about the murderer who receives 'therapy' through religion, or by other means, and is then thought to be 'cured' and allowed back into the community?"

"Therapeutic attempts to support weak or anomalous value sensibilities, which have failed to protect the subject from his own feelings, often sexual, are potentially dangerous and unreliable as a criterion for allowing freedom to live in society. But, of course, if there has been great provocation, or if there is evidence of remorse (indicating that feelings had over-ridden values), then these must be taken into account and are evidence that 'therapy' may help. Also futile is the attempt to change dominant, uncontrollable feeling sensibilities."

"Another point, which may explain some of these cases. Some subjects do not seem to be aware of the difference between their strong feelings about an incident and their ethical response to it. They tend to think that strong feelings *are* what make their ethical judgements right. Is that due to lack of education, or an impaired sense of values?"

"It may be either, but there is an important additional reason for confusion. The Utilitarians, Bentham and Mill, held that the highest value equates with the greatest happiness[25]. Equating Values with Feelings leads to dangerous errors. Kant was aware of this confusion and his solution was to assert the existence of God as the over-riding authority (23, 24).

"Why do humans fight over colour, customs, race and beliefs as well as natural resources?"

---

[25] *Utilitarianism* Reprinted in *The English Utilitarians* J Plamenatz, Blackwell 1949

"A feature of the Sensibilities is that, although the patterns laid down cannot be altered, all are responsive in variable degrees to educational and general cultural influences. In fact, these are what primarily distinguish a community that considers itself civilised from others. People who fight over colour etc have not learned to accept the tolerances that are the norm in a civilised community.

But this field is so obscured by belief systems that it has only been possible recently for certain western democracies to establish a core set of values that characterise a culture that is not dedicated to specific beliefs. In this field of discussion, there are eggshells all over the place! And when immigrants with a different belief system appear, a delicate balance may be upset.

A more difficult problem arises when a community is threatened by war, or decides to make war. An individual may decide that to kill is evil and therefore wrong. But the circumstances may appear to make war justifiable and therefore right for the community as a whole. There is no way at present of resolving differences between the individual and the communal positions. In theory, the evil of war will diminish or even be resolved when the expression of ethical opinions by individuals comes to have a global reach, rather than be restricted to ethical profiles in the interests of the tribe, community, nation, or religion.

An ethical system based on common beliefs, as we have seen, exists when the *value status* of another is accepted as equal to that of the subject. By extension, ideally, this ethical profile then becomes the profile of the community and even the wider global community. You may think that far-fetched, but we do think globally today about many things.

It will now be obvious that without values, social relations based on benevolence, tolerance, altruism and forgiveness would instead be based on lines similar to the aggressive, destructive self-interest of the animal kingdom. **Hobbes** (1588-1679)[26] thought that the latter applies in human societies, but fortunately it has been found since then that the number of humans with a sufficiently well developed awareness of values is such as to make relations based on

---

[26] *Leviathan*   Hobbes (1651)

common values possible for most educated communities.

These cultural factors have been confused over millennia due to lack of knowledge of the facts about human biological inheritance. This is another area in which beliefs have totally obscured the biological facts. These aspects of ethics have been regarded variously as determined by hidden powers and religious doctrines.

Strife due to these factors is on account of failure to endow other categories of beings with equal value status, so the actions of the subject become largely based on subjective feelings. In fact, it is primarily sexual feelings that are the glue that hold herds, primitive tribes and modern human societies together. But, despite this, motives for strife do arise from other feeling sensibilities and also from value sensibilities, particularly when faith based beliefs strongly influence the outward expression of all three Sensibilities.

This is a convenient place to mention some other properties of the Sensibilities. I emphasised that all three contribute to motivation and choice. But we have also discussed examples of the exchange or substitution of one sensibility for another. For example, we may use the language of values but be motivated primarily by aggressive feelings. Also, it is possible for one value sensibility to be substituted for another. Thus, it may be thought right to kill one person if ten others will be saved. Or, it is justifiable to kill in war to save the community. These are difficult ethical problems that we cannot pursue."

"Allied to this is what causes an individual to become a suicide bomber? He strongly believes in the rightness of what he does. Belief in supernatural guidance appears to place his own values above everyone else's."

"Such an individual has an intense *religious* belief that after death there is an existence infinitely better than that on earth. There is a failure to grasp some of the basic points now built into the ethical profiles of Western Democracies, especially the value status of other beings and the need for tolerance that this brings about. It is an example of the harm that religious beliefs can do."

"What about the growing number in the West without religious beliefs?"

"There is no evidence that the sensibilities in such people are any less strong or long-lasting. Those without religious beliefs are still dependent upon beliefs in order to behave ethically. We have seen that all understanding works on the basis of beliefs that are held to be true, at least for a period of time.

You will appreciate now that it is impossible to describe, discuss and even practice science without mention of the sensibilities. The history and philosophy of science does not therefore make sense without considering its relations to the sensibilities."

"Many philosophers and scientists, especially during the 20th century, seemed to believe that understanding the universe hinges on confining their attention to sensory experience and the application of logic and mathematics."

"They take the view that for statements to be accepted as true the proof had to conform with methods applicable to sensory experience, but as we have found, they ignore aspects of consciousness that I have described and normal people are clearly aware of. My approach has been to include all aspects of consciousness in understanding, for if you leave anything out, you can be sure that error will follow. In fact the problem has been to tease out from initially confused, or unclear ideas more accurate descriptions of the subjective phenomena of which we are aware. It is true that the origin of the sensibilities, like the origin of sensory experience, is unknowable, but that does not justify ignoring whatever appears to be inconvenient."

"Much of this discussion seems to have been more about psychology than philosophy."

"That is because, in order to convey the properties of the subjective, it is necessary to illustrate how the mind operates"

Discussion 13

We have approached the problem of consciousness by considering its various elements, but what we need is a unified description. The *advancing edge of consciousness*, which gives the sense of 'being alive' at each instant, is sensory experience. The related events that we immediately become aware of are the *responses* to sensory experience in the form of *Ideas*. Memory enables these to be retained and re-called. Both of these are clearly functions of the brain about which a great deal more will become evident with further research. Although the ideas with which we respond to sensory experiences are in themselves mysterious, it is essential to describe their properties correctly.

The first point to note is that ideas cannot be communicated to other persons until they have been converted into a linguistic and/or mathematical form and this is discussed later (28). Having appeared, ideas are never 'free-floating' as it were; they are always in the embrace of the Sensibilities, as already described. And this applies also to strictly scientific ideas because these also are never formed in isolation. There is always the striving for new ideas, the sense of success or failure; the search for the solution to a puzzle, even a crossword puzzle.

The content of the ideas is primarily visual and/or auditory so that it includes musical notation and composition. Ideas may have a content of supernatural phenomena. But these also must relate to sensory experiences in some way; otherwise they would be fictional or irrational. We have then a wide variety of ideas that together comprise the extent and content of consciousness. Those that are accepted as true in some sense we call beliefs."

"But where do they come from?"

"This is where I must introduce the concept of the Minome.

The Minome

We are able to describe ideas but not the hidden events that produce and control them. The minome (6) is the description of all those aspects of consciousness that are the *hidden* engines of everything that happens. I have used the term 'Sensibilities 'to describe hidden properties that control and direct all ideas. And whatever it is that produced the increasing complexity of the

Sensibilities during evolution is also hidden. Philosophers have used various terms to describe other hidden properties and these include *agent, apperception, motivation* or *will, logic* and *mathematics.*

It is at the advancing edge of consciousness that the so-called '*agent*', 'I', or 'self' operates to bring ideas into being and once in existence the Sensibilities determine their fate. This awareness of an agent is coupled with the sense of the mind being able to regard itself, that is, to be able to compare and contrast ideas and systems of ideas. It has been described as *apperception* and implies awareness that there is *control and direction* of actions focussed on specific objectives. This sense of control creates a fixed decision-making focus in an otherwise ever-changing sequence of ideas and sensory/responsive events. *It is this focal point that creates the familiar sense of the self, or I.* Clearly it is not inaccurate to speak of such a focal point as 'I', for all are very clearly aware of it.

Motivation was described earlier as a property of the Sensibilities (9) and this implied the impulse to act: to accept, reject or believe. 'Will' enters such discussions at various points but my conclusion is that it is a redundant term since it has been given various ill defined meanings in the past."

"What are we to make of these hidden properties that comprise the minome?"

"Like causation and energy in the physical world, they control ideas and makes things happen. In consciousness we are not aware of them directly, but only indirectly by what they do, that is, through their effects. They are invisible and indescribable. This subjective evidence of dynamism is somewhat reminiscent of the objective dynamic phenomena we are aware of in the physical universe: the dynamism of the sub-atomic particles that is also unknowable. Flux is a feature of all life."

"But how is subjective evidence from the minome and objective evidence from the genome related?"

"That is what neuro-scientists are busily investigating.

Energy is the term scientists use to explain, or rather describe the dynamism: of the very active processes observed in the world of quantum physics. This ceaseless motion of particles becomes indirectly evident in the motion of the common objects observed by the unaided senses in everyday life."

"How do these relate to the agency that we have been discussing?"

"You have to remember that everything we have discussed pertaining to consciousness is *also* the product of these busy particles. The quantum world describes the dynamic processes in all brain functions. It is not surprising therefore to observe the continuous flow of ideas into and out of consciousness and an invisible agent controlling and directing ideas. When the scientist investigates brain function, it is the *objective* dynamism of the quantum world that is being described. We, on the other hand, are describing the *subjective* dynamism behind all thinking. These activities appear functionally to be quite distinct, yet research is revealing close links between them.

The Implications of the Minomic Structure

We need to do some tidying up. Terms are introduced in order to achieve greater clarification or understanding, but often over time the result is overlap and redundancy of terms. So let us go back a little and review the position at which we have arrived.

Scientists have demonstrated that inanimate objects observed and the motions they display are constructed of matter; that is, atomic particles, combinations of atoms, or molecules, and the unknowable energy that moves them. From this dead world developed the living world, which is also constructed of the same matter and energy."

"But what is distinctive about the living world? We found that the simplest unicellular organism is a multi-molecular structure, but that does not make it 'alive'. So how does it differ from the dead matter around it?"

"Because its matter particles have developed the capacity to interact with other matter, alive or dead, around it. The distinctive feature is that the matter particles of the living cell are able to absorb the chemicals needed for survival and excrete other chemicals not required. How these two key processes developed we do not know. This was at first passive, but the organism soon became sufficiently complex to develop a new trick, the reflex. The organism became able to sense the nutrient it needed and actively retrieve it. Thus evolved the simplest sensory-motor axis.

This axis principle persisted, but became infinitely more

powerful when organisms with brains had evolved. Choices then became possible. The development of sensory organs and motor dexterity of many different kinds in a wide variety of species appeared and thereby increased the efficiency and effectiveness of the axis mechanism. This apparent 'inventiveness' made it appear as though one species vied with others for survival and the Darwinian theory described this principle as 'the survival of the fittest'.

We found that the axis mechanism, which had been so fruitful, gradually became more powerful through enhanced brain functions that put humans virtually in charge of their own destiny. This enhanced mechanism has taken over in some measure the 'blind' process in the animal kingdom of developing new mechanisms to meet new challenges to survival. And so one must assume that the evolution of the axis mechanism itself together with all its consequences must be driven by the hidden forces, or energy of the universe "

"So far, so good! But I have a few problems. The brain and body that became detached as a living unit with an axis mechanism, now has a minome that has taken charge and a brain that does what? Neuroscientists are finding ever more correlations between brain and mind or minomic functions. Some people are horrified that what is being discovered is a 'mechanistic' relation between brain and mind, so that the idea of god, for example, may be reduced to a function of nerve cells and the mind to a mere mechanism."

"We are a long way from knowing how brain/genome and brain/minome functions relate, even when such investigations have gone to completion, should that ever become possible. You will recall that genome and gene/brain relations exist but are not remotely 'mechanistic'. I suspect that similar, but probably looser correlations will apply to brain/minome relations on account of the major environmental factors that operate. After all, the machines that humans have made are nowhere to be found in nature.

We said that ideas *'represent' something unknowable in the sensory world.* The scientist works in that quite different dimension, so it is clear that ideas and brain function can never be logically related.

Responsive knowledge from the minome is the consequence of its functions. Consciousness differs from the minome in that it includes additionally the sum of *knowledge* that has been accumulated by an individual."

"It could be argued that what is unknowable can be ignored. How do the unknowable dimensions influence matters?"

"I must stress that nothing could be more important than these! Paradoxically, it is precisely *in the unknowable* that human feelings, aesthetics, and values reside. These dimensions we can neither ignore, nor understand. Hence it is this that has led to beliefs of religion and it is the management of beliefs that is our main concern. They were once described in terms of gods and unknown forces, but scientific enquiry has replaced these with energy (unknowable) as the dynamic agency. The counterpart of this in consciousness is the minome.

The unknowable inherent in subjective knowledge is described by many in terms of beliefs about the supernatural. But, like the gods of Homer and many other beliefs before and since, these tend to fade over time and become replaced by others, as was vividly described by **Matthew Arnold**[27]."

"How is it then that Hume (21) rightly claimed that, however carefully the subjective is examined, nothing identifiable as 'I' is detectable?"

"The paradox is brought about by the clear awareness that, on the one hand there is a control property, the agency, that is self evident, but which Hume ignored, presumably because he correctly took the view that it did not seem to refer to anything one could be directly aware of, but I think I have made the reason for that quite clear.

This is the point at which the unknowable, subjective 'I' and the unknowable objective properties of particle physics meet. It remains possible that some properties of the mysterious 'I' may be

---

[27] And you, ye stars! / You too once lived- / You too moved joyfully / Among august companions / In an older world peopled by Gods, / In a mightier order,/ The radiant, rejoicing Sons of Heaven! / But now you kindle / Your lovely, cold shining lights, / In the heavenly wilderness / For a younger, ignoble world. / And renew by necessity / Night after night your courses / Above a race you know not, / Uncaring and undelighted.   Matthew Arnold

discovered, but others will remain hidden. We have found that the self, or 'I' is merely the fixed reference point for all the dynamic events of objective experiences and subjective responses. It is not possible to 'prove' it exists. One cannot meet 'I' in the manner that Hume expected, but one can recognise that awareness of a control locus is simply part of the description of how the understanding operates. It is evident that without a control locus, the result would be chaos. In fact, many of the aberrations of mental activity take the form of loss of control of powerful subjective motivations in response to provocations from objective events.

The unfolding of the future, although a continuous process, is not all instantaneous. First, at each instant there are new sensory experiences that are immediately followed by sensibility responses. As explained, these will usually include elements from all three Sensibilities. But a final decision on motivation is preceded by the use of commonly used *enabling words* such as accept, reject, control, influence, choose, change of mind, recall, contrast, decide and compare. The use of such linguistic expressions is evidence of the ever-changing sensory experiences and responses to them that is a continuous feature of consciousness. This is a rapid assessment process that may also involve a review from memory of relevant sensory experiences, especially when continuing actions on the part of other individuals are involved. Also, there may be the recall from memory of past responses to events. Thus, the enabling words are used to allow appraisal of sensory experiences and the responses to these at the leading edge of consciousness and thereby arrive at acceptable adjustments, or changes of opinion, prior to motivation. Settled choices may take seconds, hours or days to arrive at, especially in the case of difficult ethical decisions.

The complexities of sensory and responsive knowledge are reduced by enabling words to arrive at relatively simple choices. This gives *perspective,* that is, we do not review objective or subjective evidence piece-meal, but as formed, objective/subjective, motivating units. In other words, we are barely aware of considering the responses from *each* Sensibility individually, but in the light of prior experience, rapidly arrive at a unified view.

When you consider that all these adjustments are carried out within a rational/logical framework, you can appreciate that the subjective is not an easy dimension to describe and our description is not yet complete. The logical muddle to which Ryle refers (see 14) was created in part by Locke who thought the subjective could be understood as 'machine-like' and methods could be applied similar to those of the scientists of his time. This must not be confused with the fact that modern psychological methods correctly use scientifically based comparative studies of the subjective to compare selected groups of individuals.

The essence of the minome is the active processes of reason/logic/mathematics that relate sensory experience to the Sensibilities. These relations were described above in terms of all properties relating to the 'self'.

These properties appear to have two functions. On the one hand they respond to sensory experiences to give the tentative beliefs of everyday life and of science, as described (9-12). On the other, the Sensibilities expose us to their unknowable dimensions, which brings within reach a range of unverifiable ideas and beliefs including those of religion.

You can appreciate now that the description is one of a continuous interaction between the subject and the environment. This results in a *cycle of beliefs and actions* that begins at some point in early childhood and continues while consciousness exists or until memory fails. The ideas from sensory experience and the knowledge that flows from it never ceases; it merely changes. The actual content of the knowledge acquired, in each case, changes in response to (1) new sensory experiences and (2) new responses, such as a change in ethical ideas and objectives.

It follows from these considerations that the strength of the motivation to act in a certain way depends upon,

1. Individual beliefs and their origins.
2. The Sensibilities and their motivating powers, which vary greatly from person to person, but remain constant throughout life (12).
3. The environment and its powerful influence on behaviour."

"How are objectives to be described?"

"In the case of sensory knowledge, we are always striving for some kind of truth or certainty. Why? Because we act under the impulse to respond to objectives set to achieve responsive knowledge. The objectives are commonly a better life, and in the end, even hoped for perfection, (perfect happiness, beauty and goodness).

Objectives and associated beliefs vary enormously from those at one extreme of the terrorist, whose idea of perfection is to achieve his immediate salvation at the expense of others, to the majority at the other extreme, whose beliefs aim to improve human welfare and support the norms of the community. Rarely, you will recall, there is the apparently benign person with no evidence of strong beliefs who suddenly commits an unprovoked murder. This problem is not one of strong beliefs or wrong beliefs. I concluded that the value sensibility in such a person must be anomalous and hence, for example, such a person may simply not be aware through accepted beliefs of the norms of society, or has a distorted idea of these norms (9, 12). We concluded that ethical beliefs may be strong yet remain hidden until some event occurs that is regarded as a provocation.

Levels of minomic function

The description given has assumed that all minomic functions operate at one level; that there is only one stream or system of 'ideas/ reason, logic and response of the sensibilities' existing in consciousness at a time. But in reality several systems operate in parallel. There is the level of immediate everyday events. At another level there are the past and future events pertaining to a job or profession. Then at other levels there may be concerns about a disease, a marriage, unemployment and so on. As life progresses, each person develops a web of interrelated levels of these functions. The knowledge accumulated in relation to each is a measure of the extent and complexity of consciousness in an individual and the vigour of minomic functions.

Psychologists in particular may need to investigate the details of minomic function in individuals. For example, the terrorist, the potential murderer or the paedophiliac may appear normal and quite harmless at one level but have other levels of functioning that are highly dangerous in society."

"How is progress to be made?"

"It takes the form of choices between sets of beliefs. These can only be finally judged to be good or bad in retrospect from past experience. It necessitates bringing into consciousness several alternative possibilities. The understanding appears to do this because it is possible to be aware of several alternative possibilities at the same time, which is the phenomenon of apperception. *If we could not do this, we would not be able to make choices.* But, viewed more broadly, such choices determine how societies evolve over centuries.

The beliefs of the Scholastics spearheaded the objectives of power, authority and influence of Medieval Christianity, which reached its peak around 1300, when it almost matched that of kings and emperors. The ideas of Aquinas and others were meant to strengthen the theology and therefore the power of the Church, but elements of realism and empiricism were creeping in and these ideas contained the seeds of its decline. These destructive elements became more evident in William of Occam and Roger Bacon.

But that was the beginning of the changes that characterized progress at this time. A further extension of these and similar ideas formed the driving force, in terms of beliefs and motivation that heralded the new ideas of the post-Renaissance scientists and philosophers. Each age breeds both the ideas that support and strengthen what exists *and* the ideas that undermine and may destroy it.

This is not an entirely avoidable accident of history: It is impossible to see the future and thereby form objectives without discovering motives through criticism of the present, a process that may risk destruction of what exists. And you can appreciate from the medieval experience that even the strongest of supernatural beliefs were not proof against this process."

"In view of that, do libertarian ideas strengthen the democratic ideals of today, or do they weaken them and even risk their destruction?"

"Progress is brought about by the abandonment or modification of old beliefs and their replacement with new ones. This applies to the scientific theories that define knowledge, the beliefs that define democracy and beliefs about good and evil that may or may not flow from religious doctrine. These different kinds of belief should not be thought of as neat and circumscribed entities that will endure forever. They are not like that: they are ragged, ill-defined entities from which parts may be removed over time and others inserted. We preserve what we think is true and remove what appears to be false or inaccurate. We mould and modify our beliefs in order to progress. That is what Einstein did and scientists understand. But sceptics of the libertarian West ignore or destroy beliefs, or invent their own, while the rest of the world clings to old ones in self-defence.

Sociologists, politicians and some philosophers are also frequently not aware of the importance of preserving what is good and modifying or discarding *only* what appears to be at fault. In short, humans have not yet learned to understand and manage their beliefs, a fact that threatens their welfare and even their existence".

Part 3
Consciousness, Recent Literature
(Discussions 14–28)

Discussion 14

"Do views in the literature about consciousness differ significantly from those you have described?"

"Yes, and some differ quite dramatically so I would like to describe these now and return to a review of earlier literature in more detail later (Part 4). As the knowledge of sensory phenomena has increased over time, ideas about the unknowable dimensions obviously have changed. I suppose, to a considerable degree, we are discussing those changes."

"I read the book by **Gilbert Ryle** (1900-1976), written in 1949 called *Concept of Mind*[28]. His aim was to eliminate what he described as the 'logical muddle' that had been created by attempts to deal with the unknowable dimensions. He thought that philosophers since Descartes had produced this muddle by creating complex metaphysical constructions for which there is no evidence. He claimed that these could be avoided by describing in plain language what had formerly been, as he said, 'ghosts in the machine', that is, in the subjective, or mind. Now what is the matter with that? It seems to get rid of the false beliefs that you are anxious to discard together with metaphysics."

"I do not disagree with his linguistic descriptions, but by ignoring the subjective, the minome, he leaves the fundamental problems unresolved. But before I answer your question, there is a further reason for this exercise. As you are aware, scientists have started to correlate events in consciousness with biomedical functions of the brain, as mentioned earlier, and the ways in which these are affected by disease. Add to these, contributions from physicists and geneticists, and you can appreciate that a vast

---

[28] *Concept of Mind* Gilbert Ryle Hutchinson &Co Ltd 1949

explosion of knowledge is occurring. Attempts to find philosophical correlations, as Kant did, between the subjective and objective dimensions of experience will become irrelevant and the emphasis will be on the accuracy of description of the events in consciousness, which is what I am attempting to achieve.

Now, to answer your question: Ryle's only concessions to the subjective are to explain the non-awareness of 'I' as due to the fact that we are only aware of 'its coat tails' because it operates at the interface between the past, which is memory, and the future at each instant of revelation. Also, he does admit that mathematics belongs to the subjective, but he is unable to explain how it relates to other functions. This approach, however, leaves all the important problems unanswered and in any case, he gives a grossly inadequate description of the agent, the subject, or 'I'. We need a detailed description of what happens at the interface and this I have described.

It is not true to assert that the subjective is 'hidden' and therefore cannot be usefully investigated. As we shall see, Kant thought that logic could remove all subjective muddle. Later, **A J Ayer** (1910-1989) described the position of the Logical Positivists who dismissed the subjective because the verification methods of science could not be applied[29]. Then Ryle decided to abandon ship, like some other modern philosophers to be considered later."

"Many scientists and philosophers are today investigating brain function and consciousness. I have been reading *Consciousness Explained* by **Daniel Dennett** (1942-) (5) who has summarised recent work on consciousness and brain function by philosophers, neuroscientists, psychologists, and others [30]. He criticizes Cartesian dualism and in particular the idea that 'I', the agent or 'Boss' in charge perceives the external world as it really is. He produces evidence that it often happens that we become aware of more than one 'draft' of an objective event and do not necessarily know which one is true. Experiment shows that different parts of the brain become active in response to a peripheral stimulus, giving

---

[29] *Language ,Truth and* A J Ayer

[30] *Consciousness Explained* D C Dennett 1991 Penguin Press

multiple 'drafts' in consciousness that show, for instance, location, shape, colour etc to objects perceived.

He conceives of the brain as a computer-like machine with specialist activities designed to achieve certain ends. He argues against the idea of a 'Boss', or agent directing operations at the centre of what he calls a 'Cartesian Theatre'. He builds his case for a computer-like brain that can make discriminative choices. This would make redundant the ever more complicated models of other investigators who try to describe how the brain might work. But all these are surely metaphysical approaches?

His aim is to examine all subjective brain functions, such as language production, to see if a computer could achieve similar results, but a particular difficulty is motivation, or the 'Boss' function. He claims that there is no single 'stream of consciousness', but multiple streams or drafts. He suggests that the basic brain functions of primitive man have been adapted from the simple roles of predator avoidance, berry picking and throwing a weapon to perform their present very different functions today. He complains that neuroscientists, cognitive psychologists and many others continue to construct 'models', to relate brain functions to specific parts of consciousness. But for whom and about what, he asks.

He says that it is not necessary to postulate subjective centres described in the literature by various authors as 'intrinsic properties of conscious experience', the qualitative content of mental states' or qualia (Latin for quality of things). These have been thought necessary in order to record redness, specific sounds or smells, for example. But he regards this as an error and proposes that qualia do not exist.

The brain-machine has evolved, he claims, under the influence of the inherent 'phenotypic plasticity of the brain', (the theory that it has the capacity to respond to changing environmental stimuli over time), also in response to genetic factors and the effect of 'memes' as described by **Dawkins** in *The Selfish Gene*[31]. He examines brain function starting with the basic computer model

---

[31] *The Selfish Gene* Richard Dawkins Paladin Books 1979

developed by Turing[32] and von Neumann."

"I agree with Dennett that the brain does have discriminative powers and makes choices as already described. But the powers I am concerned with do not depend on the kind of discrimination required to distinguish between colours as a super-computer might do. We already know that fundamental differences between individuals in their Abilities and Sensibilities are of genetic origin. So we already know that on this basis, parts of the brain are broadly speaking responsible for all that I have described as 'subjective'. But I do not wish to enter further into controversy over the relations between mind and matter because a great deal more progress has yet to be made on understanding these relationships by experts in the field.

Much has been written about the relations between neurological events and, for example, the awareness of pain. Macdonald has reviewed some of this work in *Mind-Body Identity Theories*[33]. But there is one danger that is always present. The scientist relies on accuracy of observation and logic. But the scientist never allows logic to distort his observations. The great temptation that is an important cause of inaccurate scientific reports is to allow logic to 'bend' the facts to fit a theory based on a faulty hypothesis."

"Surely, this must be equally true of philosophy?"

"Agreed. Logic was the nutrient for post-Renaissance physics. But it was also for the metaphysics of Kant and the Logical Positivists. The computer is a purely logical construction held together by metal and plastic, so we must treat it with extreme care, both in theory and in practice! In other words, it must never be allowed to bend accurate observations.

A fundamental difference between my position and that of Dennett's and those who produce brain-mind relation theories is that they regard the mind as a *closed ended system* in the sense that a machine operates as a closed system. If this were not so, a machine could not achieve the objectives for which it was designed. The

---

[32] *Computing Machinery and Intelligence* A Turing 1950 Mind 59 p433-460

[33] *Mind-Body Identity Theories* Macdonald 1989 London

difference between our approach and Dennett's is that he has not allowed for the fact that both sensory experience and subjective experience from the Sensibilities must be regarded as *open-ended* because they both have unknowable components. Therefore any system, such as the one I describe here, must reflect this. And when you build that in, you have not got anything machine-like, or computer-like."

"Another point he makes is that many philosophers regard the method of *introspection*, (what he calls Descartes 'first person phenomenology'), to observe what goes on in the mind as flawed and unscientific. He therefore uses a third person perspective in his method of what he calls 'heterophenomenology' to make it scientific. The third person, the scientist/philosopher asks a group of subjects to answer specific questions and problems that they are aware of subjectively and these are subsequently analysed. This is thought to avoid errors due the fact that introspection allows the subject to make unverifiable statements."

"But this method could never harvest the details of the minome that I have described. I keep stressing the need for accuracy of description, and such descriptions over time, will be accepted or rejected by other workers. Moreover, it would always be possible to do the experiment of taking the introspective analysis that I have used a stage further by analysing the reasons for any significant discrepancies between my results and those of others. In other words, when I give a linguistic description of the minome, I am exposing it to critical appraisal by others in possession of their own minomic experiences. The test will be whether there is or is not sufficient agreement to approximate to verification."

"As you said, Dennett does not seem to confront the unknowable components. How does the scientist deal with these?"

"When the scientist stumbles over something unknowable, he does not hesitate to invent a mathematical solution. He can afford to do that because his end-point of scientific knowledge does not depend directly on the unknowable: he can still achieve the standards of verification he sets himself. For example, he invents stuff called 'energy', that is unknowable, builds it into his equations and ends up with anti-matter that is also unknowable (I quote Dirac), yet does not lose any sleep over it and publishes papers that are convincing to colleagues! **Paul Dirac** (1902-84), who postulated anti-matter said, 'Mathematics is the tool specially suited for dealing with abstract concepts of any kind and there is no limit to its power in this field'[34]. But the scientist never 'bends' his observations, because he knows that the whole validity of his methodology, including the mathematics he uses, depends on the accuracy of his observations."

"So he cheerfully builds these unknowable elements into his hypotheses and if these are verified, the result is published as new scientific knowledge? That sounds like sleight of hand!"

"Not quite. After all, scientific knowledge is a set of beliefs about the way the world is thought to work, but they are never certain and only differ from the beliefs of the layman in being more secure. Now this knowledge from sensory experience also includes the record of how other humans think and behave and is established by the science of psychology. The subjective responses from the Sensibilities are applied like imprints to all varieties of sensory knowledge to give the complex flavours to life that make us human. These imprints are about Feelings, Aesthetics and Values. Note that there is nothing logical, deductive and hence metaphysical about this; it simply *describes* what is observed and is then applied to sensory experience, animate and inanimate. Also, to complete the description, when we say that X is good, or Y is beautiful, the commotions in consciousness are quite distinctive, but have an element of mystery about them on account of unknowability."

"If these responses are forms of 'knowledge' and there is an unknowable dimension to them, then this knowledge must be accompanied by beliefs?"

"I agree. There is no getting away from beliefs! And of course, these were always religious in primitive times."

"What then is the difference?"

"The beliefs of religious knowledge are validated by faith. The tentative beliefs in knowledge from the Sensibilities are normative and remain true while the originator accepts them as true. The tentative beliefs in the knowledge that is science are true only as

---

[34] Preface to *The Principles of Quantum Mechanics* P Dirac Oxford 1930

long as they are in agreement evidence from sensory experience."

"So what is our objective?"

"To achieve a minimalist philosophy of values because, to anticipate, only in this way can we hope to minimize errors in the application of beliefs of the first two kinds, which often result in intolerance and violence in society."

"We seem to be a long way from home!"

Recent Literature
Discussion 15

The Ethical Dimension (component 7)

"This is a large and complex subject and we have touched on some of it already. It is not our primary concern, but some points must be mentioned. The ethical dimension comprises the ideas that describe the relations in terms of values between one human and other humans or animals. All ethical knowledge takes the form of beliefs that are normative and in this it differs from scientific knowledge that is based on tentative beliefs, as we have found. Scientific knowledge has no absolute certainty, but comprises beliefs that, by virtue of verification, have the probability, but never the certainty of truth. Ethical knowledge, on the other hand is normative: it only remains true in so far as the subject believes it to be true.

The failure to make this distinction has caused considerable confusion. The Logical Positivists failed to do this and thought that Responsive Knowledge should be verifiable by the same methods as science[35]. Since it cannot be so verified, they regarded it as nonsensical and its conclusions simply emotive, or expressions of emotion. **G E Moore** (1873-1958) decisively resolved this confusion by describing what he called the '*naturalistic fallacy*' in his book *Principia Ethica*[36]. He described the mistake of confusing ethical knowledge from the Value Sensibility that is not verifiable, with knowledge from sensory experience that is verifiable. He asserted that if good does not refer to natural properties, it must refer to non-natural properties, that is, to Responsive Knowledge from the Sensibilities. For this reason, I have made no attempt to 'prove' and have been content to 'describe' as accurately as possible.

Let me expand on that. When the scientist makes observations, sensory knowledge is derived from it based on comparisons, contrasts and relations between sets of data. In parallel with this process, the Sensibilities essentially guide and control the use that is to be made of this knowledge. Otherwise there would be

---

[35] *Language, Truth and Logic*   A J Ayer 1936 Victor Gollancz Ltd

[36] *Principia Ethica*   G E Moore 1903 Camb Univ Press

no motivation at all to achieve sensory, or scientific knowledge.
The ethical dimension is the value judgements that inevitably form, even though these may not be immediately evident. All these events describe sensory and responsive knowledge acquisition."

"But the ethical dimension is about *relations between people.*"

"Correct, but that happens within an environmental frame made up of the physical environment of sensory experience, knowledge derived from it and the response to this from the sensibilities. The above analysis shows how the subject responds to observed events with the formation of objective and subjective forms of knowledge. But it is worth noting how these are utilised in practice: for example, in an attack on X by Y, the decision of a third party observer is the product of the Sensibilities: (1) the subjective *feeling* response of the observer maybe one of anger that an attack has been made. (2) The *aesthetic* response may be that the individual attacked appears to be well dressed or aggressively armed, or poverty stricken an defenceless. (3) The *values* evoked take account of these responses and determine what, if anything is to be done; what action, if any, is right or wrong.

But occasionally anger, or a similar feeling response, is such that it may over-ride other sensibilities and may largely determine the actions that follow. In these cases the subject will often modify the value decision to justify, for example, injuring or killing someone in a fit of anger. He might claim, 'that it was right to kill X because he was a danger to other people'. It is a small step from this to the subject who fails to distinguish between values and feelings, and contends that his strength of *feeling* is evidence for the *rightness* of an action."

"Bur religions claim that ethical decisions are from the supernatural, from belief in god."

"Before language existed, primitive humans may well not have been able to distinguish between beliefs and simple awareness from the sensibilities. Even after this distinction became possible, they still needed the aid of friendly gods to help them escape from their animal-like existence and offer the possibility of a better future after death. But achieving these two objectives necessitated the idea of sanctions. Since humans were prone to 'evil' there had to be heaven and hell in the life to follow to mirror good and evil on earth. It is that ancient belief system that has remained at the heart of ethics. But it is now evident that the Sensibilities are not dependent on the supernatural and one of our objectives is to explore the consequences. There can be no doubt that when there is no belief in the supernatural, the Sensibilities remain undiminished in power.

The ethical Profile

The collective experiences of each individual I have described as the individual's *ethical profile* because this tends to remain stable over at least a period of years. The balance between the contributions of individual sensibilities may be dramatically altered, however, by the use of drugs. Each has distinctive actions that I don't need to go into, but the temporary effect of drugs on the ethical profile has recently come to have important social consequences. The general effect of drugs taken by the younger generations is to diminish or distort the strength of the value sensibilities and usually to accentuate the feeling sensibilities in response to specific experiences. This, of course, may have disastrous consequences.

Value sensibilities are evoked in the form of a spectrum of possibilities from good to evil with near to neutral responses between, as we have found. There is no absolute good, or evil and all judgements are evaluations of *differences*. It follows that there is no certain path which points to ethical progress.

Although the truth or falsity of Responsive Knowledge cannot be verified by the methods of science, useful properties can be investigated by these methods. The ethical profiles of individuals may be compared: how they think and act in specific situations, may be investigated and compared with responses in the past, or by other groups of individuals. Analysis is confined to establishing similarities or differences, for that is all the sensibilities make it possible to become aware of. But this kind of analysis aids the accuracy of ethical decision-making."

"In that case, isn't it impossible to make progress? Yet religions are always very clear about what good and evil are and how progress is to be made."

"That is true, but when ethics are hitched to supernatural beliefs we are then at the mercy of fallible ideas and you know what havoc these have caused in history. Today, as already mentioned for example, we have people in many countries who are prepared to kill others as well as themselves in response to their religious, racial, or nationalistic ethical principles."

"Where then do ethical principles come from if not from these kinds of beliefs?"

"You will appreciate now that statements about things unknowable are necessarily 'faith based' beliefs. Statements about sensory and responsive knowledge on the other hand, are tentative beliefs, or hypotheses and these I call 'science based' beliefs. So your question is about the former. The very process of believing motivated humans to indulge in acts of violence against other humans (the enemy) and animals (for food and sacrifice). The various major religions did little to alter this state of affairs, except to control the lives of individuals, often in cruel ways, in the interests of preserving true belief. Religious wars were frequent. But in Christianity, the element of violence has now largely diminished, due as we have seen among other factors, to the relentless pressures we have discussed. War and terrorism, however, continue to affect other faiths. Violence diminishes as the value status of other individuals' increases within and between communities, and in the end comes, hopefully, to have a global reach.

In the distant past, and still for many today, beliefs must always be there, and when one belief is discarded, another takes its place. Even today, the idea of extra-terrestrial powers is built into the great religions and is sought through prayer, ritual, dietetic observances and even sacrifices. In the mature religions, Islam and Christianity, for example, belief in the supernatural includes the idea of 'being saved'. Without this idea there would be little point in religion. And presumably it derives its force from the fact that, for most people, survival after death in some form hinges on this belief.

The question, which then arises is, who is to be saved? If the answer is nobody, again religion is virtually redundant, and if it is everybody, it is also irrelevant. Therefore, it was long ago concluded that only some are saved. Only by the appraisal of an individual's ethical standards was it possible to arrive at a qualification for entry into heaven. This was how ethics came to be incorporated into religious belief systems. Then the awkward questions arose: what happens to the survivors and to the dammed? This is how fears and hopes are generated by religion, which I will discuss later (34, 35).

The idea of the *spiritual* avoids these difficulties by reducing belief in the supernatural to the single belief that there must be some unspecifiable, god-like power over the universe, past, present and future. For others, everything distinctive about religion must be removed in the interests of individual freedom. The spiritual then becomes subjective and intuition the basis of ethics. That at least is harmless and has two consequences,

1. It eliminates the motives for religious strife, wars and faith-based terrorism.
2. Ethics are transferred from the supernatural to the natural, the human. Although an individual may claim spiritual guidance, that does not present a problem because the ethical objective is human welfare. It then becomes a matter for all individuals who have a sense of values. And since human relations form the subject matter of the ethical, each person becomes an agent for the regulation of society. Ethical principles are then derived from relations between individuals and between each individual and society; that is, all members of a community."

"The situation we have arrived at appears unsatisfactory to many people. Mortality remains as an unanswered problem and generates fear and foreboding. In general, the greater the fears, the stronger the beliefs."

"That question about destiny is different from the ethical problems we have been discussing although in the past, and often today, they were conflated. I think there can be no doubt that the rich baggage of beliefs stretching back into the mists of pre-history stems from the fact of mortality. Every tribe and nation has its mythology. Without exception, these belief systems ruled the lives of those in their sway. But beliefs were used by rulers and priests to control their lives as they struggled to survive, not only in the face of death, but also pain, disease, the loss of loved ones and the lesser trials such as poverty and ill-fortune."

"And as you mentioned, the forces of nationalism and racial hatred must have compounded the fanaticism, for example, of the Crusaders. There must have been ever-present threats and curbs on physical and intellectual freedom imposed by vicious rulers, feudal barons and/or the church; for example the Inquisition in the Middle Ages. Yes, on reflection, I think we have made progress."

"The quarrel in the 17th century between Galileo and the Papacy is one example among countless others. It was assumed by the Church that Responsive Knowledge from supernatural beliefs should equate with the (scientific) knowledge being described by Galileo and others, and when it did not, then Galileo was judged to be wrong. He had to recant before the Inquisition. After all, such departures from accepted teaching had been treated as heresy throughout the Christian era – so what had changed? Only that Galileo was applying methods to achieve knowledge from sensory experience that the Greeks had discovered long before the Christian era, but this had been long forgotten.

Primitive beliefs are historically where ethical values came from. But now they come from members of the community in the form of laws and customs. All members contribute to codifying, whether they do or do not have specific beliefs. An ethical problem only arises if such beliefs threaten harm to others in the community, or in other communities.

There is a great advantage in basing ethical standards on a communal basis. It points the way to ethical progress, freed in part from the dragnet of beliefs. It does not prevent those with strong religious beliefs from contributing, but does prevent such views from over-riding all others.

It remains a fact, however, that ethical knowledge still takes the form of beliefs derived from the community, from personal convictions, or from a particular religion. Such beliefs tend to become more inflexible with age, and following the adoption of a specific religious belief system at any age. These points are important because inflexibility militates against ethical progress, which is so crucial."

"So again I ask: how do we make ethical progress today?"

"This is determined in Western societies by the community as a whole, as already mentioned. Members with religious beliefs find the idea of progress difficult, especially when confronted with changed conditions due to advances in technology. This is not necessarily disadvantageous, for it acts as a counter-balance to those who want to progress too fast: they are often too keen to destroy and re-build, which is when they may lose their way.

Ethical foundations based in the community tend to be regarded by those with religious beliefs as rootless, secular and therefore not ethical, or at least as inferior. But there is no evidence that the value sensibilities of individuals who contribute to what I call *pragmatic ethics* are any less active and effective than those with strong beliefs.

The consideration of the sensibilities and how they interact illustrates how we form objectives in life, whether these are to climb a mountain, seek pleasure, or save a life. Some philosophers have asserted that which of these objectives is acted upon is a matter of *will*. But 'will' must be regarded as a figment because no such thing can be observed in consciousness; one is able only to observe the consequences of decisions. What *is* observed is that we *choose* one course of action or another as a consequence of the relative strengths or balance of the sensibilities in response to environmental events and these decisions also take into account past ethical experiences.

Responses leading to ethical progress are therefore in terms of choices. The sensibilities provide the motivation to act as well as make available a wide range of value possibilities that meet the needs and desires of the subject. Sensory knowledge determines the possibilities that are available. The subject acts by making choices that are possible. The composer, for example, chooses musical notation to describe aesthetically meaningful sounds in response to the ethical and other sensibilities of the listener. An activity thought to be good, or evil may be chosen as an objective to be attained. All choices in work and play have ethical implications in some measure.

Clifford (1845-1879), a philosopher and mathematician, gave a lucid analysis of how ethical values are formed in an essay in 1879[37]. He took the view that what makes an ethical belief right is the strength of the evidence for it. He shows how motivation from each of the sensibilities contributes to specific ethical decisions. He emphasises that it is incumbent on each individual to ensure that the evidence for a belief is carefully examined. Otherwise, he says

---

[37] *The Ethics of Belief 1879* W. K. Clifford   Pub Amherst N.Y.1999

'Every rustic who delivers in the village alehouse his slow, infrequent sentences, may help to kill or keep alive the fatal superstitions which clog his race', and later, 'we have no right to believe a thing true because everybody says so.'

On the strength of beliefs and their dangers for society, he states, 'It is the sense of power attached to a sense of knowledge that makes men desirous of believing and afraid of doubting'. Power, he claims, gives pleasure and it is power and pleasure together that induce powerful motivations, (from the Feeling and Value Sensibilities). Then there soon follows the potentially dangerous idea that this new found power must be shared with others so that soon '*we men* have got mastery over more of the world.'

Beliefs vary enormously in motivating power. Belief in a supreme being supporting an ethical objective is perhaps the most powerful and potentially dangerous. The warlike god of the Crusaders persists today in other guises. The degree of toleration of the 'heretic' or 'infidel' today is evidence of progress. The objective is a *Value Status* acceptable to society and then between societies, but mankind is far from that position today."

"But in the case of religious beliefs, what is believed came in a revelation, so that there is no evidence for or against its validity."

"Clifford would agree with that but claims that it is even more important in the presence of beliefs of supernatural origin to assess with greater care the *practical* effects of ethical principles on the community. Clearly, Clifford's ethics come from the community, not from the supernatural."

"So in a democratic society today, we have some, perhaps the majority of ethical principles derived from individuals that are of what might be called 'communal' origin. Each principle is tested by its effects, for good or ill, on members of the community. But we may also have individuals with unshakable beliefs of supernatural origin derived from one or more religions. How then can ethical principles acceptable to the community *as a whole* be arrived at, for if they cannot, then surely there may be conflict?"

"These are, I agree, irreconcilable ethical positions, but fortunately history points to the solution. The medieval church, fashioned by the theology of **St Augustine** (354-430 AD), assumed that all were believers so that this ethical dilemma did not arise, for non-believers were hunted and punished as heretics. But the effect of the Enlightenment (19) was to place much greater emphasis on natural as opposed to supernatural ethical principles, so that the excesses of heresy hunting declined and have now gone in the West. And, of course, communal decisions are now on a democratic basis so that the opinion of each individual carries equal weight. If members of other faiths join such a society and have not been subjected to similar modulating effects over hundreds years then, as you say, there may be conflict.

It is a matter of accommodating to the democratic principles that evolved during the 18th and 19th centuries. After all, it is precisely the *resolution* of such differences that motivates people to form societies in the first place. But I would agree that this kind of progress did not come without bloodshed. It may be, however, that experience will help again if we learn the lessons of history."

"And when resolution of conflicting principles fails, society falls apart?"

"Returning to Clifford, he distinguishes between the 'instinct' of beneficence, for example, (motivation from the Value Sensibility) and the 'intellectual conception of benevolence' contained in the question that he says should always accompany arousal of the 'instinct': 'is this [action] beneficent or not?' 'By continually asking and answering such questions, the conception of benevolence grows in breadth and distinctness'. Only thus, he claims, did the beneficent tradition of throwing money to the beggar turn into true beneficence, namely, 'that which helps a man to do the work which he is fitted for, not that which keeps and encourages him in idleness.' He makes the important point that the testing of principles must be a *continuous* process, for if that ceases, 'we shall be left with a mere code of regulations which cannot rightly be called morality at all'. Morality reduced to a code of practice is, I agree, an inherent danger in a democracy.

This last point has resonance in the context of today, for in the absence of such questioning, the beliefs that went to form the laws of today become obstructions to progress tomorrow. This cardinal principle of responsive knowledge is precisely the same as the principle adhered to in the search for scientific knowledge. It is inevitable because, in each case, we are dealing with *tentative beliefs*

that must sooner or later be replaced by others that never turn out
to be final and absolute truths.

The thoughts of Clifford were written down at a time when
the seeds of the welfare state were being sewn and democratic
principles were forming. Over a century later the demand for goods
and services provided by the state has grown beyond all
expectations, especially to improve social conditions, health and
education. The motivation to raise standards of living and increase
happiness is primarily from the Feeling Sensibility and the
satisfaction of these requires finance, but no great skills to provide.

The desire for better health and education is from Values and
makes much greater demands on the professionals concerned to
meet exacting requirements and maintain the necessary research to
ensure progress. And if the expectations of the consumers of these
services exceeds the capacity to supply, then the discrepancy tends to
induce in the professional providers demoralization and loss of the
essential ingredients for success, namely enthusiasm, dedication and
loyalty."

"But these are surely all problems that, although ethical, in
the end are also political?"

"They are and that is why, over the last half century, there
has been a great interest in political philosophy. A major figure in
this field has been the American philosopher, **John Rawls** (1921-
2002). His main works[38] attacked the Utilitarian model – 'the
greatest good of the greatest number' of **Bentham** (1748-1832)[39]
and **J.S.Mill** (1806-1873)[40] - as simplistic and inaccurate. Instead,
Rawls described a 'thought experiment' that asks 'what principles of
social justice would be chosen by parties thoroughly knowledgeable
about human affairs?' He believes that once a society has been
organised around a set of rules that ensure justice and fairness, then
people can be free to 'play the game' that has been discovered and

---

[38] A Theory of Justice, 1971, Harvard University Press 1999 and
Political Liberalism, 1993 Columbia University Press, 1996

[39] *An Introduction to the Principles of Morals and Legislation*   J
Bentham

[40] *Utilitarianism*   J S Mill 1863

established in the community. He goes into great detail as to how this could be established if a set of principles were to be be agreed to include rights, liberties, opportunities, income, wealth and self-respect. Thus it should be possible to arrive at a 'reflective equilibrium' within society."

"But how does this relate to reality because once a democracy has been set up, do we need theory? Democracy seems to have an in-built momentum and reflective equilibrium of its own and the problems that arise are practical rather than theoretical. Rawls's model could only come into action once a universal franchise has been established, but would not allow for value differences *between* communities."

"I agree. But it seems to me that the ways in which democracy functions today have become much more complex than any comprehensive theory could cope with. Like science, democratic societies change and develop in quite unexpected ways. The continuous three-sided debate between the people, the media and government takes place against a background of endless problems of population flow, religious conflict and biogenetic advances. Ethics have to focus on *specific evolving problems as they appear*."

Discussion 16

"I have a problem here, in fact a few problems! Everything in consciousness appears to have perspective, as already mentioned. This appears to stem from me: the 'I' or 'self', the agent at the centre of operations. This applies in particular to the ideas you have been talking about. Yet you have described the Sensibilities as the motivating agents. There cannot be an indefinite number of 'selves'."

The Idea of the Self

"We have seen that the ideas that appear on this subject are about the subjective response of the Sensibilities to the objective world. And as you say, this leads naturally to identification of motivation with the idea of the self. In the past, the self had long been regarded as a distinct metaphysical or philosophical entity, the soul, which is probably where the idea of perspective came from. However, as we shall see, Hume abolished the self!

But that is not necessarily the way in which 'I' need be thought of. Consider the evolution of the idea of the self. In the Middle Ages, each person was created by God, and by implication was immortal, yet appeared to be mortal. But, since immortality was not questioned at that time, the self had to have a mortal part and an immortal part, the soul. Descartes' idea of the self was a res cogitans, the thinking element we are now considering. Then Hume said the self does not exist, which seemed only to add to the confusion. And Kant further complicated the situation by giving dominion to the 'will', as we shall see. So you can appreciate that, although the subjective has perspective in everyday experience, and we think of ideas as issuing from something called 'I', this is because the I had become attached to one or the other of these vague metaphysical roots just described. But this is clearly a habit of thought rather than a property of the subjective.

I suggest that we change that habit to align the self with all the active properties of the subjective, as follows,

1. Intuitions (formation of new ideas), rationality and logic leading to the creation of new ideas in the lay and scientific spheres in respect of sensory *objective* experience

2. Motivations from the Sensibilities that lead to new ideas in respect of the *subjective* experiences of feelings, aesthetics and values.

These form the content of the minome. Note that it does not make sense to say that the 'I think so and so' has to be 'spatially positioned' in consciousness in order to give perspective. It is therefore incorrect to regard 'I' as a free standing and separate agency, but it *is* appropriate and correct to align it with the motivating elements of the understanding in respect to sensory experiences and subjective experience from the Sensibilities. I will take this further in a later discussion (28)."

"That scheme satisfies me and may even satisfy some philosophers! But I think nobody else will notice! Now I should like to know where 'will' and 'choice' fit into this scheme of things that now includes the self, or 'I'? They usually are linked to the idea of the self."

"The motivation to choose is the dynamic aspect of the understanding that is inherently unknowable. It stands at the interface between the past that is known and the future that is as yet unknown. It is a continuous and inevitable process of moving from the past into the future. Everything happens at this frontier, which is where questions of choice arise. We sometimes have the impression that we control what happens, (we feel we have freedom of choice), and at other times events seem inevitable, (as if we are in the grip of a mechanism).

Motivation must be understood in the context of the agency/sensibilities complex, as described. There is no evidence of a free standing 'will' such as Kant described. Will is a lay term that has many meanings, so it is best avoided. It arises primarily from motivation by the Value Sensibility, modulated as described earlier by the other Sensibilities. The motivation to act ethically in a given context results from this process of appraisal by the Sensibilities

The will is to be regarded as identical with the self when it is motivated to act. Choice arises out of the same process of appraisal, during which it may become evident that there are several alternative ways in which the subject could act, or the 'will' could operate. The actual course of action will depend in some measure on the subject's ethical profile, as already described.

<u>Personal Identity and the Ethical Profile</u>

Now we are in a position to clarify a little further the ideas you posed about the self and perspective in relation to the subject's ethical profile and objectives. I suggested earlier a tentative definition of the self. Now I want to add that each individual assembles, as a consequence of daily experiences, a unique portfolio of sensory experiences together with his/her ethical responses to these. This I call the *personal ethical profile*. Moreover, that profile changes slowly over the years with new experiences. It used to become the 'wisdom' that was said to be associated with age, but this only happened when little changed within a community from generation to generation. However, nobody pays much attention to the idea of wisdom these days. And the reason is that we happen to live in a fast moving age. By that I mean that changes due to advances in technology and the movement of peoples have brought the need for rapid ethical progress in many fields in order to 'keep up'.

When this happens, youth takes over! One of my grandchildren in the 'teens said recently, "the opinions of old people don't matter; they won't be here for long anyway". The fact is that individuals find it difficult to change their ethical profiles rapidly at all ages in order to adapt to new circumstances, and this is especially true when there are strong beliefs and as age advances. A novelist recently said that the elderly 'lose velocity', but it could also be said that the young have too much velocity, little experience and less wisdom!

But it is the *uniqueness* of each individual's ethical profile that constitutes *personal identity*. Every person differs from others in respect of Abilities and Sensibilities, just as the face and behaviour differ, and these are the keys to identity. When one perceives the uniqueness that accompanies one's *own* identity, one is then aware of *perspective*. The subject, being aware of his/her own identity and perspective, and then conversing with other people, becomes aware of *their* unique but different profile and hence they also come to have their own perspectives with respect to others.

We have now completed a description of the human understanding. It makes clear those aspects that are unknowable. The history of ideas reveals that this dimension has become obscured by imaginative ideas that over time have turned into fixed beliefs. Philosophers in Greek times, and since the Renaissance Locke and Hume in particular, sought to expose false metaphysical beliefs. Kant used logical methods to grapple with the unknowable, but became entangled in new metaphysical beliefs."

"What then are the merits of the philosophy you have outlined?"

"I hope it avoids some of the pit-falls of the past. It does not depend upon metaphysics, that is, on permanent systems of ideas, whether established by faith or reasoning. It does, however, depend upon beliefs that are transient, tentative and serve a purpose, for it is impossible for the understanding to function without them. What are described are all the elements of consciousness of which we can be aware. Doubtless the descriptions could be more accurate. There has been a long tradition in Western philosophy along these lines that commenced admirably with John Locke, followed with major contributions by David Hume and in the 20th century most notably by Bertrand Russell and Ludwig Wittgenstein.

I suppose the main lesson is to be content to *describe* and not try to *explain*. The scientist describes the world of sensory experience, but as Newton said, 'Hypotheses non fingo'. A less satisfactory tradition in European philosophy has been to do more explaining than describing, and that applied in particular to Kant and the Idealists who followed him, but the later Wittgenstein became content to describe."

"And the purpose of accurate description?"

"To minimize the risk of falsity[41].

---

[41] A point emphasised in an essay by William Kingdom Clifford, 'The Ethics of Belief' 1879 and attacked by William James in 'The Will to Believe'. 1997 Burger

Part 4
The Failure of the Enlightenment Quest for Values
(Discussions 17-28)

Discussion 17

"I would like now to discuss how the ideas so far described compare with ideas from the past. How did we arrive at the current situation? The comparison will enable me to appreciate how far we have moved on and provide a contextual background for what has been discussed and what is to follow".

Post Renaissance Europe

"The Hundred years War, commencing 1337, and the ravages of the Bubonic Plague in the middle of the 14th century brought about a pause before the onset of the High Renaissance. Leading figures included the polymath **Leonardo da Vinci** (1452-1519) and **Copernicus** (1473-1543), a mathematician and astronomer. The latter produced convincing evidence that, contrary to the geocentric theory of **Hipparchus** (c 310-230 BC) and **Ptolemy** (2nd century AD), the earth and planets move round the sun. This heliocentric theory was contrary to current scientific opinion and, more significant, the Church had taught the Ptolemaic theory throughout the Middle Ages, since it was fitting that the earth should be the centre of all things and Man the reason for creation.

This was the first major conflict in the modern age between science and religion. It foreshadowed a centuries long conflict between the dominance of beliefs and the facts about the sensory world that were being revealed by science.

Galileo (1564-1642) used experimental methods to investigate the effect of gravity on bodies and established the laws of motion. Whereas Copernicus had been guided by the a priori principle of mathematical simplicity, Galileo, using a newly invented telescope, began to make accurate observations. His methods combined observation, experiment, and mathematical deduction. He was able to use precise mathematical concepts to describe motion in space and time in place of the vague teleological ideas used by the scholastics, which were based on the one thousand years old physics of Aristotle. Hence he was one of the first of the moderns to refine the methods required to investigate the sensory world. It had proved to be a long and arduous journey since the time of **Archimedes** (287-212 BC), one of the first scientists to use experimental methods, for after him Greek science virtually came to an end until the 15th century.

Galileo thought that objects had primary qualities that could be measured accurately and were a part of the objective world. They had secondary qualities such as colour, touch, taste and sound that are not part of that world and are therefore subjective.

Isaac Newton (1642-1726) extended Galileo's investigation of gravity to show in precise mathematical terms that the force that causes an apple to fall could also explain the movements of the planets. He invented the calculus in order to aid in the mathematical investigation of these and many other phenomena. He made hydrodynamic investigations of fluids, including tidal movements, and produced a wave theory for fluid movement. He made many advances in optics. He produced a wave theory for the transmission of light, but realised that light also behaved in particulate fashion. He produced evidence to show that it has a finite velocity. He performed many chemical experiments, reflecting an early interest in alchemy.

Contrary to subsequent views, he did not believe that he was discovering a wholly mechanical universe. He did not suggest explanations for what he discovered. His metaphysical view that God is everywhere and determines everything he kept quite separate from his scientific investigations.

We do not need to describe the work of these and many other post-Renaissance scientists further in order for you to appreciate that the world view being created was poles apart from that of the Scholastics and has since been extended immeasurably during the succeeding centuries. But I do want to illustrate briefly how this came about, which is a point you raised earlier about how scientific progress is made.

Galileo and Newton realised from their work that bodies are inherently inert: they continue in a state of uniform motion in a straight line unless an outside force produces a change. This is

Newton's first law of motion. Newton developed equations to describe the movement of matter due to the force of gravity and the energy involved was measured as the product of the force and distance. Advances in other fields soon made it evident that in addition to the kinetic energy of motion, there is also chemical, thermal and today, nuclear energy due to the decay of large atoms with release of radiating particles. All matter contains stored energy, which is its mass.

Countless experiments on mass and its relation to energy were performed by many scientists, such as **R. Boyle** (1627-91), **J Dalton** (1766-1844), **J P Joule** (1818-89) and **H L F von Helmholtz** (1821-94). They established the principle of the conservation of energy and this applies whether changes are produced by mechanical, electrical or thermal means. By the end of the 18th century it seemed that mass and energy were constant features of objects and the laws governing the gain or loss of energy had been established. But in the 20th century, **Einstein** (1879-1955) showed, as a consequence of his work on relativity, that all matter is associated with mass that could be regarded as another form of energy, (mass being the energy required to cause a body 'at rest' to accelerate)[42]. This principle of equivalence had enormous implications. Consider some of these.

Humans move about at a relatively slow pace on foot and even in cars or aeroplanes compared with the movement of planets and stars. The fastest moving objects, however, are the smallest, sub-atomic particles such as photons that transmit light, gamma rays, and X Rays, for example. Even these have been shown to have mass and perhaps this limits their ability to go faster. Einstein found that if a human were subjected to an accelerating force, then as the speed of light is approached, the mass increases indefinitely and the velocity decreases so that the speed of light is never attained. This seems to make the speed of light a barrier that cannot be exceeded. Mass–energy equivalence has now been worked out and quantified for all manifestations of energy, kinetic, chemical, thermal and nuclear. By

---

[42] *Einstein* - Jeremy Bernstein   Fontana Press (Collins publishing co) 1973

comparison with these other forms of energy, the nuclear energy locked within large atoms, such as uranium and plutonium is enormous by a factor of millions. It can be released in a controlled chain reaction to produce power, or rapidly to produce a nuclear explosion and hence nuclear weapons.

The future seems uncertain. In the sub-atomic world, is our description of matter going to dwindle into a mere granularity or 'soup' with our description of the recipe made up largely, or even purely of mathematical equations?"

"That does not sound very attractive and will certainly not be understandable to most people."

"But you have to remember that the products of the technology that follows have a habit of being extremely powerful and impinge on all aspects of life for good and ill. These have transformed the human situation. I will return to the philosophical implications later (29).

The Break with Scholasticism

By the 17th century, a new world appeared to have opened up in which the possibilities of knowledge and progress were boundless. What science had achieved in the material world could surely be replicated by investigation of the mind, and this would throw new light on social and political questions? Rational answers to ethical questions now seemed possible. The Rationalist philosophers thought that the truth about the universe could be arrived at by reason, whereas the Empiricists thought equally strongly that it could be arrived at by observation and experiment. The Rationalists were convinced that *reason* would remove all irrationality in religion and empiricism and abolish superstitions. All knowledge could then be harmonized to remove all the theoretical and practical problems that had bedevilled humanity. Eternal truths could thereby be uncovered and pernicious beliefs would disappear.

This spirit of optimism could not be sustained however, but nevertheless it unleashed a flood of diverse, new ideas once the atmosphere of freedom had taken root. The break with scholasticism became decisive when philosophers no longer were constrained by the need to ensure that their ideas conformed to the beliefs of the Church. Reason became the dominant weapon used to construct a description, not only of the sensory world, but also to provide a rational explanation for human existence. **Descartes** (1596-1650), **Spinoza** (1632-1677) and **Leibnitz** (1646-1716) were the main Rationalist philosophers. But reason when unfettered by theology, to the surprise of many, produced three utterly different solutions in the hands of these three major philosophers!

Descartes was a philosopher and mathematician who, contrary to scholastic views, accepted that the philosopher's ideas must conform to the findings of the scientists and not to theological doctrines. He sought for certain knowledge and adopted a system of doubting until he found ideas that he could accept with certainty. He concluded that he could only be certain of the self, the 'I' that thinks. But he included in the *cogito*, the thinking process, everything of which we can be aware in consciousness. This led to a duality: the existence of the subjective self that is not extended in space, and an objective world that is extended in space/time. He had to postulate the existence of God to explain the latter.

Spinoza found that he could only link these by adopting a metaphysics of pantheism. God is everywhere and is everything. The universe is mechanistic, as the scientists had discovered. Therefore we must learn to live in harmony with it, and he developed an elaborate ethical system to achieve this end.

Leibnitz rejected dualism and resorted to an elaborate metaphysical system. At the extreme of the rationalist/empiricist spectrum of opinions, his philosophy exerted a powerful early influence on Kant, as it did also in his native Prussia where he taught philosophy. His philosophy did not start from the perspective of the individual, but from the general question of how we obtain knowledge of the world.

He accepted the Greek idea that the world must be made of tiny particles or atoms, but anticipated the modern idea that these are units of energy, which he called monads. Each monad accounts for the physical and spiritual dimensions (thereby removing Cartesian dualism) and God set each in motion simultaneously. The goal of creation is to develop a state of perfection, an Aristotelian concept, and the moral objective for man is to live in accordance with this plan. His premise was that our basic awareness is of substance and by logical steps he built up a rational structure of knowledge of the world. Mental and physical events have no influence on one another and both are embedded in the monad in a state of pre-established harmony. This clearly left no room for Kant's less radical metaphysics, or for Newtonian physics (with which he quarrelled). Leibnitz believed that reason could solve all problems, dispel all beliefs and thereby remove all evils."

"The break with scholasticism seemed to release human endeavour in all directions. The 17th century has been called the 'age of genius' because so many notable figures appeared in literature and the arts as well as philosophy and science. They included Bacon (1561-1626), Descartes (1596-1650), Shakespeare (1564-1515), Galileo (1564 1642), Hobbes (1588-1670), Locke (1632-1704), Newton (1642-1726), Milton (1608-1674), Bunion (1628-1688), Dryden (1631-1700), Spinoza (1632-1677), Leibniz (1646-1716) and Boyle (1627-1691)."

"It was a remarkable century and marked the beginning of the Enlightenment, a decisive move towards an entirely new concept of man's place in the universe.

Discussion 19

The Enlightenment

The launch of science and the break between reason and belief marked the beginning of the Enlightenment in Western Europe[43]. It continued until the 19th century, by which time the foundations of the modern age had been established.

The first major philosopher was **John Locke** (1632-1704). His publications soon came to dominate philosophical, political and social thinking and brought about irreversible changes in these fields because his ideas chartered new territory."

"How did he come to exert such a dramatic influence over political and philosophical ideas in England and Europe?"

"Men of genius do tend to think the unthinkable and achieve the seemingly impossible. Locke had the advantage also that he was in the right place at the right time. He was ten years old when the civil war broke out and was exposed to political turmoil until the glorious revolution of 1688. He was born into a puritan family in the south of England, his father being a country lawyer. He went to Westminster school and Christ Church College, Oxford, where the teaching was Aristotelian and Scholastic. But John Wilkins, Cromwell's brother in law at Oxford, exposed Locke to 'experimental philosophy' and to other scholars who later were to form the Royal Society. Robert Boyle introduced him to experimental science, the concept of atoms in motion and the structure of matter. He studied medicine and became physician to Lord Ashley, later the Earl of Shaftesbury. Ashley appointed him secretary to the Board of Trade, which gave him great insight into socio-political events throughout the Empire and in N America.

But in addition to all this experience, Locke was in the habit of meeting with friends for discussions and he recounts that they often could not agree when it came particularly to questions of morality and religion. This caused him to pause and examine the

---

[43] *Enlightenment (Britain and the Creation of the Modern World)* Roy Porter, Penguin Books 2001

limits of human understanding. It led him to compose 'An Essay Concerning Human Understanding,' that took the next 20 years to complete. It has been examined intensely ever since, but still stands as a landmark in philosophical thought.

At the outset he tackled the fundamental question that confronted Enlightenment philosophers: is the future to be based on the old Aristotelian/Scholastic method, or is it to be derived from the radically different method of the New Sciences that rely on observation and experiment? Locke had been exposed to both, but had no doubt that he had to base his quest for understanding on the new sciences"

"How did he make a start, for there were no previous guidelines?"

"In **Book 1**, he states that nearly all existing knowledge consists of a series of established principles. These are the principles that underpin Aristotelian science, the validity of the Cartesian cogito, the teachings of the Catholic Church, the claim that a king has the divine right to his throne, or the despot to rule. These claims had all been derived by deduction from a priori, or supposedly self-evident truths or truths given by revelation. Locke dismissed these metaphysical approaches as false because they could not be substantiated empirically in a rational manner. He came to the view that at birth the mind is like a clean slate and that all knowledge must be from observation, reason and experiment: there are no innate principles."

"Why did he take such a radical stand?"

"Some of his critics asked that question; was he attacking straw men, they asked. But John Yolton[44] pointed out that these ideas were crucial because they were prevalent in Locke's day so for example, innate principles were assumed to be necessary for the stability of religion, morality and natural law. Locke's motives were therefore quite fundamental for his philosophy and were also in keeping with his puritan upbringing and subsequent political views. In summary, he *was against authoritarianism of all kinds.*

---

[44] *John Locke and the Way of Ideas* John Yolton (1956), Oxford University Press.

On the political side he, like Shaftesbury, was in favour of the Protectorate during which Cromwell removed the authority of the King, the House of Lords and the Anglican Church. Locke was against the re-instatement of Charles 2nd and his catholic brother James 2nd. As a result he, like Shaftsbury, was regarded as a revolutionary and they became refugees in Holland. Here he finished the Essay, but Shaftesbury died there. Locke was able to return after the revolution of 1688 when James abdicated.

In **Book 2** he asks how humans come to understand the world in which they live. Boyle taught that the fundamental units of matter are atoms and these combine to form all the objects of which we are familiar. Locke argued that the brain and mind must function similarly and used '*idea*' as the fundamental and minimum unit of thought. Ideas for Locke are simple, indivisible units that are from experience, a concept that he accepted as self evidently true. All knowledge is from the mind after reflexion and is about the agreement or disagreement between ideas. The 'empirical way to knowledge' is a theory of knowledge based on the methods of the scientists. It begins with observation and ends with a system of ideas in consciousness. Locke thought that, since the scientists were discovering a sensory world composed of particles of matter that obey laws, the same principles could be applicable to the mind. Therefore, it must be appropriate to examine the phenomena of consciousness just as the scientist examines nature. This empirical system contrasted with that of the Rationalists who began with a system of ideas accepted as true and then tried to fit them by deductive argument to the world observed.

Locke's was the first attempt to describe the phenomena of consciousness in this objective fashion, free from belief systems and the innate principles that had ignored observation, the nature of ideas and the way they form and function. Locke's work has been criticised on many counts, but it was massively important as it set in motion numerous trends of original thought that are still being explored today. The methods used in our project follow Locke's lead and explore it further.

The importance of this view is that, whether the subject is philosophy, psychology or metaphysics, inaccuracy will follow if observation or description is faulty, as they have often been. One source of such errors, as Locke pointed out, is that many problems in philosophy occur on account of linguistic confusions. These he examined in book 3 and they were re-examined rigorously in the 20th century, as we shall see (27).

Upon the receipt of *simple ideas,* and after reflection, the subject combines simple ideas to form *complex ideas.* He says that philosophical knowledge is about the origin, growth and assembly of simple and complex ideas. This way of thinking immediately separates him from the Schoolmen and the Rationalists."

"How is knowledge obtained from single ideas?"

"Locke says the mind has three capacities.

1. It combines single ideas to form complex ideas of two kinds. There are ideas with *independent existences* and he lists God, angels, humans and animals. Thus we can obtain clear ideas of such existences, whether from sensory experience or the mind. Such ideas could not form if sensory experiences did not exist. Secondly, we can have complex ideas of *dependent existences,* or *modes* and here he includes mathematics, morals, religion, politics and culture. These distinctions do not fit neatly with the system I have developed, but in general *modes* are the responses from the Sensibilities (9-12) to sensory experiences.

2. It is possible to hold two or more ideas in the mind and compare their relations. This is what I have called *apperception.*

3. By the method of *abstraction* it is possible to use words to arrive at general principles, or knowledge.

Book 3 is about the relations between ideas and language, and deals with the kind of linguistic problems I examine later (28). These have caused much confusion in philosophy and that little word 'idea' is a good example. It is important to appreciate that 'idea' is used by Locke to perform two different functions. In the first it stands for *intuition*: the arrival of new thoughts in consciousness. In the second it stands for *communication*, as when we convey our thoughts to another person. Common usage does not make this distinction and that creates confusion."

"But where do ideas come from?"

"Aristotle and the Schoolmen searched for 'real essence'

without which a thing could not be said to exist. All physical and mental events were assumed to be sustained by an invisible 'substance'. Locke knew that 'idea' could not stand for hidden substances, which he described as 'I know not what'. But idea had to stand for something of which we are aware if it is to have meaning. We will find that 'idea' does have an unknowable component, a property displayed by other subjective and objective phenomena. Although it has meaning, it only acquires its capacity to refer to events in daily life when converted into language and it then performs a communication function (28). Locke rightly contends that ordinary people are the makers of language."

"What are Locke's views on the impulses that reach the sensory organs to give all sensory experiences?"

"This is where Locke got into difficulties. He followed Galileo and asserted that *primary* qualities of material objects that are extended in time and space are properties of the object, but *secondary* qualities of colour, taste and sound are subjective. But this is logically untenable as Berkeley and Hume were to show."

"So Locke accepted that we do not have access to the ultimately real and therefore his description of empirical knowledge, based on a system of ideas, does not have a secure foundation?"

Book 4 "Yes, but what we *do* have is his description of the ways in which ideas are manipulated in consciousness to give knowledge. Locke defines knowledge as *'the perception of the connection and agreement or disagreement and repugnancy of any of our ideas'*.

Locke then considers the *probability* of the truth or falsity of items of knowledge and defines three categories.

1. Knowledge by intuition. Relations between ideas not formerly in the mind appear clearly, immediately and are accepted as intuitively true, no reflection or analysis being required. This he believed is the most certain form of knowledge.

2. Knowledge by demonstration. The agreement or disagreement between ideas that appear to be intuitively true is not immediately apparent. The truth or falsity is verified by reason and experiment in two possible ways, (a) by searching for a relationship based on a logical, deductive

process and (b) by analysing for constant co-existence between ideas by the method of induction, which is now the standard method for establishing scientific knowledge. The significance of induction, however, was not fully appreciated by Locke but was explored later by Hume. This is a less certain form of knowledge and the existence of God comes into this category.

3. Sensitive knowledge is the least certain form of knowledge, yet we cannot deny it exists since the senses undoubtedly convey awareness of something, although we do not know what it is.

These are all forms of relations between ideas that for Locke comprise knowledge. What Locke and other empiricists failed to do satisfactorily is to describe how we *respond* to sensory knowledge. This I have described as Responsive Knowledge from the Sensibilities (9-13). Locke has been criticised for his representational description of knowledge: his use of relations between ideas in which to present all knowledge. He is said to have trapped human knowledge within the mind, since he admits we do not know where ideas come from. But, as Locke says and his critics now admit, *all* ideas come from outside the mind in the form of Sensitive Knowledge, which is the core of the empiricist's claim; but I would now divide this into knowledge from sensory experience and from the responses to this from the Sensibilities.

Locke discusses *faith,* which applies when reason fails: faith is the assent to any proposition 'upon the credit of the proposer, as coming from God in some extraordinary way of communication'.

In Locke's *Two Treaties of Government* he applies his anti authoritarian principles to all forms of government. In the first he refutes the divine right of kings. In the second he examines the many versions of the natural rights of individuals circulating at that time and the notion of a social contract (see Rousseau 29). Locke says that since God sets the course and end of life, the means must include the right to life, liberty, health and property. From the right to property, Locke develops a version of the *social contract theory* (see Rousseau 29). Notice how close these come to the principles that underpin a modern democracy.

The initiatives brought about by the scientists, Locke and the

Rationalists continued apace during the 17th and 18th centuries in Europe. The Age of Enlightenment was a period when the intellectual life of Europe was extremely fruitful and brought about dramatic changes. We shall see how Bishop Berkeley made a valiant attempt to break through the barriers he thought had appeared as the empiricists attempted to establish knowledge based on observation Then we will discover how David Hume retaliated by making striking advances when describing the degree and extent of these barriers. Immanuel Kant then entered the fray when he 'awoke from his slumbers' relatively late in life. After a career in science, he realised that philosophy appeared to be in ruins and, by contrast, science was steaming rapidly ahead and discovering a whole new world.

In France a group of philosophers, influenced by Locke and the advancement of science aimed to define and propagate the ideas that were to characterize the Enlightenment. Chief among these ideas were the following and it is interesting to note that some have become woven into current thinking.

1. Reason is sovereign: sapere aude. According to Kant 'enlightenment is the emergence of man from his self-imposed infancy. He defines infancy as the inability to use one's reason without the guidance of another.'
2. Humanity is able to progress to perfection.
3. Humanity by nature is rational and strives towards good.
4. Tolerance is to be extended towards all creeds and ways of life.
5. Beliefs are to be accepted on the basis of reason, not the say so of priests, sacred texts and tradition.

Voltaire (1694-1778) excelled in literary talents; satire, rhetoric and invective aimed at the political, aristocratic and ecclesiastical establishment figures of his day. He was a towering figure who became the main driving force behind Enlightenment ideas of the 18th century. He had unbounded admiration for Locke because he believed that his philosophy laid a sound scientific and philosophical foundation for the ideas Voltaire wished to express and apply.

Voltaire's contribution, which encapsulates the spirit of the Enlightenment, is summarized in one forceful sentence by **Isaiah**

Berlin (1909-1997): 'He, and the generation which he had done so much to educate and liberate, believed that by the scrupulous use of genetic psychology – although they did not call it that – the functioning of everything in man and in nature could be explained, and an end put to all those dark mysteries and grotesque fairy tales (the fruit of indolence, blindness and deliberate chicanery) which went by the names of theology, metaphysics and other brands of concealed dogma or superstition, with which unscrupulous knaves had for so long befuddled the stupid and benighted multitudes whom they murdered, enslaved, oppressed and exploited.'[45]

Francis Bacon (1561-1626)[46] presaged the new intellectual climate of ideas: 'the desire to seek, patience to doubt; fondness to mediate; slowness to assert; readiness to re-consider; carefulness to arrange and set in order'. **Fontenelle** (1657-1757) realised that it was dangerous to pick and choose between the former beliefs of trusting to faith and fanaticism. Instead, **Montesquieu** (1689-1755) presented new ideals of justice, truth, liberty and tolerance. To accomplish their ideals the French philosophers set out a programme of public education and propaganda to encourage critical examination of ideas so long held and never questioned. **D'Holbach** (1723-1789), a German and an atheist, was one of the leaders of mechanistic materialism.

Diderot (1713-1784) and **D'Alembert** (1717-1783) published an *Encyclopedia* (1745-1772) by multiple authors. It attempted to expose to public view the immense advances in science and 'free thought' that had been hidden from public view by despotic rule for years; but the encyclopaedia was suppressed at first.

---

[45] *The Age of Enlightenment* - Mentor Books Isaiah Berlin 1963

[46] *Proemium,* 1653 Francis Bacon

Discussion 20

George Berkeley (1685-1753) was born in Ireland and became bishop of Cloyne. He wrote his main works before the age of thirty, including, *A Treatise Concerning The Principles Of Human Knowledge*. Although a Christian, his views formed a bridge between Locke's attempt to break free from the metaphysics of the scholastics and the scepticism of Hume who followed. His empiricism was more radical and logically consistent than that of Locke. He denied something called matter, or substance, which he claimed to be atheistical and unintelligible because it is not perceptible to the senses, or the imagination. He claimed that what exists is what is perceived, and that for Berkeley is the meaning of 'existence'. Matter and the properties of matter are the figments with which philosophers have peopled the world from Plato to Locke, all the products of rationalism and its end product, materialism. He claimed that the age of atheism in which he lived was the consequence of philosophers listening to the scientists who saw the world as a vast machine composed of chunks of matter having the innate characteristics of recognizable objects; these all being part of an unseen, unknowable medieval substance or substratum.

Berkeley's approach was utterly different from materialism. The world is a spectacle of continuous spirit in the mind of God and of man. This is not established by reason, but is a direct vision, something of which we are immediately aware. In the 'Principles', he argues that it is the particular thought process, which he calls 'abstraction', that leads to the mistaken view that objects exist quite detached from the mind that perceives them, and he continues: *'Hence as it is impossible for me to see or feel anything without an actual sensation of that thing, so it is impossible for me to conceive in my thoughts any sensible thing or object distinct from the sensation or perception of it'*, and he continues,

'Some truths there are so near and obvious to the mind that a man need only open his eyes to see them. Such I take this important one to be, viz., that all the choir of heaven and furniture of the earth, in a word, all those bodies which compose the mighty frame of the world have not any subsistence without a mind; that their being is to be perceived or known; that consequently so long as

they are not actually perceived by me, or do not exist in my mind or that of any other created spirit, they must either have no existence at all, or else subsist in the mind of some Eternal Spirit: it being perfectly unintelligible and involving all the absurdity of abstraction to attribute to any single part of them an existence independent of spirit. To be convinced of which, the reader need only reflect and try to separate in his own thoughts the being of a sensible thing from its being perceived'. In essence he claimed: *to be is to be perceived – esse est percipi.*[47]

And later he says, '*the only thing whose existence we deny, is that which philosophers call Matter or corporeal substance. And in doing of this, there is no damage done to the rest of mankind, who, I dare say, will never miss it. The Atheist indeed will want the colour of an empty name to support his impiety; and the Philosophers may possibly find they have lost a great handle for trifling and disputation'.*

All that I described earlier under Rationality, Logic and the Sensibilities (6) are manifestations of Berkeley's subjective Spirit."

"Berkeley was obviously a master of prose and logical thought. How did people come to use abstract ideas in the way he describes?"

"Berkeley thought it was due to the misuse of language. When we refer to cats, we 'abstract' something we call 'cats' that stands in the mind for each individual cat. This is manifestly different from naming or describing each particular cat on a one by one basis. But this process of abstraction, inventing a universal term to apply to all cats, does not refer to anything that actually exists, that can be perceived. This Berkeley found objectionable, since all manner of objects can be given fictitious existence in this way, which he rightly claimed leads to much philosophical confusion.

He thought that a 'universal' is arrived at by thinking of a particular cat and then assuming that in some way this represents all cats. But this we cannot know. It seems clear now that such general terms are used not to *describe something that exists* but to *form*

---

[47] *Principles Concerning the Treatise of Human Knowledge* G Berkeley (1710)

convenient categories of things observed. This is crucial to ways of thinking in everyday life and in science, but caused much confusion in philosophy. Thus, for example, in order to discover how samples of 100 cats behave when subjected, to changes in diet, the scientist resorts to such abstractions. In other words, the universal is the description of a defined category of objects of unlimited number. Our understanding cannot comprehend an unlimited number and so takes a short cut to make the idea manageable. Samples are approximations, yet the application of logical methods to these enables humans to reveal the sensory world in ever more detail. But these scientific methods of investigation had not been worked out in Berkeley's day."

"So these descriptive belief systems conveyed by language are the essential pre-requisites for the application of logic and lead to new knowledge?"

"Yes. As we have seen, these procedures are how we endlessly extend the sphere of what can be known. And the universal is the first step in this process both in everyday life and in science. But this descriptive/logical definition of universals never frees us from the necessity for hypotheses, or beliefs.

One function of language is to attach names to specific objects. Another is to categorize or invent universals, for these then become crucial weapons in most, if not all of the business of living. Berkeley argued that the first is legitimate, but the second is not because universals do not refer to or describe anything perceived. The latter are ideas that are not from sensory sources. These, he says, are from the Imagination, the Will, or Spirit and are a manifestation of the Self (Soul), which is no other than the Spirit (God) that causes all sensory ideas. He allows that the former, the universals, from the imagination, are less distinct and definite than ideas from sensory experiences, which appear to be more real and orderly.

David Hume (1711-1776) was born in Edinburgh and wrote his most important philosophical work, '*A Treatise of Human Nature*'[48], in France in his early twenties. He set out to describe the 'Science of Man', which he thought of as a psychological counterpart to the scientist's science of nature. As this book was not well acclaimed, he wrote the *Enquiry* 1751, which he hoped would be more attractive. His philosophy proved to be controversial. Recently, however, John Passmore has disentangled some of its intricacies[49].

The contents of the mind, Hume said, comprise impressions (sensory information) and ideas from the memory and the imagination (thinking). Simple ideas are copies of impressions, but the latter are distinguishable in that they are more vivid and 'lively'. Impressions may not be followed by ideas, but simple ideas are always preceded by impressions. Complex ideas are assembled from simple ideas.

Thinking is characterised by a process of forming associations between ideas. Ideas are attracted together to form a sequence, which then comes to have 'meaning'. There is a kind of attraction between ideas that acts like gravity. You will recall that I described this process, not as one of attraction between words, but of establishing rationality (6). The individual uses of words to describe events then come to have meaning on account of agreement with descriptions of previous similar experiences.

Hume held that the concept of *causation* follows from the common experience that certain events follow one another. The reason why event A is always followed by event B had never been closely examined. The association had perhaps been thought of as akin to 'will' or muscle power, which gives a vague belief in the idea of a hidden power described as 'causation'. On analysis of the psychological elements involved, Hume concluded that there is no

---

[48] *A Treatise of Human Nature*   David Hume   first Published 1739/1740,

[49] *Hume's Intentions.* John Passmore, Published by Duckworth 1980

evidence to explain causation: all that is observed, (omitting details), is that three conditions must be satisfied, spatial contiguity of the two events; priority of the sequence in time (A always occurs before B); and a constant conjunction or connection between the events in time. Those observed facts are all that can be said about causation. There is no room for belief in hidden powers. He concluded that causation is a figment.

He accepted Berkeley's view that there is no evidence for the existence of physical objects in space and time: all we are aware of is a sequence of impressions. Because these appear and disappear in rapid succession, how can we know that an object repeatedly observed has a constant *identity*? He applied his explanation of causation to explain identity. We have the impression of identity because the three conditions applicable to causation also apply, so that an object seen on different occasions is simply assumed to be the same object.

Hume's conclusion about causation in no way upset the scientists. But Hume brought to light a further problem that did upset both scientists and philosophers, and still does. If there is no evidence of a logically secure connection between regularly occurring events, in what sense is the principle of induction secure? This states that unobserved instances, past, present and future, will behave exactly like currently observed instances of 'causation', such as those a scientist might observe. Hume concluded that there is no principle that makes induction as secure as deduction. Induction leads to conclusions that depend only on the probability of truth, and probability cannot be used in the attempt to bolster the likelihood of all possible examples of the event being true. He concluded that the *inductive method* of science reveals probable, but not certain truth.

He then turned to the existence of the mind or soul. Both Descartes and Leibnitz thought that there is a soul substance, which persists unchanged throughout life and afterwards. But Hume had already concluded that, for want of evidence, substance does not exist. Hence the mind, or soul could not come from 'mind substance'. Therefore, the idea of mind must come from sensory impressions only, since these are the source of all ideas.

He then asks what impressions could cause the idea of mind? This move from substance to impressions caused him a great deal of trouble. The only thing we are aware of is bundles of perceptions or impressions passing endlessly into and out of consciousness. But he had already shown that the only causal connections between these could be no more than contiguity, priority of occurrence and conjunction. He was left with the question, that in view of all these separate elements of sense data, what gives the impression of the *identity* of the self? And this problem he was never able to resolve. Towards the end of the analysis he remarks:

'For my part, when I enter most intimately into what I call myself, I always stumble on some particular perception or other, of heat or cold, light or shade, love or hatred, pain or pleasure. I never can catch myself at any time without a perception, and never can observe any thing but the perception.'

In the case of objects in space/time, Hume thought it of little consequence that the images as they appear to us are a sequence of separate images seen in consciousness as a unified object. But it was totally unsatisfactory that the 'self' is no more than a series of images."

"Is there not something wrong with this? Hume seems to be seeking evidence of the self from objective sources, perceptions, whereas I should have expected him to search among subjective phenomena such as you have described – Rationality and the Sensibilities."

"There are several points to be made. Whatever the 'self' means, it certainly does not remotely relate to awareness of objects in space/time and its existence cannot reasonably be determined by the arguments that are applied to these 'objects' from sensory experience. Therefore his criteria for identity do not apply. Secondly, as you say, if self has any meaning, it must be about subjective phenomena: such as rationality, logical reasoning and the sensibilities. You will notice that in the quotation above stating what Hume observes in his mind when searching for the self, he lists a mixture of subjective and objective phenomena. Heat and cold; light and shade are sensory in origin. Love and hate are subjective feeling sensibilities. Pain is a sensation, whereas pleasure is a feeling sensibility. The Aesthetic and Value Sensibilities are not mentioned and his ideas on this subject seem to be confusing and erroneous.

My only comment at this stage, as I have said before, is that if you do not start with accurate descriptions, logic will never produce the right answers. Accurate description is as crucial when describing the minome as it is in science.

Passmore points out in the epilogue to his book that Hume's *Treatise* was an attack on the philosophy of his day with its emphasis on metaphysics. It is ironical therefore that when Hume's philosophy famously awoke Kant from his 'dogmatic slumber', the result was to provoke Kant into constructing the very kind of system to which Hume most objected."

Discussion 22

A Crisis in Philosophy

"Hume's philosophy appeared to many to be destructive. What was left for philosophy to discuss? To 'think', which Descartes emphasised, is to create ideas from immediate experience, or review ideas from memory. But we know from hard experience that some ideas are 'true' and others 'false'; some 'right' and others 'wrong'. How are we to arrive at 'truths?' To decide is to be critical, rational, or logical, but apparently that tends to be fatally destructive."

"I followed Locke and defined 'ideas' as the simplest units of which we are aware in consciousness. Reason acts on ideas to form, modify, amalgamate or abolish them. We are not aware of anything in consciousness that corresponds to the process of reasoning, but only the effects it has on ideas. Ideas and the operating tool 'reason', is all we have. And reason itself is indifferent to truth or falsity. But it does enable us to assemble sets of ideas and makes possible comparisons between one set and another in terms of agreement, contradiction, contrast, equality and so on, using a rich store of logical techniques. That is what science was and still is doing so successfully.

The term metaphysics has come to mean any system of ideas that comes *after* consideration of the ideas from sensory experience, which includes physics, and the sciences generally. Over millennia, metaphysics has produced countless belief systems to explain the universe, taking into account whatever scientific knowledge was available. After the Renaissance, philosophers, now free from the scholastic belief systems, set out to explain how the world works. It soon became clear that the scientists, applying reason solely to ideas from sensory experience, were establishing rapid and relatively secure knowledge. But philosophers, straying beyond ideas from sensory experience, were producing diverse and often conflicting systems of ideas."

"So how did they get out of these difficulties?"

"Although Locke's ideas had been broadly constructive, Berkeley's had become otherworldly: his explanations were 'beyond' physics and in the realm of metaphysics. And Hume's philosophy appeared at the time to be wholly destructive. This led philosophers to turn attention increasingly to how the mind works. It led Kant to attempt a synthesis of ideas based on the 'self-conscious', or subjective phenomena on the one hand, and objective, sensory experience on the other. These were his premises: the existence of the self and empirical realism, (acceptance that sensory experience is 'real'). These he thought were the only legitimate premises for metaphysics; all other metaphysical questions could not be answered.

This was the first real crisis in philosophy, but we shall find that it was not the last."

Immanuel Kant (1724-1804) was born in Königsberg, Prussia, and worked there as an academic until he died. His work created a revolution in philosophy, the consequences of which are still influencing thought today. Most of his relevant ideas for us are contained in the first and second editions of his *Critique of Pure Reason* and the *Critique of Practical Reason*; the first being concerned with epistemology, or what we can know, and the second with ethics.

He regarded his main work, based on metaphysics, as the prelude to a critical examination of ethics, which was his real and underlying interest in philosophy. He kept a portrait of Rousseau on the wall of his study because it was Rousseau's views that had convinced Kant that morality was being abused by reason when applied solely to the pursuit of scientific knowledge. He therefore saw his task as to offer a rational explanation for ethical knowledge. But he realised that Rousseau's own ideas could not be sustained philosophically and therefore Kant planned a new metaphysical basis for morality, This would provide the rational support that morality had been denied by the new sciences and the accompanying philosophical ideas that have just been reviewed. He developed these ethical ideas in the *Critique of Practical Reason* and the *Critique of Judgement.*

Critique of Pure Reason
In his major work, the *Critique of Pure Reason*, he claimed to have shown that metaphysics could be used to set out in a logical manner how the subjective, the 'I', and the objective world in which the 'I' lives, relate to one another. He thought that he could successfully cross the Cartesian barrier, and thus remove the duality inherent in the idea of distinct subjective and objective dimensions; also that he could remove the destructive effects of Hume's scepticism and Berkeley's idealism. Additionally, he thought that he had countered the false metaphysics of Leibnitz, that the world could be explained on a purely rational basis from the single premise of the existence of substance as 'Things in Themselves'. It must be added that in later publications, Kant modified these views.

Kant was appalled that the empiricists, on account of their

scepticism, had reduced philosophy to the point at which it failed to give a satisfactory account of the subjective dimension of consciousness and of the objective world of sensory experience. He began with an examination of consciousness but does not describe it in the manner that I did earlier because he applies logic and thereby ends with metaphysics.

He asks what can I, as a self-conscious being, know and what can I do; how is it possible to know objects from sensory experience? From this subjective standpoint, he describes a system of ideas, which he claimed the empiricists had ignored. These ideas are a priori, that is, are prior to sensory experience as opposed to the a posteriori, empirical world of sensory experience. They are the ideas I described under the headings of rationality and logic (6). He sets out to investigate the place of reason in the acquisition of knowledge from sensory experience. But he extends my description of rationality to the subjective and describes what he calls *concepts of the understanding*. Knowledge, he claimed, is only possible when these concepts are applied to sensory experience. Here I follow Gardner[50].

Kant said that the empiricists had ignored this aspect of understanding. His extension of the mind's role in understanding he called his *Copernican Revolution* in philosophy. He explained that 'hitherto, it had been assumed that all our knowledge must conform to objects' and suggested that 'we might have more success if we suppose that objects must conform to our capacity for receiving knowledge'. And he likened this change in the approach to knowledge acquisition to the revolution that Copernicus had brought about when he suggested that the solar system is heliocentric, as opposed to the long-standing, contrary belief that the earth is at the centre of the universe and the sun revolves around it. This change suggested by Copernicus was revolutionary in that it led immediately to modern views about knowledge of the solar system.

Kant's 'Copernicanism' reverses the relation between the object perceived and the subject perceiving it, so that the subject

---

[50] *Kant and the Critique of Pure Reason*   Sebastian Gardner Routledge 1999

does not merely record what is out there, but also determines what can be perceived and the forms in which it is possible to perceive it. For Newton, objects in space and time are real existences and independent of the subject's awareness, so that the observing subject simply records what is there. For Kant, objects in consciousness are 'intuitions', that is, transcendentally ideal appearances of objects that have undergone a transformation before appearing in consciousness.

Kant accepts the position that objects experienced do have a real objective existence; that is, they are not products of subjective imagination. Acceptance of the sensory existence of objects is called *empirical realism*. And Kant leaves open the question as to whether these objects do have an unknowable dimension of 'things-in-themselves', which Hume had denied. Kant calls all sensory information we are aware of in consciousness *'transcendental'*, meaning that this is the way we experience objects following the process of perception, which I described earlier (5). The burden of the Critique is to discover what the process of perception entails.

Kant begins his new critical, transcendental philosophy with acceptance of the self-conscious by which he means the subjective awareness of understanding. The whole argument is couched in terms of the *perspective* of the individual, the 'I', the cogniser or person seeking knowledge. The Critique starts by summarizing the *Elements of the Understanding.* Under this heading he describes our capacity to be aware of, or know anything under three headings.

The *Aesthetic,* (from 'aesthesis' the capacity to perceive), describes sensory experience, including the 'intuitions' of space and time, mathematics and geometry. Knowledge is grasped by these (self conscious) *Concepts of the Understanding.*

The *Analytic,* describes the metaphysics of the understanding, which is a logical verification of the methodology of the Aesthetic.

The *Dialectic* is a description of transcendent metaphysics; it is about things *not* from sensory experience and includes ontology, the soul and God. These are described in the Critique of Practical Reason. This work is about things not verifiable in any rational manner, whereas the Aesthetic and Analytic aspects of the understanding are concerned with knowable, verifiable things.

Reason is included in the faculty of understanding and when this is applied to sensory experience the result is knowledge. But, when applied to ideas divorced from empirical, or sensory experience, such as the ideas that comprise religions, the result is illusion. This may seem surprising, but later we will find that it *is* surprising! So the first necessity in the acquisition of knowledge is that reason, and this means the concepts of the understanding, must be directed to sensory experience.

Kant claimed that the subjective process of understanding gives true, a priori knowledge because, unlike empirical knowledge from sensory experience, it does not require explanation, or validation and is self evidently true in the manner of mathematical truths. Although these truths are usually regarded as analytically true in the sense that on analysis the subject of a proposition entails the predicate, he claimed that this truth is grasped by two elements of the understanding: one is in the form of concepts or ideas that can be thought about logically, and the other is by intuition, the way in which we become aware of the objects of sensory experience. Note this definition of intuition differs from the one I used when describing intuition in science (58). Intuitions relate to objects and represent them on a one to one basis. He claimed that the process of understanding, or cognition requires a synthesis of these two elements, (logically based ideas and the intuition of sensory experience).

These two elements are contained in a new proposition that he called *synthetic a priori*. He regarded such propositions as equivalent to mathematical truths in that they are self evidently true, and that the intuitive knowledge from sensory experience they contain is therefore logically secure, that is, both necessary and universal. This conclusion is important because it is the foundation for his claim that his new metaphysical, Critical Philosophy makes knowledge secure from the ravages of Humean scepticism. However, it must be said at this stage that despite Kant's analysis of mathematical (analytical) truths, synthetic propositions are simply different from the analytical truths of mathematics and this weakens the force of his conclusions. He thought he could pull off this sleight of hand amalgamation because, as we shell see, he proposed that we are only aware of certain appropriate, or allowable sensory experiences, (the Copernicanism that distinguishes him from Newton).

The Aesthetic

The main objective in this section is to establish that space and time are different from all other aspects of sensory experience. He claims that they are a priori intuitions: the forms in which the mind receives sensory experience. They are therefore subjective and not features of objective reality. All spatial and temporal properties of the outside world, all the objects of experience, are but appearances: the subjective 'forms of appearance'. Here he describes how objects can be sensed. In the Analytic he describes the act of cognition: how they can be thought of, or known.

Kant emphasised that knowledge begins with self-consciousness and is from the perspective of the self. But the awareness of the self, or I, is not primary, as Descartes had said: it arises out of an awareness of the distinction between subject and object. In turn, this distinction is possible because transcendental knowledge is based on his premise of empirical realism: the claim that there *is* an objective dimension, so that all knowledge begins with sensory awareness. What he thought it essential to disprove was Humean scepticism: the abolition of objects (substance), causation and the idea of the self. In fact, Kant's strictly rational structure of the Critique re-instates all of these!

Kant claimed that his critical philosophy minimized or eliminated most of the mistakes of pre-Copernican philosophy. He said that the world couldn't be explained by reflection and reason alone, as the rationalists, and in particular Leibnitz, had tried to do, or by the description of sensory experience alone, as the empiricists had said. A judgement by the understanding delivers knowledge only after the receipt of sensory experience. A mind without concepts of the understanding would be unable to think and therefore to make use of sensory information. A mind with concepts but not exposed to sensory experience would have nothing to think about. He stressed that the receipt of sensory experience is not a two-stage event: data do not arrive and are then converted into knowledge. Sense data have *already* undergone a process of transformation to form the percepts we experience in consciousness. In Kantian terminology, concepts of the understanding plus sense data deliver knowledge. You can appreciate that the essence of Kant's endeavour is to explain the process of perception on a rational basis.

We are only aware of space and time in the act of intuiting objects. These are ideal representations that conform to the conceptual, a priori space/time frame set by the mind. Since the objects of intuition cannot be known and presumably are not in a form we can be aware of, then what we are aware of must be a priori. Since we have no knowledge of the properties of the objects cognised (things in themselves), they must be assumed to be unknowable."

"Why couldn't the objects as they appear be as they really are?"

"What is given to us as objects is a product of the 'ideal' space/time conceptual frame and the sensory experience of specific objects. The conceptual frame makes the cognition of objects possible. To this extent Kant accepts empirical reality. He refers to your question again in the Analytic. Kant's position contrasts with Newton's, who regarded space and time as real existences. It also contrasts with Leibnitz's view that objects appear spatially related because space is a structure in which objects have logical relations with each other.

He set out several arguments for his view of space/time. An important one was from geometry. Geometry tells us what the spatial properties of objects *must* be as defined by geometry in order to be objects of sensibility, since the postulates of Euclid are true, a priori. But science today has shown that at least the fifth postulate (parallel straight lines do not meet and enclose a space) is not necessarily true and this has been thought to undermine the transcendental project.

The Analytic

Whereas the Aesthetic gives an account of how objects are intuited, the Analytic investigates how this process happens by logical verification. It investigates how sensory experience is converted into thoughts, or ideas: and thus how empirical knowledge is possible. The assumption is that the fundamental features of objects are derived from the mode of cognition, (that is subjective), and not from the objective properties of things as the empiricists said.

Concepts of the Understanding transcend the limits of sensory experience, and are subjective, that is, a priori. Kant describes how these function under the heading of *Transcendental Logic*. Ordinary logic is about the relation of thoughts to one another, whereas transcendental logic describes how thoughts relate to objects in space and time. This step is metaphysical and forms a part of the arguments in the *Transcendental Deduction* to follow. Kant uses 'deduction' in the legal sense of the right to land, or in this case, the right to apply as correct certain concepts or categories of the understanding in making judgements of how objects are cognised.

But the visual cognition of an object, a human face for example, involves unifying a collection of shapes and colours. The empiricist might contend that this unity is *given* in the apprehension of an object as a unitary whole, but Kant claims that it is the 'I' that is essential to this unity because it gives perspective, which all are aware of, to the act of cognition. Since the self or I cannot be empirical, because it is not from sensory experience, Kant speaks of *A Unity of Apperception,* meaning a self-conscious awareness of self. However, the status of this 'self' is uncertain and certainly conflicts with Hume's empiricism.

Kant agrees with Hume that the self is not empirically evident and hence he asserts that there must be an a priori self-consciousness, a transcendental apperception of the self. The 'I think' must accompany all representations of objects. He is then confronted with the question as to whether the 'I' is to be thought of as a separate, free standing agent, but this creates further difficulties for him for it would then become another, (but this time subjective) 'thing in itself'.

He divided Concepts of the Understanding, expressed in the form of a priori synthetic propositions, into specific categories, which are active in the sense that they have to be applied to sensory experience in order to make knowledge possible. He said that the empiricists had failed to understand the role of 'Concepts of Understanding' and had described them as though they were sensations. For Hume, the idea of a concept is a faded impression. Kant aimed to show in the Critique that a priori synthetic knowledge (of concepts) is possible, a claim that Hume would have rejected, since all knowledge for the empiricist is from sensory experience only. But Kant claimed that if cognition depends solely on sensory experience it leads to Humean scepticism: the abolition of objects and the self, the 'substance' in which they were supposed to 'inhere'. And at the opposite, rationalist extreme of Leibnitz, Kant claimed that pure reason alone, operating outside the constraints placed upon it by sensory experience, leads only to illusion: a world full of monads, a result produced when reason attempts to explain the universe.

The transcendental deduction is a theory of the understanding, or process of cognition under which heading Kant claims that it is possible to identify twelve main concepts or *Categories of the understanding*. These are the a priori concepts to which sensory experience *must conform* for us to know objects. Therefore the concepts necessary for experience are not from experience, but from the understanding. The question then arises: how do the conceptual and the sensible come to match, or fit in order to make cognition possible? Kant's answer in brief, is that it is sufficient to know what is conceptually possible. But he strengthens this position by speaking of a 'transcendental object', which seems to be a half way house between the ideal representation of an object in the mind and empirical objects, or things in themselves, or as you said, things as they are."

"So really the argument is a bit of a cheat?"

"His critics do argue about it and I comment on this later. He divides concepts of the understanding into categories that all operate within the space/time frame. The categories describe all the ways in which knowledge in the sensory world is possible and known with certainty, that is, through *synthetic a priori propositions*. Amongst these categories are causation and substance. An additional complication is that the contents of Categories have to be modified in order for us to become aware of them. These are the ways - he contends the only ways - in which it is possible to receive sensory experiences. He proceeds as follows.

Kant seeks to establish the objective validity of the categories or concepts by two procedures. First, they must be modified, or *schematised* for them to be applicable to objects of sensory experience as categories. This determines what sort of content the categories must have in order to become objects of experience. It means that the sensible and the conceptual must connect, or become matched, and it is the schemata that make this possible. But instead of using Kant's theoretical, logical method, one could simply describe, as I did, what is observed: the young child learns to match concepts with sensory experience in early life and until he learns to do so, the objects remain meaningless and the world is chaotic. Schemata and the application of categories are metaphysical inventions to explain what is not understood at present, and when you do this, you simply create new problems.

As explained, all sensory experience through the categories is in the dimension of space/time and all objects that change inevitably with time must retain their identity or permanence and in order for this to be so, he postulates they must inhere in *substance,* which of course, is another metaphysical, medieval invention.

Under the heading of the *Analogies of Experience* he then describes how the modified (schematised) categories make it possible to have sensory experiences.

The *First Analogy* aims to establish the permanence of substance despite any changes in the positional appearance of a moving object. This is essential to give the sense of time, since we are not able to perceive time directly. He concludes that it is through changes in the appearance of objects that we become aware of time and this must be due to changes in substances. Kant does not wish to imply that substance is real as the rationalists had contended, nor does he want to imply something unknowable that the empiricists had abolished.

The *Second Analogy* aims to establish causality, the law of cause and effect. Kant argues that the concept of causation is essential in order to explain our experience of the world as continuously changing, as distinct from the subjective representations of change. What is experienced is a necessary and irreversible succession of events and objectivity is established by demonstrating that it must imply both substance and causation."

"But that wasn't the basis on which Hume abolished causation."

"Agreed. He was not referring to all events but *only* those where a 'regularity' in the succession of events could be demonstrated.

The *Third Analogy* extends the idea of causality to assert causal interaction or reciprocity between all substances. It deals in particular with the causal relations to which you have just referred, but extends it to explain how all objects are interrelated. He claims that it is from these kinds of events we can know how objects relate to one another. It is how we piece events together so that appearances become ordered as opposed to chaotic. The objects of cognition are simply appearances: they are transcendentally ideal and empirically real. There is harmony between the capacity of the knower to know and the nature and extent of what can be known. These laws are a priori and necessary and are metaphysical since they are not from sense data. But he distinguishes these from all other metaphysical propositions, which he claims must be false because they are not established as a consequence of sensory experience."

Discussion 24

Commentary

"Did Kant's Critical, Copernican philosophy succeed?"

"In some respects it did and in others it did not. He did create a Copernican scale revolution in philosophical thinking. Prior to him, philosophers had been searching for the key to knowledge in many different directions, yet no obvious direction for future progress had emerged, as it had in science. He worked on virtually virgin territory when he made his critical analysis of the events that occur in consciousness in the process of acquiring knowledge.

From the purely logical perspective Kant was a very acute observer of the subjective. For example, he was not content to assert as Hume had done that sensory experience is received without explaining how or by what means it is received. He correctly claimed there must be conscious awareness of a subjective something, commonly called 'I' to communicate with the outside world because the process is perspectival.

Philosophers until Descartes and Locke had largely ignored the subjective dimension but Locke sought to describe it in terms of the mechanistic principles being applied so successfully in science. Kant's work is distinguished by the fact that he realised that this was not satisfactory, that the subjective could not be ignored and also that it is essential for any such investigation to include the relationships between the subjective and objective. He had written on scientific subjects earlier in his career and appreciated the importance of reasoned arguments. Hence it is perhaps significant that his Critique of Pure Reason investigates subjective phenomena using strictly logical methods. But the success or failure of logic depends upon its premises and this is where he went wrong.

Science is logically and mathematically based, but the success or failure of an hypothesis is crucially dependent upon the accuracy of its premises, that is, the observations upon which hypotheses are based. These principles accounted for the success of Newtonian physics, based on the inductive method of science that Hume was to describe, and which led to the relatively secure knowledge of science.

Kant ignored the inductive nature of this knowledge and

assumed in the Analogies that the causal relations between objects were necessary and that changes in substances and their relations are what we perceive as ideal representations. Bur this is a metaphysical illusion for there is no evidence that the world is like that. There is simply no evidence as to how the vast array of objects are related and neither deduction nor induction can be applied to arrive at a proof. In fact, as pointed out earlier, it is *because* most objects do *not* display regularities in their relationships that scientists are able to detect those that *do,* and *that is why the inductive method of obtaining knowledge works* (see discussion 8).

One can only respond to sensory experience by recording events with maximum precision, not by perceiving them through a manifold of deductive logical propositions. The layman navigates towards a successful conclusion in a rough and ready way. The scientist employs inductive logic, aided by mathematical/statistical methods to achieve much greater precision in the attempt to establish the truth or falsity of an hypothesis, but as we have found, the conclusions are probable, never certain. Kant had a very different objective, for he was trying to explain how the understanding grasps the truths of Newtonian physics as *necessarily* true.

Crucial to Kant's project was not only the relationship between the subjective and the objective, but also the status of the latter, which so far is ambivalent. There are two possibilities:

1. Things are as they appear in consciousness, a state that Kant calls 'transcendentally ideal' and these are from empirically real objects, a position of empirical realism (accepted by Kant and denied by Hume).

2. Things are as they are: what are observed are things as they really are in the objective world (so called transcendental realism that Kant rejected).

'Things are as they appear' (1) refers *only* to those aspects of whatever constitutes the objects that are cognisable for us, (whatever it is that precedes perception is postulated by Kant as the origin of sensory experience). Kant's contemporary, Jacobi, claimed that critical philosophy fails unless it is accepted that (2) is true. Otherwise, he said, Kant's description of objects as transcendentally ideal, (as they are 'in the mind'), is tantamount to Berkeley's idealism, 'esse est percipi', (page 133) since it essentially refers to a subjective reality and nothing more. This was incompatible with the empirical realism that Kant had accepted as a premise: (the assertion that the objects of sensory experience do exist).

In defence of the Critique and against a Berkeleyan interpretation, Kant wrote '*The Refutation of Idealism*', claiming that Berkeley's idealism is not the same as transcendental idealism. Kant asserted that objects only become knowable *in so far as* they have properties that are cognisable for us, and that is determined by the categories of the understanding.

The difficulty for Kant was that he wished to affirm empirical realism (a), the idea that something objective exists, yet reject the idea that things really unknowable do exist. Some think his views were ambivalent, for in places he accepts (b). Certainly he rejected Humean scepticism, which claimed that the only evidence we have, is from sensory impressions, that is, Kant's transcendental ideal. He needed stronger evidence than that, yet not so strong as to assert the existence of things unknowable. Yet (b) is unknowable according to Hume. And that was the dilemma left by the Critique. He certainly rejected the Cartesian idealism that the only secure knowledge is the subjective res cogitans, for Descartes failed to establish any evidence for external objects except by invoking the Almighty. The question that remained was, had Kant managed by means of his Copernican philosophy, to create a bridge of logical construction between the subjective and objective? And the answer must be no. The Critique seeks to explain how knowledge is possible at all and as such must be regarded as an hypothesis and not a proof.

Kant's analytic method depends upon his invention of the synthetic a priori proposition in his search for certainty. But it does not work. In the 17th and 18th centuries, it was assumed that the 'new sciences' were revealing a certain and final picture of reality, which was replacing all the old beliefs. For this to be so, there must be a secure philosophical link between the knower and what can be known. Kant concluded that this link must be in the form of the logical proposition he proposed: a secure a priori, subjective component linked to a synthetic component from objective experience. This made scientific knowledge secure, as he believed it to be. It no longer depended on Humean causation.

But as it turned out, Hume was right. His analysis and

criticism of the inductive method revealed the true status of scientific knowledge. This immensely important conclusion illustrates well how the conflicts within and between science and philosophy in the post Renaissance period contributed to real progress.

Kant was clearly trying to hang on to assumptions about the nature of science and the status of scientific knowledge that the work of Hume had already shown to be false. The Critique was designed to re-establish by means of the synthetic a priori proposition and other elaborate logical means a concept of knowledge that was already out of date. In support he gave as an example the proposition, 'every event has a cause'. But this is a metaphysical statement that may be true or false and does not yield the necessary truth that synthetic a priori propositions are meant to deliver.

Kant asks us to accept that space/time is subjective as opposed to the objective dimension of sensory experience, so that we perceive the world through a logical manifold that delivers certainty. But this is a false premise. As stated earlier, we are no more aware of time and space than we are of causation and energy. All we are aware of is things in motion."

"Why did Kant pursue his Critical method so ardently?"

"In adult life, the immediate sensory impressions are sufficiently stable and repetitive to give 'meaning' to rational and logical experience. By these means, science and technology extend our overall conception of what the world is like. It is possible that further research will throw more light on perception and any rationalising/logical processes involved and this knowledge will come from the biological sciences, not Kantian logic. However, an uncrossable barrier will always remain between the knowable and the unknowable."

"In that case, to what extent is it possible to put Humpty together again?"

"It will not be possible to do that without including all the faculties of the understanding, which I have described, and in particular the Sensibilities, that is, human values and ethics. This is a huge subject that Kant ignored in his first Critique. We cannot embark on it here, but there are aspects of it that must be considered because it will illuminate further my criticism of Kant's inappropriate application of logic and his neglect of accurate observation. I now wish to consider briefly Kant's ethical theory in his Critique of Practical reason.

Critique of Practical Reason

Kant accepted the common view in the 18th century that the universe is mechanistic. But since he was religious, he had to provide himself with an escape hatch and this he did in his *Critique of Practical Reason*. He calls it his second Copernican revolution. The ethical, he claims is in the subjective, transcendental domain. Therefore it is not empirical, that is, not from the mechanistic world of sensory experience. Nor is it from a transcendental reality, God. Good, he claimed, is not from any outside source, but from the *subject* and from his/her power of willing good or evil. But reason per se does not determine ends, for in practice, we tend to pursue ends set by our 'inclinations', or in Hume's words, 'reason is the slave of the passions', or in my terminology, motivation from the Feeling Sensibility (10). Therefore, according to Kant, there must be a guiding ethical principle that overcomes the effect of the inclinations.

It follows that when reason leads to actions *not* in accordance with the 'inclinations', the individual acts morally. Action then, must come from a principle that enshrines a sense of duty, irrespective of the inclinations. Kant sought a moral principle of action, which is a priori and universal. And this he found in the *categorical imperative;* which variously stated, is: '*I ought never to act except in such a way that I can also will that the motive should also be a universal law.*' Therefore one should always act from a sense of duty, not from inclinations. Since the will can determine actions from a sense of duty, the will is paramount in Kantian ethics.

But here he has to assume that there is the (transcendental) freedom so to act. This he asserted does exist, since 'reason' in the transcendental domain has no empirical roots. Therefore, morality for Kant is founded on the concept of the agency of the noumenal self, where duty and the will originate.

The structure of experience outlined in the First Critique (of pure reason), tells us what *is* the case, (such as, evidence about a specific set of human relations). The second Critique (of Practical Reason) tells us what *ought* to be done under the action of the will. And since there are no empirical constraints in the transcendental sphere, the moral law can command in an absolute manner. Actions imposed by the will, in accordance with the categorical imperative, are paramount. Kant calls this a moral world of knowledge that exists alongside the mechanistic world of sensory experience. It is detached from the latter world, where freedom does not exist, and all we can do is discover the ways in which that mechanistic world works.

Although the ethical appears to be detached, Kant maintained that it is morality that brings the ethical and sensory worlds together to form a unity. As moral beings, we are not bound by the restrictions that apply in the physical world. By applying practical reason to objects in the sensory world, the moral order, grounded in the noumenal, transcendental world becomes implicated in the world of experience."

"But was the moral order he had created self-sufficient?"

"It was except that Kant found that he could not explain happiness, (an 'inclination'), on a moral basis, yet clearly it is to be desired. This antinomy he could only resolve by postulating a supreme authority, God. And the freedom of the moral realm allows this 'upward' extension of the noumenal to provide a rational solution. The effect of introducing God ensures what Kant called the 'highest good'. And since happiness is often not attainable in this life, there is the necessity for a modest further extension to this realm to include the assurance of immortality and permanent happiness.

It follows from all of this is that it can now be appreciated that the ultimate objective of reason, (despite the first Critique) is not to gain knowledge in the world of experience, but to achieve the highest good.

Rousseau, heading the Romantic backlash to the Enlightenment (of which Kant through his philosophy was also an exponent), had complained that 'civilisation' and the exercise of reason had brought neither happiness nor virtue to mankind. Kant had no satisfactory answer to this criticism, so that his endeavour was to answer it through his philosophy.

A cardinal error in his philosophy is that everything is based on logic to the exclusion of those aspects of the subjective that are the foundation of ethics, namely the Sensibilities. This premise was wrong and as you know, I have maintained that 'will' is a figment.

The Critique of Practical Reason is unacceptable because it is highly metaphysical and as you know, my views on ethics are radically different.

I conclude that Kant's description of knowledge from sensory experience is incorrect. Also, his description of the link between sensory knowledge and ethical knowledge via the transcendental and emphasis on the 'will' is inaccurate and metaphysical.

I have approached the subject in an entirely different manner. I have separated those elements of consciousness of which we are aware (3, Forms of Knowledge), from those of which we are not aware, the minome (6-13), which is the hidden machinery that produces all knowledge and the actions that follow.

Discussion 25

The Idealists who followed Kant included Fichte, Shopenhauer and Hegel. They started from Kantian idealism and developed in a variety of directions that we do not need to follow. But the motivation of these idealists was similar and widespread in Western societies: 'The crisis that Hegel was trying to describe [was] the crisis of a civilisation that has discovered the God upon whom it depended to be also its own creation'[51]. Existentialism and Phenomenology are more recent developments that were sparked by Kantian ideas but developed many different strands of thought.

The Existentialists Kierkegaard, Husserl, and Heidegger were the main instigators of the movement that developed between the mid 19th and mid 20th centuries. They tackled head on the question of the meaning of life and emphasised its origin in the unknowable subjective and objective dimensions. They lamented that we are 'trapped in existence' without access to the knowledge felt to be essential to give any sense of meaning or purpose. Nietzsche had similar views and Sartre developed Existentialism further in the 20th century. They accepted that sensory experience does not offer a solution. They rejected supernatural beliefs. I will discuss some of this work later, but it is not central to our objectives

The sensory-motor axis has guided humans from pre-historic times and we have investigated the implications of this mechanism for the present day. The main consideration was to describe in some detail the content of Responsive Knowledge (page 26). But the Existentialists do not know how to respond to the demands of this knowledge; that is, to motivations from the Sensibilities and the unknowable components that it contains. These are contained in the streams of ideas that continuously confront them. These streams tell them the ways in which it is possible to live. Sartre described one response in a novel called Nausea, but apart from this there are not many alternatives apart from suicide, or seeking treatment from a doctor."

---

[51] *A Short History of Modern Philosophy,* Roger Scruton 1995

"They seem to have gone beyond belief, or to extreme disbelief, whereas Galileo in the 17th century suffered from the opposite – the excesses of belief emanating from the Papacy (15). Was philosophy not losing its way at this juncture?"

"I think so and an important reason is that the philosophical principle that had driven it from the Renaissance came into question. **Isaiah Berlin** (1909-1997) points out that from Socrates to Kant, the German idealists and the Utilitarians, the basic assumption throughout had been that *reason*, as opposed to the age-old resort to *beliefs* would, given time and new knowledge, finally produce a solution to the objective of an ideal society. This in the opinion of some major figures at the time such as **Mill** (1806-1873), (Essay on Liberty)[52] and **Constant** (1767-1830), (Ecrits Politiques)[53] would require a maximum degree of non-interference with the subject, compatible with a society government by laws that make minimum demands. Berlin reminds us that the basic assumptions behind the faith in reason may be at fault; in essence he suggests, because there may not be a *single* solution based on reason that embraces the needs of all humans. He asks, '*Can it be that Socrates and the creators of the Western tradition in ethics and politics who followed him have been mistaken for more than two millennia, that virtue* [which they sought] *is not knowledge* [which they assumed it was], *nor is freedom identical with either? That despite the fact that it rules the lives of more men than ever before in its long history, not one of the basic assumptions* [which Berlin spells out] *of this famous view is demonstrable, or perhaps even true?*'[54] Berlin concludes that the solution must be some form of *pluralism*, a conclusion that became starkly evident by the end of the Romantic period and was later built into the structure of Western democracies."

"It is evident that the crisis in philosophy at this point had

[52] 'On Liberty', John Stuart Mill, Thinkers Library, 8th impression 1948

[53] 'Ecrits Politiques'; Benjamin Constant, edited by Marcel Gauchet, Paris 1997

[54] 'Two Concepts of Liberty' page 200, Isaiah Berlin, in Liberty, edited by Henry Hardy, Oxford University Press 2005

not been resolved. Philosophers were evidently becoming uncertain of their reliance on reason."

"That is so, which is why the search for knowledge led to the exploration of other possibilities that we must pursue in the next discussion (26). But we will also find that during the 19th century philosophers and scientists were looking for new solutions (27). This will bring us to the modern age at the beginning of the 20th century. Then I will be in a position (28) to start finding solutions to all the turmoil by utilising the knowledge gained in the previous discussions.

Discussion 26

Phenomenology

Many philosophical strands of thought developed in the 19th and early 20th centuries and most of these come under the heading of phenomenology. Some of these are worth reviewing briefly because they have an important bearing on the description of the subjective that I have given.

The subject of phenomenology has been formed primarily since Brentano. It is defined as the elements of all that is experienced in consciousness. **Brentano** (1838-1917) first introduced the cardinal feature of *intentionality* (from 'intendo', pointing towards) into the description[55]. I have used the term *motivation* and the development of this idea as the approximate equivalent because it is less recondite and does not contain other implications of Brentano's terminology (16).

Husserl (1859-1938) was a mathematician, who applied logical principles to the analysis of the subjective.[56] He wrote major works on all aspects of phenomenology. He tried to apply the logical rigor of science and mathematics to the phenomena of consciousness. He treats the flow of ideas through consciousness as a series of units that he called *intentional acts or experiences* that represent something. They exhibit *intentionality* and this is a property of consciousness that gives *directedness* (what I also called *motivation*) towards objects. Intentional acts and their contents he attempted to treat independently of objects. He 'bracketed' the objective dimension of sensory experience so that, for purposes of analysis, he could consider the subjective dimension separately (see *Ideas*)[57], although in this he was not consistent. He describes all these functions as first hand relationships with 'I', as he says 'in the interest of accuracy', as I have also done because that makes it

---

[55] *Psychology from an Empirical Standpoint* 1874 and *The Classification of Mental Phenomena* 1911

[56] *Logical - Investigations 1901* Routledge revised ed. 1913

[57] *Ideas* 1913 Husserl

central in the subjective/objective analysis. That is sometimes appropriate instead of the third person, agency (16).

In my analysis, I deliberately described the subjective and objective dimensions as quite distinct, but added that functionally they are inextricably linked in the sense that one cannot exist without the other. Also, it is the Sensibilities and their motivating properties that account for so called intentionality and directedness. The relationships between these subjective properties and sensory experience are clearly described in my account, whereas Husserl was ambivalent about these relationships.

Heidegger (1889-1976) was a pupil of Husserl's, but in contrast with him, asserted that we, and all our activities, are 'in the world'[58], and meaning is wholly derived from relations with sensory experience. The discovery of the meaning of 'being', *Dasein,* is derived from the subject's contextual relations with things in the world. Dasein refers to our own existence. Heidegger looked for deeper levels of the personality than is being revealed by technology in the modern world. I have made it clear that these deeper levels are to be found in the depths of experience derived from the Sensibilities.

Merleau-Ponty (1907-1961) was another Phenomenologist, whose existential view can be summarised in a quotation from his *'Phenomenology of Perception'*[59],

'Insofar as when I reflect on the essence of subjectivity, I find it bound up with that of the body and that of the world, this is because my existence as subjectivity (=consciousness) is merely one with my existence as a body and with the existence of the world, and because the subject that I am, when taken concretely, is inseparable from this body and this world'.

This does not accord with my views because, although subjective and objective are inextricably related as described, responsive knowledge is from the Sensibilities and points both

---

[58] *Being and Time* 1927 Heidegger New York, Harper and Row

[59] *Phenomenology of Perception* 1945, and 1996, Merleau-Ponty Routledge

towards the sensory experience of everyday life and *also* away from it on account of unknowability."

"We have already distinguished between things potentially knowable, as in science, and those that are potentially unknowable."

"You will recall that the first category is always about relations *between* things, such as A and B in the sensory world, both of which are observable and are therefore knowable, or potentially knowable. In this dimension, the unknowable arises out of the sensory experience of say an object X, of which we are aware, but there is no Y (Kant's Things in Themselves) to which it could be related and have its origin, and we are left asking what does that mean? Or, where did it come from?

The subjective unknowable arises out of the *response* to such sensory experiences. You may have sensory knowledge of a Grecian Urn, X, and decide that it is beautiful. Although you are aware of beauty, there is no definable Y to which the X could be related that is telling you where beauty comes from, or what it *actually is*. There is no perfect, or supernatural beauty. We are again aware of sensory experience and aesthetic experience but cannot get beyond these limitations. This may clarify the problem, but of course, does not solve it! The important point is that a clear recognition of these human limitations is what matters because it prevents confusions and in particular, the formation of beliefs that aim to explain things unknowable."

"Where do 'I', the subject, or agent fit into this scheme?"

"If I use the word 'agent', I use a word that the lay person may not understand. Moreover, it does not convey meaning. That meaning is to some degree added when I use 'I', 'self' or 'subject' instead. Ideally, one is trying to convey by the term 'agent' what it would be like to be in the place of 'I'. And what is meant by 'I', for our purposes, I have carefully defined (16)."

"Does that get one nearer to the truth?"

"If you put yourself in the place of 'I' and consider sensory experience, which is analysed 'horizontally', as it were, the subject is looking for verifiable relationships between observed events (as in science and everyday life). Subjective events, however, are experienced 'vertically' and are not analysable: they simply appear in consciousness from the various sensibilities. As we found, several different combinations of the sensibilities usually appear as alternative possibilities for action, so that the options to choose become possible when attempts are made to 'fit' these to the objective scenario. In such situations, the subject's and other peoples' past experiences are compared and contrasted before the subject chooses to act."

"When you use the term agent or an alternative term, I take it that you are trying to convey what is happening at the leading edge between the future and the past that gives the sense of living. Now surely, all the descriptions given by philosophers of how the world works must be attempts to put into words events that are beyond that leading edge? As I see it, they must all be beliefs summarising how each thinks the world works. Thus, empiricism, idealism, phenomenology and pragmatism are beliefs that describe this situation. One could say that beliefs are getting in the way or, to paraphrase Wittgenstein, 'we are being bewitched by such beliefs'. How do we get beyond this situation?"

"Other philosophers that we have not mentioned yet are seeking in the same way for solutions. But apart from philosophers, we are also dealing with an unlimited number of people, each with different ideas of how the world works, such as Muslims from Asia, as well as academics from Harvard."

"But your current description of the 'truth' in that case is only another belief. Are we getting any nearer to THE TRUTH?"

"Yes and no! Not in the sense that we are up against the unknowable. Yes in the sense that, for example, to identify the process of 'bewitchment by beliefs' is a step forward. It leads to an appreciation of the fact that every step taken is a further attempt to discard beliefs that are untrue, or 'get in the way'. When I speak later about the management of beliefs, I am referring precisely to this process in the context of the welfare of societies. But we will find that although we have to live with beliefs, it is possible to become less dependent upon them, so that they have a minimalist role in society as a whole. The problems we shall discuss next are motivated by these objectives.

Towards the end of the 18th century, philosophers were casting about for solutions. Some were loath to accept that Enlightenment philosophy had been a failure.

Ernst Mach (1838-1916), a philosopher and physicist, feared that the great benefits of the Enlightenment were in danger of being submerged in a welter of metaphysical philosophy during the Romantic period that followed.[60] The French Encyclopaedists had thought they could give a final explanation of the world through physical and mechanical principles (e.g. Laplace). For Mach, sensations are the only elements from which knowledge is possible because such knowledge can be validated and communicated between people. He did not accept the validity of private experiences accessed by introspection, such as the Sensibilities. But of course, this caveat prevented the development of any account of how the 'mind' works.

Mach set out to draw a clear distinction between physical science and everything else. Physical science, he claimed, does not pretend to be a *complete* view of the world; it simply claims that it is working toward such a view in the future. The highest aim of the scientific investigator is precisely this *toleration* of an incomplete conception of the world."

"But science cannot be isolated in this way, for it is surely an integral part of human understanding and welfare."

"At that time, the future of critical enquiry was still uncertain. Could language itself hold the key to secure knowledge?

Confronted with an impasse, philosophers turned from metaphysics to the analysis of language. Could this resolve the crisis? After all, the Greeks knew that the basic medium for the acquisition of all knowledge is language, for without this the storage and transmission of it is impossible. As usual, reason, logic and mathematics were the tools that came to hand, and when you think about it, they are the only tools that are available. But humans had

---

[60] *The Science of Mechanics*   E Mach Open Court Publishing Co, Chicago, 1893

become too sceptical to seek easy answers by resorting to beliefs. The first step was to ask: could a natural language like English be made logically foolproof?

Deductive, symbolic logic had been developed and was applied to the study of propositional arguments. Symbols could replace the premises and conclusions so that, it was hoped, the validity of an argument could be studied in a manner comparable with mathematics. Russell and Whitehead in the early 20th century published the '*Principia Mathematica*' in which they analysed the validity of propositions and to this end regarded mathematics as a branch of logic. They devised a method of reducing language propositions to their simplest units, corresponding to units in mathematics, and hence the name 'logical atomism'.

They hoped to arrive at linguistic propositions possessing the certainty of mathematics. Anatomic propositions express facts about which there can be no argument, whereas complex propositions do not have this certainty. **Frege** (1848-1925) is the accepted founder of mathematical logic. However, his attempt to devise a method for describing linguistic expressions in logical terms, thereby giving them the certainty of arithmetic, did not succeed. **B Russell** (1872-1970) approached the same problem by a method of denoting phrases in his theory of descriptions. But this version of 'logical atomism' also failed.

Philosophers then decided to discard everything as false that could not be verified by the methods of science. Early in the 20th century this led to the appearance of the 'Vienna school' of Logical Positivism. **Carnap** (1891-1970) and other members of this school regarded logical atomism and most previous philosophy as metaphysical and therefore wrong, (see A J Ayer, 14). They maintained that the job of philosophy is to analyse statements and these are true when,

1. The proposition is *analytic*: it can be seen to be true by analysis, as in the case of mathematical truths. It is not necessary to refer to outside evidence to establish its truth.

2. The proposition is *synthetic:* outside empirical evidence is required to establish its truth. It is true by synthesising, or joining together two unrelated statements such as the

subject 'John's hair' with the predicate 'is brown'. This corresponds to the verification principle applied in science.

The Logical Positivists maintained that all our information consists either of logically true propositions that have no factual content, (such as mathematical truths), or factual propositions that cannot be shown to be necessarily true by logical procedures, (such as, 'that mountain is 600m high'). The latter truths are arrived at by the scientific method. But absolute certainty requires a proof that the statement could never be false and this science cannot achieve, as we have seen.

Both Russell and Carnap, from different perspectives, accepted the scientific tradition, as also did the American philosopher, logician and mathematician **Willard Quine** (1908-2000). But Quine broke new ground. He pointed out that the long tradition of attempting to establish a foundation for secure knowledge in philosophy had failed. From the Theaetetus of Plato to the cogito of Descartes, Locke's sensory knowledge underpinned by 'substance', to Kant's new a priori-synthetic class of propositions, no safe haven had been found. Philosophy, he claimed, had not produced a secure foundation for knowledge. But this could be achieved by making epistemology 'naturalistic', that is, with the help of psychology, by making its foundation identical with that of science. He regarded epistemology as an extension to the discipline of science. And he took the view that the exploration of nature, including human nature, is properly done by the scientist."

"That clearly does not fit with our findings. On the other hand, computers produce secure knowledge. How can you be sure that a computer will never be able to replicate what the mind can do?"

"**Alan Turing** (1912-1954), an English mathematician and philosopher, thought that this would become possible[61]. He laid much of the groundwork for modern digital computers in the 30's and 40's. He invented an 'artificial intelligence test' and the

---

[61] *Computing Machinery and Intelligence* – A M Turing, in Mind '49 433-460

'imitation game' to compare the computer with human performance. However, when the computer invents something equivalent to Einstein's relativity theory, I will believe his claim! You will now appreciate that deductive logic does not tell us how the world works: it does not yield knowledge. As Wittgenstein said, it simply removes confusions. However, inductive logic is quite different and it is upon this that scientific discovery depends Turing thought that all of this function could be made computable by a machine."

"Where is the programme in a modern computer?"

"In *human* heads, of course! It will now be clear that the formation of objectives and motivation are both functions of the minome that controls and directs all that the logical/mathematical functions do, as well as activate all the other abilities to produce new ideas and objectives plus motor functions, (described in conversations 9-15). The current computer is confined to the performance of logical/mathematical functions.

The assumption underlying the analysis of language by logical methods was that it would reveal truths with a certainty at least comparable with that of science. But there appeared on the scene an Austrian, **Wittgenstein** (1889-1951), who trained as an engineer, fought in the First World War and during it wrote a book on philosophy, the *Tractatus Logico Philosophicus*, which changed the course of 20th century philosophy. He then taught school children and joined the Vienna Circle before moving to Cambridge to work with Bertrand Russell.

Wittgenstein based his early work in the Tractatus on a theory of how language works, derived from Russell's atomic theory. He called it a 'picture theory' because, in a perfect language, each unit gives a picture of reality: he claimed that language is like a map in that it gives the structure of, or facts about reality. And every fact describes an object and its properties. But later, in *'Philosophical Investigations'*, published after his death, he came to the view that this was wrong: language cannot be used to express the truth. Rather the opposite; philosophers are engaged in a battle against the bewitchment of our intelligence by language. The role of philosophy is to remove the confusions that arise from the misuse of language. Language is a tool, not a mirror as he had previously thought.

Wittgenstein had an intense interest in words, or ideas if you like, what they mean and how they should be used. He analysed their different usages in daily life. And his slogan was, 'the meaning is in [their] use': if you want to know the meaning of a word, don't apply logic, but observe its use in daily life. He looked for what he called 'family resemblances' in the use of words- the different meanings that had become attached to words in use. He contended that the application of reason had led philosophers to used logic to search for hidden meanings and it is that which had produced metaphysical nonsense since Plato. These he called 'perplexities' due to the miss-use of language."

"Why do you accept Wittgenstein's views?"

"I don't, but I agree it is crucial that we use words descriptively and accurately. In our next discussion, (28) I offer a better explanation for avoiding perplexities by distinguishing between the use of the word 'ideas' and 'language'.

I would add three points,

1. The words I have used I have defined as accurately as possible, as one would in science.
2. Our sensory objective experiences are unknowable because they undergo a transformation before their appearance in consciousness. Hence the use of ideas and language act as mirrors, which offer utility in science and daily life.
3. Similarly, ideas and language applied to the Sensibilities of unknowable origin gives utility in the form of ethical knowledge.

Thus, although all are aware of objective and subjective experiences and these can be described with variable accuracy, their ultimate significance is unknowable, yet each contributes crucially to human existence and welfare. It remains to be considered later in Parts 5 and 6 of our project the ways in which humans have *adapted, or more accurately failed to adapt* satisfactorily to this situation.

There were others in the 20th century interested in language and the meaning of words. **G E Moore** (1873-1958) took a common sense, realist view of objects and agreed with Wittgenstein that the meaning of words is to be found in their use (15). **J L Austin** (1911-1960) claimed that ideas, or words, must be analysed in order to discover the possible meanings for which they stand[62]. But the situations he discusses tend to shade into a discussion of psychological problems."

"All this is analytical philosophy. Is the discussion about the meaning of words leading anywhere?"

"I follow Wittgenstein and also avoid the problems of empiricism and the origin of sensory experience. It is dangerous to identify any elements of experience as prior to words or ideas. All one can say is that language conveys sensory experience to give it usefulness and meaning. I am not concerned with how it does that"

"Aren't we here verging on pragmatism – the evaluation of assertions by their practical consequences?"

Pragmatism

"The American scientist, philosopher and logician, **C S Peirce** (1839-1914), was the originator of pragmatism and considered it to be a theory of meaning and an alternative to the method of Kantian idealism. He taught that what works in practice provides a tentative standard of truth. He claimed that although the evidence may be partial, it should never bar the path to progress. He considered pragmatism to be a way of setting standards and thereby objectively monitoring progress. It is a pragmatic theory of meaning, rather than a way to truth. But Peirce was mainly concerned with scientific evidence.

William James (1842-1910) veered away from this objective and the impersonal principles of Peirce to focus on personal, subjectivist ideas of efficacy aimed at the populace at large[6364]. While Pierce was concerned with meaning, James was concerned with truth, including religious truth; for truth, he claimed, is what compels people to believe and is what pays by way of belief. James, in a major work, the *Principles of Psychology* (1890)

---

[62] *Sense and Sensibilia* J L Austin 1962, Oxford

[63] *Pragmatism A new name for some old ways of thinking* William James New York, 1907

[64] *The Principles of Psychology* William James 1890 (reprinted Bristol, Thoemmes Press 1999)

discussed many topics covered here, including consciousness and the idea of the stream of consciousness, free will, the idea of the self, choice and belief. All of this was relatively new territory and James tackled it on a broad front, incorporating psychological aspects of medicine. The method I have described can be thought of as an up-date of some aspects this early work, but it would take us too far afield to go into detailed comparisons.

John Dewey (1859-1952) extended the concept of pragmatism again to focus on morals in a social setting. He investigated the application of pragmatic principles in a democratic, social and populist context.

Pragmatist thinkers approached the subjects of truth, meaning and beliefs from these three different angles. These subjects have been mentioned at various points in our discussions and we do not need to enter further into the specific ideas of individual pragmatists. The philosophy underlying their ideas will be investigated further at the end of the next section on Postmodernism."

Postmodernism

"We have followed philosophical ideas up to the middle of the 20th century. The analytical school were still seeking to discover the keys to knowledge and truth by means of reason. But the going seemed to be getting harder and with Wittgenstein, Quine and the pragmatists, one begins to wonder where, if anywhere, the trail is going. Ryle whom we referred to earlier (14), spoke of the subjective as a 'logical muddle' and concentrated his approach to solving most problems by analysing the meaning of words. Radical changes were afoot. Rawls, you will recall, proposed a new approach to individual and social life (15). For Dennett, the subjective approximates to a computer (14). Turing machines were already able to monitor some aspects of mind.[65]

Philosophy at this point moved in a completely new direction called *Postmodernism*, driven by the failure of the other approaches. I will briefly discuss the work of a few major figures,

---

[65] *The Universal Turing Machine. A half Century Survey* 1988 Herken R. (ed) New York Oxford University Press

for you will then be able to see where our work fits into this new phase in philosophical thinking. I believe there is still a trail to be followed.

The American philosopher **Richard Rorty** (1931-)[66] in *Philosophy and the Mirror of Nature* and other publications proclaimed that traditional philosophy based on epistemology is dead. All that is left is to help people and society to 'break free from outworn vocabularies and attitudes, rather than to provide "grounding" for the intuitions and customs of the present'. In this he was following **Nietzsche** (1844-1900) who had proclaimed that god (and metaphysics) is dead and is to be followed by the advent of nihilism[67]. Nietzsche tried to find a way beyond nihilism, because he thought that traditional values were collapsing. Religion and philosophy could no longer find answers to questions of meaning and value; also science does not deliver secure knowledge[68].

Rorty began as an analytical philosopher studying epistemology, but soon became disillusioned with the 17th and 18th century view that knowledge acquisition requires something given from sensory experience plus something added by the mind. This defined epistemology and was the essence of philosophy. The mind

---

[66] *Philosophy and the Mirror of Nature* Richard Rorty, 1979 Princeton University Press

[67] *Beyond Good and Evil Friedriich* Nietzsche

[68] Schacht's interpretation of Nietzsche: 'If humanity is to outgrow its childish need for absolutes without despairing at their absence, and winding up nihilistically, willing either nothing or nothingness, we must find a new and more viable way to the affirmation of life than those that have been based on fictions, illusions, impossible dreams, and leaps of faith. We must re-think meaning and value, and find ways to attune ourselves sufficiently to attainable forms of them that this 'disillusioned' affirmation becomes not only humanly possible, but humanly compelling. Nietzsche's kind of philosophy is not intended itself to be the answer, meeting this need out of its very own resources and accomplishments, for that requires more than thought' The Oxford Companion to Philosophy, 2005 p659 Professor Richard Schacht, University of Illinois

works on empirical data to produce thoughts and representations that mirror reality, a so-called correspondence theory. Rorty and Quine came to the view that knowledge is not about accuracy of representation, for that is a matter for the scientist, but something quite different: we understand knowledge when we understand the social justification for beliefs, so accuracy of representation is irrelevant. His attitude to the 'usefulness' of science is ambivalent[69]. He concludes that knowledge is a matter of 'conversation and social practice.'

But we have been concerned with both kinds of knowledge, empirical from sensory experience and responsive knowledge from the Sensibilities. I have left questions involving perception on one side on account of insufficient scientific knowledge at present. But of course there will always be unknowable aspects to this problem.

Rorty dispenses with rationality and logic, and presents himself as a 'romantic, bourgeois liberal' and a believer in piecemeal reforms to advance economic justice and increase personal freedom. He emphasises that the primacy of 'truths' held by individuals become their own private fictions. The future he sees, not as a matter of understanding, but of how to cope. He has been criticised by academic colleagues on account of his radical 'deconstruction' of philosophy for which he found little use.

Donald Davidson (1917-2003) agreed with Quine and in some measure with Rorty, but explored the subjective and its relations with sensory experience further. He did this in a series of articles over more than twenty years during which his thought evolved. He denied 'monism', which claims that ideas in the mind directly relate to physical events in the brain, a theory that entails determinism. He claimed that this relation is not strictly necessary: he called it *anomalous*. From this he developed the concept of *'anomalous monism'* that allowed him to break out of the determinist-materialist straightjacket.

He invoked the principle of *'supervenience'* to do this. He

---

[69] *Objectivity, Relativism and Truth* Richard Rorty 1991

borrowed this term from Kim Jaegwon. In 'Mental Events'[70] Davidson uses this principle to claim that independent rationality and desires of the subjective are possible, but these activities are supervened, that is, modified or restricted by the physical environment. This, however, is not accurate, for our analysis showed that the environment is like a mould that keeps changing in response to nature and the advances of science-based technology. Hence it *permits* and makes possible as well as *restricts*. But supervenience allowed Davidson, as he says, to retain the ordinary language of folk psychology: the beliefs and desires, actions and reasons.

Since knowing depends on language, this led him to develop a theory of language in which meaning is embedded. Meaning for Davidson equates with truth. But meaning, and therefore truth, is not to be thought of as in the world, but in the *sentences of a language*. The self-knowledge to which this may lead is restricted by his concept of '*holism*'. This states that there is no such thing as private, self-knowledge. All knowledge comes from the *triangular concept* of three elements, the self, other people and the world. Incidentally, he does not explain where the intuitive ideas of Galileo, Einstein, or Beethoven came from, but presumably they are 'in the world' under the umbrella of holism.

These moves justified ideas expressed in an early paper, '*Action, Reasons and Causes*', 1963. Reason precedes action, or motivation. Action depends on the belief-desire pair, which specifies the reason for the action but is also causal; presumably belief here expresses the intention to act.

Three lectures by Davidson called *The Structure and Content of Truth* was published in 1990[71] in which he summarised the literature and gave his own thoughts on the use of language. It is worth briefly summarising his views here because they clarify recent thinking and some recent literature, the volume of which is large.

---

[70] *Mental Events*, Davidson, in Lawrence Foster and J W Swanson *Experience and Theory* published London, Duckworth

[71] The Journal Of Philosophy   ps 279-328 Vol LXXXV11. No. 6th June 1990

Following the efforts of Russell, Frege and Wittgenstein, it became clear that a natural language like English would not convey the TRUTH for which you asked at the end of our last discussion.

At this time a Polish logician and mathematician, **Alfred Tarski** (1902-1983) travelled on the last boat at the beginning of the war from the Baltic to the States in 1939. He invented a richer 'metalanguage' based on a natural language, such as English, but with added terms that ensured the preservation of the truth of a statement made by an agent and received by a hearer. Davidson says that Tarski's definitions of truth 'may legitimately be treated as conveying substantive truths by means of a language, but that, nevertheless, there must be more to the concept than Tarski specified. Thus, when the word 'truth' is used, it is necessary that the language is able to convey all other meanings of 'truth', such as the ones we have discussed. He says we still lack a satisfactory account of the general features of truth and these cannot be found in Tarski. He discussed the views of those who think that truth must be found through an epistemological, metaphysical route, essentially by means of subjective reasoning, but that solution had failed. Alternatively, through a version of realism, that is, a correspondence between the subjective images from sensory experience and something real assumed to be 'out there', to account for sensory experience. But that also had failed. Another alternative is the pragmatic view of truth; or the view of Pierce who thought it is whatever the scientists end up with. Davidson concludes that truth cannot be any of these things."

"All that sounds complicated. What is your reaction?"

"I think he has slipped back into covert metaphysics that postmodernism is supposed to have left behind. I become suspicious as soon as I encounter principles, concepts, or terms, such as 'anomalous monism', 'holism', 'triangulation' and 'supervenience'. Each implies the logical treatment of aspects of the subjective, which we have found are inappropriate on account of lack of supportive evidence. There is much that is good that can be extracted from Davidson's work, but again it re-enforces my emphasis on keeping to descriptions when trying to understand the subjective and avoiding logic in this dimension like the plague."

"If truth cannot be found via any of the directions so far

tried, where does one turn? How did Davidson deal with the problem?"

"Let me quote from the end of his second lecture, '*To the extent that realism and antirealism depend on one or another of these views of truth* [and he quotes the various possibilities that have been put forward] *we should refuse to endorse either. Realism with its insistence on radically epistemic correspondence,* [images from sensory experience that, indirectly, define TRUTH] *asks more of truth than we can understand; antirealism with its limitation of truth to what can be ascertained,* [by reason and metaphysics] *deprives truth of its role as an intersubjective standard',* [a means of communication between people].

He rightly asserts that truths are not in sentences or utterances. Sentences or utterances should serve two purposes: make possible accurate communication between people and allow them to discuss any kind of 'truth' they wish. He follows Quine and Tarski, but with modifications that allow him to arrive at a method of reliable communication.

He claims that reliability depends on (1) the preference of the agent for one sentence or another to deliver the truth desired, (2) what the sentences are taken to mean, '*This led philosophers to turn from metaphysics to language*', and (3) the probability of their conveying truth. He concludes, '*The approach to the problems of meaning, belief and desire which I have outlined is not meant to throw any direct light on how in real life we come to understand each other, nor on how we master our first concepts and our first language.*'

He says the philosophical question is: what makes communication possible at all? He responds by saying, '*What makes the task practicable at all is the structure, the normative character of thought, desire, speech and action imposes on correct attributions of attitudes to others, and hence on interpretations of their speech and explanations of their actions.*'"

"Surely, all these are the problems we discussed when describing the minome?"

"That is so, but there is more work to be done. He concludes, '*What I have said about the norms that govern our theories of intentional attribution is crude, vague and incomplete.*' This is where he leaves matters. In our next discussion, my objectives are to demonstrate why Davidson's conclusions are inevitably incomplete and unable to provide a solution."

Discussion 28

"The collapse of Enlightenment philosophy seems to have led to many post-modernist ideas. If reason has failed to deliver understanding, where do we turn? There appear to be innumerable attempts to reconstruct, deconstruct, abandon logic (regarded by many as the culprit behind past failures), etc, etc. Where are we, or rather, where are postmodernist philosophers going, if anywhere?"

The way ahead

"When you are lost, retrace your steps and review the position. With one exception I have stuck to logic-free descriptions of all the subjective components of which we are aware. The exception is the application of logic to produce scientific knowledge. This has been a huge success, as few would deny, due to its by-product, technology. We found, that sensory experience does have an unknowable dimension and we discussed how the scientist deals with that problem.

Consider next the implications of this approach. Philosophers ask what the cognitive processes of perception could be that relate mind to sensory experience? They speak of *reductionism,* the idea that mind events are the direct counterparts of brain events, which leads to one form of materialism. Also of *functionalism,* the idea that, although the awareness of pain is related to a focus of brain stimulation, pain is only one of various functional effects in consciousness that the stimulation produces. This evidence is thought to get rid of the one to one relationship between body and mind events that seemed to point to a simple mechanistic explanation. Functional relationships have been studied using Turing machine tables that aim to measure the extent and variety of the responses. I am not concerned with problems of perception. I leave that to neuroscientists who know too little about the molecular biology of it at present, but knowledge is increasing rapidly. Our concern is with the ways in which understanding grasps the information received.

In the absence of more evidence, it must be assumed that objects observed cannot be said to relate to anything definite 'out there'. Although the scientist and layperson simply accept sensory data at face value, they do need to have some kind of relation to it. Whatever the model or hypothesis, accuracy is crucial. Objects immediately detectable by the eyes and ears and the application of intelligent guesses are the beginning of understanding. Recall the invisible particles of Epicurus or the monads of Leibnitz.

But much of science is now mathematical and the 'objects' are of necessity, portrayals of what the quantum world might look like. These are not in any sense 'reality'. They are working hypotheses. As Stephen Hawking rightly said,

'I don't demand that a theory correspond to reality because I don't know what it is. Reality is not a quality you can test with litmus paper. All I am concerned with is that the theory should predict the results of measurements'[72].

The scientist works at two levels. He lives in the everyday world of objects in motion detectable by the senses, but he also is aware of another level, which is the invisible micro-world he has created from the observable macro-objects by observing instruments and applying logic. They are both parts of the subjective response to sensory experience. But there is another dimension to knowledge with which we have to contend. When we include this, sensory experience makes possible two very different subjective responses.

1. The inanimate world using the layman's logic of common sense and the scientists' method of logic/mathematics These may be described as *closed-ended beliefs* in the sense that they are verifiable.

2. The sensory, animate world of other humans activates the Sensibilities. These give rise to *open-ended beliefs* because they are not verifiable by the methods of science.

We have found that these two kinds of knowledge are wholly interdependent, that is, one cannot exist without the other. The postmodernist focus of attention has been on the first to the neglect of the second. I suggest that significant progress in human understanding will not be made until both sensory and responsive knowledge are pursued simultaneously. This is what we have been

---

[72] *The Nature of Space and Time* Hawking S W and Penrose R 1996 Princeton University Press

describing in earlier discussions.

The current project will, I hope, move postmodernism on beyond deconstruction. Reconstruction begins with the description of the subjective as the response to sensory experience to give *sensory knowledge* (lay and scientific) *plus* the response to this by the sensibilities to give *responsive knowledge*. This defines the role of logic as crucial to sensory knowledge acquisition. But its role in responsive knowledge acquisition from the sensibilities is quite different, as has been described. It is the management of open-ended beliefs in a social setting that is important and this we will be discussing.

You can appreciate now that the postmodernist philosophers have been discovering that logic is applicable to two entirely different belief systems, and Davidson has not yet made this distinction complete, so that his mistaken application of logic leads to the errors I pointed out in our last discussion. He employs what might be called a minimalist metaphysics to describe how the subjective works. His assumption, I suspect, has been that if you eliminate metaphysics, you eliminate philosophy and end with something like Rorty's 'conversation and social practice' [see his *Philosophy and the Mirror of Nature*], or as Nietzsche put it more bluntly, with the demise of philosophy, followed by nihilism."

"There are some loose ends to be fitted in somewhere, such as meaning, truth and beliefs. Presumably the postmodernists don't devote much time to these topics, yet they seem to be important in society?"

"We have discussed these apparently disparate topics at various points, but when considered together, they describe well how subjective functions work. A specific belief is formed by motivation from one or more of the Sensibilities. It conveys meaning and the hope that the content is true for events in the natural or supernatural worlds. This is simply a description of what subject X desires. The metaphysics of beliefs about the supernatural is, of course, theology.

<u>The Foundation of Understanding is Pre-Linguistic</u>

I now want to explain, in terms of our analysis, why linguistic analysis failed and in particular, despite Davidson's 'precautions', why his analysis, as he said, ran into 'deep and difficult' territory.

It is essential to appreciate that language is merely a store for information in the memory and for its transmission to other humans. There is nothing more mysterious about it than that. It is not the key to any kind of truth. Prior to words and sentences, there is a fundamental ground or foundation in consciousness that I have called 'idea' (3,7) and this plus the Sensibilities (9-12) form the basis of all understanding and of all thinking. Yet few investigators make the distinction between the ground of understanding that requires ideas, and communication, which is by means of language. The reason for this failure is that as soon as the agent makes use of the core ideas/sensibilities for communication purposes, language takes over and its precursor, the ground of ideas is neglected as no longer necessary.

If the objective of linguistic analysis is to increase the accuracy of communication, then that is laudable, but alone it must fail for the reasons I will explain. If the objective is to investigate the fundamentals of perception and understanding, those interested in the purely linguistic approach may be barking up the wrong tree. The problem is this: subjective ideas and sensibilities are locked away in consciousness and accessible only to the *subject* with whom the ideas originated. When that person wishes to communicate with others, the ideas/sensibilities have to be converted into appropriate words, symbols and sentences. Information is of course received back from others via the same language medium, which is the normal process of communication.

But the subject simultaneously forms ideas and receives images from objective sensory experiences and the Sensibilities. The content may be about everyday events and/or scientific research in this world, or about phenomena in a supernatural world. Although the core ideas may be clearly formed and powerful, they may also be vague and dream-like. They form rapidly and may rapidly be switched from subject to subject in order to appraise a problem from all angles – the process of apperception referred to later. Thinking in sentences would be painfully slow and inefficient by comparison. In essence, thinking is not like that. Also when discussing ideas, I am not referring to anything 'subconscious' that psychologists are apt to speak about."

"The foundation layer of ideas in the mind, when one thinks

about it, must obviously have been there long before languages were invented. In one form or another, they must be as old as consciousness."

"I agree and of course, because language is slow and inefficient, it takes time and effort to learn as every child knows. And some never do learn a language because it depends on very different skills from those required to establish a foundation of understanding from ideas. The extent and profundity of the latter is more related to what is commonly called intelligence, whereas language acquisition relies mainly on memory and its purpose is communication.

Attempts to understand communication between the agent and other humans clearly must start at the foundation level of ideas. But Davidson (27) starts with language and works 'backwards' towards something unspecified and not describable from the linguistic end. In our project we have started from the foundation of ideas/sensibilities. From this, communication with the world is by sentences formed with the aid of rationality/logic/mathematics as described during our conversations (6 onwards) and involves the connecting terms of belief, meaning, truth and desire or motivation. These have also been examined at various points in the course of discussing the subjective and objective dimensions.

A major difficulty in trying to achieve accuracy is the unknowable aspects of the subjective and objective dimensions. It is essential that these be clearly delineated in all descriptions because they have a bearing on the entire human situation. The descriptions in this project are designed to take these facts fully into account.

Philosophers have started with the analysis of language and Davidson took this approach as far as possible, but as he says, the end point becomes 'deep and difficult'. Clearly, the attempt to work backwards from an analysis of language is wrong. Our project starts from the opposite end with ideas and the sensibilities, which are at the heart of understanding. It is true that one then has to work forwards from what is there to describe its content in words and sentences before communication with others is possible. This we have done as accurately as possible."

"But, the essence of the method you have employed is introspection and this has been rejected by most investigators on

logical grounds as unreliable and unverifiable (14 and Dennett).
How do we answer that?"

"In fact, it is on account of this rejection that the opposite and supposedly more 'scientific' yet inappropriate methods have been employed. But this is nonsense, for as often pointed out in our discussions, mistakes are usually caused by too much logic and not enough accurate description. To reject introspection is to reject the possibility of an accurate description of the core foundation layer of ideas (as defined, 3,6,7) and the Sensibilities (9-12).

Consider how the subject moves from ideas/sensibilities to language. The first creative, intuitive process proceeds from the appearance of tentative ideas/sensibilities to the stage at which these may be replaced, modified or extended. Language/symbols then begin to form, but there may be oscillation between embryonic ideas and mature sentences/symbols as the agent casts about for an acceptable, tentative hypothesis to solve a problem in everyday life or in science. When found, it then 'matures' by becoming transformed into an accurate description with the aid of language/logic/symbols. But this transformation has become a highly sophisticated procedure, especially in science and other professions, and necessitates the employment of a specific and dedicated 'nest' of terms, comprising words, sentences and symbols.

Now this is where proceeding from within outwards, as it were, meets up with Davidson moving in the opposite direction to the point where he found communication becomes 'deep and difficult.' And the reason for this difficulty is because specialists in every field develop their private means of communication in terms of nests of specific, dedicated terms, linguistic or mathematical.

These principles apply when one tries to penetrate to the heart of any specialised knowledge. The problem does not arise, of course, when language is used to communicate relatively simple everyday events. But it does apply to the scientist, the theologian, the musician and composer; it also applies, I have to add, to the philosopher, logician, physician, lawyer and mathematician who develop their own, often complex, private nests of terminology. That is why the 'outsider' does not find it easy to penetrate to the heart of specialised subjects. Successful, detailed and accurate communication is only possible with those who have similar nests of specialised terminology by means of which they can converse. But, as I have said, beyond this point at which communication is still possible, an uninformed person cannot approach nearer to the origin of the agent's understanding."

"I can appreciate now why introspection is inevitable, since that is where all knowledge and understanding come from. Einstein must have started with embryonic ideas/motivating sensibilities that evolved into the language/symbols of Relativity; St Thomas Aquinas must have started with Aristotelian and doctrinal ideas/motivating sensibilities that became Thomist Christian doctrine; composers and poets start with ideas/sensibilities that evolve into the mature products that we come to know. Einstein makes the point eloquently in the frontispiece to this work."

"In fact, all progress then is from new ideas/sensibilities that then have to evolve into mature statements that may become accepted (or not accepted) by the community. Let me see if I can summarise this discussion.

The Spectrum of Understanding

Newly invented concepts in science, religion or any other discipline come from the idea/sensibility, embryonic end of a spectrum of understanding. This is initially available only to the agent originating the ideas. At the other end of the spectrum is knowledge expressed in the mature and communicable form of language and symbols. Knowledge must be in this mature form for it to be stored in the memory of the agent and transmitted to others. And of course it is in this form that the agent receives knowledge from others. It may not be possible to start with mature knowledge and proceed from there to its embryonic origin. The nearest approach is to employ the appropriate nest of dedicated linguistic terms and symbols necessary for communication. But new, original creations can only come from ideas."

"And of course, in the conversations of everyday life, the transitions between language and ideas are simple and go unnoticed.

The Minome and Consciousness

Let me now introduce the role of the minome. You will appreciate now the limitations of language: the idea of agency, and for that matter, the use of more or less meaningless terms such as I, he/she we, self, subject, will and even the idea of consciousness itself within which some or all of these terms are assumed to have meaning. These have all received their share of criticism in our discussions. However, since they are all terms in daily use, we cannot abolish them wholesale without the risk that we would have retreated into nests of dedicated terms that we have just described that only have meaning for specialists in science, philosophy and many other disciplines."

"In conversation, you have frequently used 'we', presumably as a conversational convenience to suggest agreement or disagreement."

"'We' like the terms referred to above are ones of convenience but do not illuminate. They tend to cause inaccuracy and confusion because they ignore the properties of the minome as these exist for each individual, (you cannot turn a bad tempered person into someone not like that – at least not yet). The concept of the minome makes it possible to focus on illumination. Language gives legitimate expression to the relevant elements of understanding and relates the subjective and objective dimensions of experience correctly, which Rorty notably failed to do, (page 172). This is a real problem that cannot be ignored and I suggest that the failure to resolve it is perhaps the main reason why philosophy appears to have lost its way. This happened when the limitations of language had become apparent.

I want now to make a clear distinction between the concept of consciousness, incorporating the many familiar, outdated and ill defined lay terms just mentioned on the one hand and the minome on the other. Consciousness comprises all the elements described in (6).

The minome does not necessarily exclude all these, but focuses on a description of the essential elements of understanding. These are, the continuous flow into consciousness of *'embryonic'* ideas. These ideas always have a reference to sensory experience of the physical world, including the world of other humans, their behaviour and linguistic communication with them. The flow of ideas for most people is quickly converted into the linguistic form and is about everyday events used for communication purposes, or storage in the memory. A few individuals retain ideas in their embryonic form and these become the new, intuitive ideas and hypotheses in science and philosophy, for example.

Reason/logic is the means whereby the ideas from sensory experience are converted into a usable, or meaningful form. The *Sensibilities* accompany all ideas and determine their utility, the uses to which they are to be put. That is the executive side of the sensory-motor axis and their activation is initiated by sensory experience.

Apperception determines how sensibility-motivated ideas are to be brought into operation. The conventional way of describing motivation has been to resort to the Cartesian cogito and the linguistic method used in describing consciousness (6). But this is the Humean 'I', or 'we' that he claimed does not exist and to speak of 'agency' is a fudge. The solution is to consider apperception, of which there is clear awareness, but its role in cognitive motivation has not yet been fully described (7). It makes possible the coordination of all the activities that comprise 'thinking'. Apperception allows the review in rapid succession of all sensibility-loaded ideas that have entered consciousness, thus making choice possible. A balance of possibilities, involving all of the relevant sensibilities is arrived at to give a single objective derived from them that is the *'best option'"*.

"How is this arrived at?"

"There is a sequence of steps. Feeling sensibilities plus ideas form the basic initial response aroused on encountering sensory experiences of things and other people. But these, we found, are rapidly modulated by aesthetic and value responses. Apperception makes it possible to review the various alternative possibilities that also appear.

This review may lead to changes in the *intensity* of the sensibilities evoked. For example, strong aggressive feelings may be inhibited by values that preclude aggression.

Apperception also makes a further choice possible: what might be called *the degree of subjective exposure*. The outward expression of all the contents of an individual's store of knowledge and beliefs is strictly controlled so that, for example, exposure to other people is limited and partial. Exposure varies from subject to subject content in a given individual. For example, feelings of happiness might be freely revealed but feelings of sexual deviance may be kept hidden. Another motive for variation may be self-protection, but these matters are in the province of the psychologist.

Once more, it suggests that the executive side of the sensory-motor axis operates to protect the subject. Exposure also varies from person to person, so that some are more 'extravert' than others."

"These new ideas help to minimize confusion. But how does all this relate to beliefs, for these have been a prominent part of our discussions."

"Belief is but a part of the mechanism of 'understanding'. Beliefs, whether they refer to a scientific theory, the aesthetic attraction of a piece of poetry, or a supernatural world, are the practical end products of understanding and help us to find our way about in the world and give it some kind of meaning."

"In that case, I think most people would say that they believe 'I' exists in some form, even if unknowable. But only philosophers seem to believe in an agent!"

"I see nothing wrong with those conclusions. We all have to keep ourselves afloat by beliefs as we travel over a treacherous sea of infinite extent, knowing that beliefs that are as safe as possible are minimal, or tentative, whilst those that promise certainty may cause the ship to sink! We each build our own private ethical profiles of beliefs that are tentative because they evolve and these determine who we are and what we do in society."

PART 5
A Philosophy of Human Values in the Community
(Discussions 29 – 31)

Discussion 29

"There is an impression that science has forged ahead while philosophy has not. It seems strange that philosophy, which has been a major discipline for two and a half thousand years, should be in danger of self-destruction at the hands of its own professionals. Why is that?"

"Central to all our discussions has been the problem of beliefs. We have discussed them from all angles and found that there is no getting away from them. We have described various categories of belief and the significance of each. We have discovered that most, but not all, relate to the unknowable subjective and objective dimensions of what we are aware."

"But since beliefs won't go away, the American philosophers we discussed must be right?"

"No. These philosophers are wrong. The history of philosophy since the Renaissance has been that every possible device of reason and logic have been used to discover truth without the need for beliefs. But this battle has been lost. What we have done is to accept the situation and describe the consequent position as accurately as possible. That does not entail the demise of philosophy, but the opening of a new chapter. This will be what the remainder of our discussions will be about. Since humans have adapted the sensory-motor axis to new purposes (3,6-8) we have to maximise the opportunities that come into view for the future of civilisation.

You are aware that science is advancing rapidly, so that what becomes possible through technology, confronts humans with ever more ethical and hence individual and social problems. Moreover, there are movements of populations that bring clashes of cultures and conflicts between long established belief systems. My aim in what follows is to outline how some of these problems might be resolved, but I would emphasise that these are only preliminary ideas. There is plenty of work for philosophers, but it cannot be done in ivory towers and in linguistic terminology that is not widely understood."

"Before you rush on, I would like to consolidate some aspects of past discussions. When we discussed Davidson's analysis of language, you drew a distinction between ideas and the expression of these in linguistic form. My understanding is that once ideas are expressed in words and sentences, they take the form of beliefs."

"Not necessarily. For example, if you recall, when we discussed the Value Sensibility, I did not assert the belief that something called 'the Value Sensibility' exists. I simply stated that we are *aware* of human values and I described them in linguistic terms, which is not the assertion of a belief. If on the basis of this awareness I assert that X is good, or Y is right, I *have* formed beliefs and these give meaning to X or Y.

Social and political implications of beliefs

I want next to examine the social and political implications of the investigations so far because these do involve beliefs. We have found that subjective functions are greatly influenced by the characteristics of the environment. The events during the 18th, 19th, and 20th centuries shaped the world of today. We have been considering scientific and philosophical changes in the intellectual life of Western Europe, but in parallel there were enormous social and political changes due to beliefs that had far-reaching consequences."

"At the end of the 18th century we still seemed to be a long way from the world of today. It is obvious from our discussions that practical, everyday events on the one hand and the two dimensions of sensory and responsive knowledge on the other are closely inter-related. As I understand it now, these forms of knowledge unfold continuously in response to events, so how did we arrive at the position today?"

"In order to fit these ideas to the practical problems of today, we need to consider how the ideas from the Enlightenment and the Romantic Age that followed came to have such importance for the world of today. The 18th and 19th centuries were   minefields of beliefs and confusions.

In the first half of the 18th century the forces that held society together in France were the church, the aristocracy and the state (19). But Enlightenment rationalism and science-based ideas increasingly conflicted with the restrictions on freedom that these old institutions imposed, until the dam finally burst at the French Revolution of 1789.

Scientists and philosophers were in many ways the engines that drove the 18th century Age of Reason. Most members of the bourgeois classes had accepted that fundamental questions, ethical and aesthetic, social and political *could* be answered, if not now, then at some future date. It was an age of confidence and it was thought that most objectives could be achieved by reason. Voltaire and his friends wanted to abolish the old regime because they believed that, once the religious and political roadblocks to progress had been removed, then reason alone could solve most, if not all the remaining problems of significance. After all, Locke had been showing them the way. But in addition to Les Philosophes, other dissenting voices had appeared and these, on the rising tide of Romanticism, took matters in entirely unforeseen directions.

Giambattista Vico (1668-1744) should be mentioned in this context. He was born in Naples and spent almost all his life there. His views were in advance of his time, but that is how change comes about. At first he agreed with Descartes that the only path to certain knowledge was mathematics and the methods of science derived from it. According to Descartes, the humanities were not worthy of serious attention. This rationalist, Enlightenment view was based on the idea that knowledge once gained is something objective and never changes. But this was precisely what concerned Vico, who had received a Catholic upbringing and realised that this Cartesian view completely ignored the humanities.

He believed that all true knowledge, including that of mathematics could be shown to be true by demonstrating how it came about. He developed the concept of outer and inner knowledge in his book, the *New Science*[73]. He believed that he had discovered

---

[73] Summarised by Isaiah Berlin in '*Three Critics of the Enlightenment*' (Published by Pimlico, 2000)

the path to all knowledge. Inner knowledge, like that of mathematics and geometry, we know to be valid 'because we made them', that is, we know through their causes, and these we work out. He then extended this idea of an inner access to knowledge to the concept that the mind plays a fundamental role in the acquisition of *all* knowledge, including those of science and the humanities. He believed the main sources of knowledge to be history, mythology, literature and law.

This meant that all that appears to be objective has come about by virtue of the subjective elements of brain function summarised earlier (6). This was a valuable contribution, and we found that it is never possible to by-pass these to arrive at something objective, changeless and real in the manner that the Rationalists thought possible.

The accuracy of this knowledge (that we know to be true 'because we made it') he claimed has decreasing certainty according to the subject matter considered. In Vico's view, mathematics and geometry are the most certain; then come mechanics, physics, psychology, history and the humanities in that order. He says, 'The rule and criterion of truth is to have made it. Hence the clear and distinct idea of the mind (i.e., the Cartesian criterion) not only cannot be the criterion of other truths, but it also cannot be the criterion of the mind itself, for while the mind apprehends itself, it does not make itself, and because it does not make itself, it is ignorant of the form or mode by which it apprehends itself'.

He later extended the capacity to 'know' to historical knowledge. We know history because we create it. He claimed that history is an ever changing and developing subject. Even human nature is not fixed, but evolves.

It is clear that Vico's approach to the problem of knowledge is vastly different from the relatively simplistic ideas of the Rationalists and came at a time when Enlightenment ideas were beginning to come under attack. It seems paradoxical that when science was forging ahead, philosophy was beginning to fall apart. Vico, followed by the Romantics, brought a deluge of completely new ideas to bear upon the problems of humanity in a dead universe. We are still in the process of recovering.

Vico correctly realised that the acquisition of knowledge is much more complicated than had been appreciated. We found that the cerebral functions involved are not simply the application of Cartesian logical principles to sensory experience. Although Vico pointed in the right direction, he was unable to supply a detailed description of the subjective and objective dimensions and how they inter-relate. Crucially he, like most others at that time, did not appreciate the dangers of the metaphysical trap: that every statement is a belief that requires some kind of validation. If it is about things unknowable, there is no method of validation, and if about things knowable, it is still only tentative knowledge.

The Romantic Reaction to The Age of Reason

After Vico, many other dissenting voices were to be heard. **Tom Paine** (*The Rights of Man*, 1791/2), **Godwin** (*An enquiry concerning the Principles of Political Justice* 1793) among others in England called for the abolition of the institution of government, as they believed this to be essential before real progress could be made. Hamann and Herder in Germany and Rousseau in France advocated a wide spectrum of philosophical, political and social ideas to remedy the ills of mankind. Their voices, among numerous others, were the first rumblings of dissatisfaction that ushered in the Romantic Age, characterised by a torrent of new and diverse ideas. Rousseau said that solutions do not come from the head (reason), but from the heart (values). In our terminology, that translates into an emphasis on knowledge from the Sensibilities, as opposed to knowledge purely from reason and logic.

At the end of our journey we will find that neither the head, nor the heart gives anything that could be called 'true meaning', for that is not possible. Experience shows that the highest achievements of civilisation seem to require the advances of science and its offspring, technology, *plus* responsive knowledge from the Sensibilities. A civilisation with this foundation is threatened only by those who *believe that these alone do not provide access to true meaning*.

The first to attack wholesale the ideas of the Enlightenment was **J G Hamann** (1730-1788) of Königsberg, East Prussia. Since Greek times, and particularly since the Renaissance, the attempt had been made to explain life and discover how it should be lived in terms of knowledge expressed as systems of ideas that could be discovered by observation and reason. But Hamann rejected all such rational systems of knowledge, whether from science, the Church of Rome or rationalist principles of social and political life. All these are artificial, subjective constructions and are false. "Blood and gold", he railed, have ruled this world, but the Age of Rationalism is no better. All are conspiracies against faith.

Hamann admired Hume for his empiricism. Hume had said that reason alone is impotent and Hamann agreed, calling it 'a poisonous snake'. He claimed that how to live and act comes from 'instinct', or self-knowledge, which is the word of God known to each individual: 'And if you do not know what to do, then read the Bible to find out'. The guide to action does not come from some obscure metaphysical principle. It comes from instinct, which after all, is how artists and all creative people work. The individual conscience is paramount and all forms of institutional authority, whether utilitarian, moral, or aesthetic must be rejected.

Hamann likened his ideas to an archipelago of islands, but he said he could not join them by more ideas because that would create a rational system that he was at pains to avoid. It would obliterate what is most living and real. In essence, each person creates his own archipelago. Hamann went to extreme lengths to emphasise the primacy of the individual as opposed to the state. That had never before been done, but he felt it to be a matter of urgency. At the very time during the Enlightenment period when attempts were being made by Les Philosophes and others to diminish or remove the authority of the Church and State, Hamann claimed that the threat to the integrity of the individual posed by rationalism was growing and must be resisted.

He seemed blind to the aims and potential benefits of the Age of Reason in which he lived. The idea of progress was at the heart of the scientific endeavour and Locke in particular had applied a rational approach to explore new social and political objectives. Intellectuals in France and England saw the possibilities of greater equality, freedom, justice and toleration as valuable objectives. But although Hamann wanted freedom, he thought that all it was necessary to know was to be found in faith and the Old Testament. Like other romanticist figures, he was also blind to the potentially explosive consequences of his ideas, which is the main reason for mentioning him. As will be found later, this was because the main thrust of his ideas was against all forms of authoritarianism, for he did not appreciate that this seriously limits the stability of the state and is a recipe for chaos.

He also did not recognize the tentative and evolving nature of the beliefs of science, sociology and politics that are essential components of a stable state and of the democratic ideals that were forming in England, although still embryonic in his day. Instead, he returned to faith in Christianity following a conversion he underwent when visiting London. His beliefs were not very different from the pietist beliefs of his childhood. The problems with which he wrestled are with us in the democracies of today. The danger looming was state organised collectivism, for this threatens initiative, enterprise and inventiveness that are all directly from each individual."

"He seems to have been a relatively obscure figure, so why do you mention him?"

"He was the earliest anti-Enlightenment figure who exerted influence on thinkers of the period, such as Herder, Heine, Jacobi, Moses Mendelssohn, Schlegal, Fichte and Goethe. It was Heine, who lived in France in later life and said prophetically something to the effect that the French do not understand the power behind those quiet Germans to the north.

The *Revolution* of 1789 followed by the *Terror* of 1793-4 and the nationalistic aggression of France under Napoleon brought forth a wealth of new ideas throughout Western Europe. But was reason failing? The Revolution had removed the apparent roadblocks to progress, (religion, the state and the aristocracy), yet still 'The People' were not in power. The Romanticists, who had criticised the Age of Reason, became disillusioned. Was the new dawn of Liberty, Equality and Fraternity no more than a mirage? Security and freedom still seemed uncertain and perhaps a distant vision. All the instruments of government in France had been destroyed, yet the result was autocracy.

What soon became apparent was that there was a growing disintegration of the cultural unity that had been a feature of 17th and 18th century Europe. Yes, there had been wars over territory and religious beliefs at that time, but art, literature and science had advanced apace and there was much common ground and a great deal of cultural and commercial communication between the various states of Europe."

"What makes the philosophical views you have developed relevant to this discussion of the Romantics?"

"Any philosophy is only relevant to the lives of individuals in society if it can be shown to 'work' under the exigencies of current events. Therefore I now want to examine our ideas in relation to the turmoil of the Romantic Age and its aftermath in the 20th century. There was little disagreement over what the vast majority of people wanted, namely peace, harmony, freedom, equality and fraternity. The great problem was how to attain these precious ingredients of life. Goethe was clear: romanticism is disease; classicism is health. But this was not acceptable, for Romanticism revealed the huge hidden potentials of the human Sensibilities.

A philosophy based primarily on reason, as exemplified by Kant, must fail because it ignored the Sensibilities, and for this reason the Enlightenment could not sustain itself indefinitely. Reason and logic are not sufficient to meet the needs of humans. Rousseau was one of the first to analyse the subjective dimension and pointed to some fundamental flaws in the concept of the state. The Enlightenment was an achievement of incalculable importance. But the endless diversity of ideas that characterised the Romantic Age also illustrated the extent to which the period of the Enlightenment had failed because it had not recognised and accommodated to such ideas.

Prior to the Revolution, as already mentioned, there had appeared critics of the Enlightenment and prominent among these was **Jean Jacques Rousseau** (1712-1778) whose analysis of society was penetrating, covered new ground and remains relevant to the problems of today. In primitive societies he claimed that, before humans owned property and had to work for each other, they were free and lived happy, honest and healthy lives. But these 'noble' savages who lived in a 'golden age' were ruined once they became 'civilised.' The invention of tools, the ownership of land and the need to work for others produced inequalities. This was because some individuals were more talented than others, so that some rose to the top and others sank to the bottom, which led to strife. Hence, the more civilised men became, the more they resorted to violence and war to solve disputes. The final end point he claimed with surprising prescience in view of the 20th century events to come, is a despotism that destroys everything remaining of value in the state. He asserted, 'It follows from this survey that, as there is hardly any inequality in the state of nature, all the inequality which now prevails owes its strength and growth to the development of our faculties and the advance of the human mind, and becomes at last permanent and made legitimate by the establishment of property and laws'[74].

He thought that life must have been most acceptable when the savage began to live in the simplest of societies. Once this point had been passed then, as he puts it in the opening sentence of his classic on political philosophy, *The Social Contract*, 'Man is born free; and everywhere he is in chains'[75]. Since a 'Golden Age' could now never be achieved, a social contract between the common man and the elite in society had to be established. This would define the rights of each. But he realised that this would still not ensure freedom for the individual, for although a person may agree to the contract, there would inevitably be occasions when individuals thought an action right, yet the community (to which each individual had signed up) ruled it to be wrong. Since Rousseau considered the freedom and moral responsibility of the individual as paramount, such a contract must be so minimal as to be hardly a contract at all. But this would create conditions favourable to the anarchist who wished to abolish government (and there were plenty of these about). He pursued this in more detail but was left with the dilemma of a state that was anarchical on the one hand, or totalitarian on the other.

The romanticists believed that everything is what it is; in the manner experienced by each individual, as opposed to theories and ideologies that are presented as *representing* reality, irrespective of the individual. From the time of Socrates until the 18th century, the assumption had been that a view of reality *could* be arrived at by reason and man was progressing steadily towards the ultimate goal of understanding everything. But the Romanticists maintained that

---

[74] *Discourse on Inequality*   J J Rousseau (J M Dent and co, London)

[75] *The Social Contract*   J J Rousseau (J M Dent and co, London)

this was false because, if reality is as it appears to each individual, then inevitably reality is going to appear different for each. Further, since there is no way of determining which of these views is true and which is false, it had to be assumed that each is an expression of reality. Hence, things cannot be defined in a rational, logical manner by overarching ideas, as the Rationalists thought. But this romantic vision of each individual as the possessor of truth is in itself a belief and it had the devastating consequence that it split society asunder. In fact, it was incompatible with the concept of a unified society.

The Enlightenment view that an objective end point does exist was also a belief, but at least it *was* compatible with the idea of a unified society and therefore was possibly not so dangerous."

"If reality is defined as it appears to each individual, how then can society arrive at a joint opinion about anything?"

"You ask why the Romantic Age appeared so diverse and chaotic? But this was more apparent than real. In terms of our description of responsive knowledge and its relation to sensory experience and lay/scientific knowledge, the answer is straightforward, for in essence it was not chaotic, or not yet. The intellectuals of Western Europe had come to appreciate that the motivating forces of the Enlightenment were aimed at seeking new definitions of utility and the rejection of old values and their associated beliefs from the Middle Ages and before. The Romantics appreciated the limitations and poverty of these objectives and instead put the Value and Aesthetic Sensibilities into forward gear at full speed across the whole range of their possibilities. And they were not always concerned about the welfare of each individual. Indeed, this approach soon uncovered conflicts and contradictions.

The democratic ideal that arose out of all this has proved to be the best solution to social welfare so far. **J G von Herder** (1744-1803), an early German founder of Romanticism, made the interesting suggestion that language, the German language in his case, race, sex, habits and customs, all contribute to the expression of each individual's views in art, literature and everything else. He claimed it is these deeper, ill-defined sensibilities that form common opinions about everything in society. And these are what hold societies together and forms a distinctive culture that defines it. The individual also 'captures' reality in myths that remain deep in the psyche and common to each community.

This means that objects cannot be described without reference to their makers, to the society from which they came. The beauty of a Greek vase cannot be defined in terms of objective criteria, for these will be different for each group of people at different times and in different places, yet he claims these are the only criteria that are legitimate. He was correctly identifying the appropriate sensibilities and the motivations derived from them.

Each culture therefore has its 'schwerpunkt', or 'centre of gravity' in these matters. But the danger is that this concept in practice may set one culture or community against another. As Isaiah Berlin put it, according to Herder *'Each human group must strive for that which lies in its bones, which is part of its tradition.'* But the consequence of this view, *'was that one of the great axioms of the 18th century Enlightenment, which is what romanticism came to destroy, was that valid objective answers could be discovered to all the great questions which agitate mankind - how to live, what to be, what is good, what is bad, what is right, what is wrong, what is beautiful, what is ugly'*[76].

It follows from the view of Herder and the wide variety of opinions of other romanticists, that the Enlightenment concept is invalid and that each community should be free to pursue its own objectives. But this conclusion was in some respects disastrous, for it turned out to be a recipe for the wars of the 20th century. Yet Herder himself, as well as other romanticists, firmly believed in egalitarianism and were against coercion and a strong central authority in the state. And so, in romanticism are to be found both the sources of war and the seeds of democracy.

Surveying the scene, **Coleridge** remarked in the 9th of his Philosophical Lectures in 1819, *'But assuredly the way to improve the present is not to despise the past; it is a great error to idolize it, but a still greater to hold it in contempt'.*

G Shenk reviewed many facets of the ideas dominant at this

---

[76] *The Roots Of Romanticism*, Isaiah Berlin   (Pimlico 1999)

time[77]. In summary he describes a widespread air of foreboding for the future and nostalgia for a past golden age; Chateaubriand foresaw the advent of military dictatorships; others spoke of a malady of the soul, of nothingness, nihilism, the longing for extinction; the fear of atheism and the loss of god; the transcendental had been eliminated and man became the measure of all things. But at the same time, others were more sanguine. A mood of optimism could also be detected; a new religion of progress seemed possible, such as that of Schleiermacher who advocated a religion without dogma. Heine spoke of the enfranchisement of humanity. Many emphasised individuality and the dominion of The People. Others were less optimistic since the spectre of death meant that all earthly hopes were inevitably doomed. Yet another romantic reaction to this state of affairs was to believe that earthly love could not perish since death removes the barrier to eternal bliss. The finale of Wagner's Tristan und Isolde is an example.

The primitive axis mechanism in modern societies creates problems that humans have not yet resolved, do not fully understand and in some respects may never resolve. The communities in which people live have the effect of encouraging or inhibiting the objective goals of each individual. At best they would allow the development of individual talents to the full. In practice, that frequently does not happen, for the subject's aspirations may be severely inhibited by an overbearing, authoritarian regime. Yet too weak an authority would lead to a state of anarchy.

Following 1789, the hopes of the proletariat disappeared under the heel of the Napoleonic Emperors. During the period of German unification in the 19th century, revolutionary movements existed in Europe and Russia. But disappointment followed when the collapse of the German Principalities was not followed by rule of the people, but by rule, as always, of kings and emperors. Even new wealth from the Capitalist led Industrial Revolution was going to the bourgeoisie. Yet, the ideas spawned by these political events produced ideas highly relevant to the 20th century Communist

---

[77] *The Mind of the European Romantics* H G Shenk (Oxford Univ Press 1966)

Revolution that appeared to be the way, at last, to a bright future, but turned into a disaster. Much more important, however, were the emergence of ideas of fundamental importance for the democracies that thrive today.

Berlin put this well in his essays on *Russian Thinkers*[78] when reviewing **Alexander Herzen** (1812-1870). Herzen was from a well-off family and went to Moscow University. He came to London in 1847 where he published articles in his journal, the 'Bell', that were circulated to fellow revolutionaries in Russia, who were plotting against Tsarist oppression. Although they looked to him for leadership, he could not agree with their objectives. He was torn by the modern predicament of how to reconcile the conflicting social objectives of *equality* and *excellence*. The objective of equality was to reign in the excesses of free enterprise, of which capitalism was a dominant one at that time. Excellence was the achievement of a relatively small number in all communities of those with ability and enterprise. Herzen believed that the essential precursor for excellence, upon which all progress depends, is liberty of the individual, which, however, is threatened by the objective of equality. Individual liberty was his constant refrain, but the conflicting aims within an ideal society led him to think that the basic problems of society are perhaps not soluble; all one can do is to try to solve them. And, it should be noted, that these conflicting principles have still not been resolved.

The solution will necessitate defining clearly the role of government in its task of exerting minimum overall control. But its second role is to encourage the pursuit of professionalism at all levels of expertise. This will vary from the expert who, once trained, brooks little interference with his work, to the majority who are trained to work to prescribed professional standards. The first create, practise and teach professionalism; the majority learn to acquire and practise professional standards. The frontiers of professionalism are not fixed, but move as the subject advances.

Berlin comments, '*the dogmas of socialism seemed to Herzen, no less stifling and erroneous than those of capitalism, or of*

---

[78] *Russian Thinkers* Isaiah Berlin Penguin Books 1978

the Middle Ages or of the early Christians'. Herzen objected violently to the demands of the socialist revolutionaries of his day who *'called for supreme sacrifices and sufferings* [of the masses] *for the sake of nationality, or civilisation, or socialism, or justice, or humanity – if not in the present, then in the future.'*

Herzen appreciated the injustice of elitism, but equally valued intellectual and moral freedom. As Berlin puts it, while refusing to sacrifice excellence to equality, unlike the ideologists of the left, the socialists of yesterday and today, he understood with J S Mill something that has only become clear today: the common mean between these values, is not arrived at by the opinion of the masses; it is not the best of both worlds. More frequently the result is, in Mill's words, an aesthetically and ethically repellent *'conglomerated mediocrity: the submergence of the individual within the masses."*

"Surely there is a fallacy there. It assumes that societies neatly divide into the elite who show excellence and the rest. But who is to decide which members show excellence?"

"I agree and it remains an unresolved problem to which Rousseau and others referred. In the democracies of today, *all* need the freedom to seek their own measures of excellence. But in practice, this would lead to chaos. Tolerance is the principle that makes this possible, but ideally one should only curtail freedom when the limits of tolerance have been reached. The Romanticists forced us to seek and apply these principles. When there is a choice, excellence should always be chosen. Otherwise, any kind of progress is not possible".

Values In The Community
Discussion 30

"How are we to understand this profusion of ideas that erupted during the Romantic period?"

"I begin by summarising their short and long term consequences.

The romanticists exploded the classical ideal of a single answer to all things, one route to knowledge, and it became necessary to replace it with a plurality of routes and values. But it was obvious to some at the time, such as Rousseau and Chateaubriand, that there could be conflict among those with different and powerful ideals. There were therefore three possibilities and each came to fruition in the 20th century.

1. In a potentially explosive situation, an individual motivated by powerful feeling sensibilities could be prompted to take strong action to seize control of the state. This action could become irresistible if the community as a whole condoned the action as right. Such was the position in Germany during and after the Weimar republic. The Germans felt humiliated by the Versailles Treaty; the economy was weak, unemployment high and morale was low. In these circumstances, it was not difficult for Hitler to seize power.

2. A common romantic ideal was rule by 'The People'. Karl Marx constructed a powerful academic argument for this principle that came to fruition as communism. But, instead of rule by the people, the result soon became rule of the people by a rigid, hierarchical elite that brought about disastrous results in Russia and elsewhere.

3. If societies were to survive, then a peaceful resolution of the conflicting ideals of romanticism was essential through tolerance and compromise, which 19th/20th century Britain just managed to achieve. This model became the essence of the democratic ideal of today. But it is not an end point, for early in the 21st century there are signs that this 19th century model of democracy is not working well and will need to evolve into something better.

These three consequences summarize the effects of

romanticism on European culture. They contributed to the disasters of the 20th century, but inadvertently contributed also to the birth of democracy during the 18th and 19th centuries."

"In the 19th century the intellectual, social and political life of Western Europe was in turmoil. How was this resolved?"

19th Century Romanticism and 20th Century Democracy

"You will appreciate now that the wealth of new and diverse ideas made any resolution of the problems difficult. There was a melting pot of religious ideas from the schisms of pre-revolutionary times; the objectives of the Enlightenment coupled with Locke's novel ideas on civil government and then the potentially diverse and explosive ideas of the Romantic Age. There was no obvious way of resolving this situation and it is not surprising that it ended in the disasters of the 20th century. The solution had to come from elsewhere.

The men of the Enlightenment, as well as the romanticists, assumed that their knowledge was secure, which is what made Romanticism particularly dangerous. The principle that had to emerge was one of toleration. Only when it came to be accepted that all claims to knowledge should be regarded as tentative, could the valuable ideas of the romanticists be incorporated to form a vital part of the democratic method of government.

In human relations, the possible effects of different beliefs can be compared using statistical methods, so that their *comparative* value can be tested, but there is no measure of the validity of beliefs held by each individual. However, this does not mean that such beliefs do not have value for both the individual and the community. Only members of the society in which an individual lives can legitimately determine these values with respect to the community as a whole.

A method of managing these problems was evolving in Britain at the time when romantic ideas began to pose threats in Europe. As Rousseau had pointed out, the interests of an individual and the interests of the community as a whole may not coincide. But methods for ameliorating the effects of this problem have been evolving within democratic governments in Britain and elsewhere during the 20th and 21st centuries. The individual is the inventor or generator of new ideas and also becomes joint arbiter of what the community decides."

"It seems strange that you make the individual as producer of ideas paramount, yet those very ideas may have diverse explosive potentials."

"And those potentials are why there have always been wars. I have only two points to make, which summarize this discussion.

1. We have agreed that all such ideas are beliefs and therefore should be regarded as *tentative*. Their temporal life is therefore limited, a principle that the romanticists had not appreciated. In practice, this means that they remain 'true' only while the whole community agrees.

2. No one member or group of fanatics must be allowed to gain power on behalf of all members, however good the ideas may appear to be. Hence government in a democracy must be strong enough to resist fanatics, yet responsive to the wishes of its members."

"It is interesting that during the critical 19th century in Britain, although there were contending forces in the form of powerful men in government, in opposition and plenty of often wild, 'romantic idealists' out in the community, yet no one man was allowed to become too dominant, but many made significant contributions to the final result."

"And it may be added, individual contributors had only the vaguest notion of what was being created; or what the final result was to be. It illustrates how important it is that motivating beliefs must be regarded as purely tentative. In other words, the values of which we are all aware, allow only very limited and incomplete views of what lies ahead. And when we try to be too visionary, the result is apt to be disastrous."

Discussion 31

"How did Europeans move beyond the Romantic Age?"

"In the 18th and 19th centuries the concept of a 'tentative' belief, was hardly appreciated, even in relation to science and in so far as it was appreciated in science, it was not applied with the rigour of today. And as we have said, those who formulated political, social and ethical principles during the Enlightenment thought they were describing 'the nature of things' and even assumed that they were discovering eternal truths. Our investigations have shown this to be false and that all 'social truths', like scientific truths, are tentative beliefs. The acceptance of this position was crucial for the establishment of stable democracies.

Many socio-political ideas in the 19th and 20th centuries were a confusing conflation on the one hand of religious post-reformation constructions of how the world works, and on the other, Enlightenment theories as to how individuals and societies were assumed to work. But in France, all the old organs of state had been removed by the Revolution, so that no guidelines were left to give stability. Also, the romanticists made the individual paramount. Initiatives then passed to individuals with ideas and enough force of character in Germany, France, Italy and Russia, to express themselves as they thought fit."

"As I understand the position now, the building blocks of a society are from two principles (1) the tentative nature of beliefs and (2) complex units described by such people as Herder, the ill-defined habits and customs of a society that characterise its culture. This is epitomized somewhat differently in the words of **Sir Walter Scott**[79] Now I should like to know where we find these two principles in democracy today, and if they are there, how did they get there? I should have thought that tentative beliefs and the rather ill defined factors described by Herder and others that describe a community

---

[79] "Let us remain as nature made us – Englishmen, Irishmen, Scotchmen, with something like the impress of our several countries upon each. We would not become better subjects if all resembled each other like so many smooth shillings" Sir Walter Scott.

are weak elements out of which to build a strong democracy. How was the transition made from the fixed beliefs of the romanticists to the tentative beliefs of today?"

"There are two aspects to this. First, consider romantic ideas. The romantic visionaries were forced to accept, perhaps aided by the disasters of the 20th century that their visions were tentative and then the bonus within a democracy was peace and freedom.

Secondly, there was the problem of how to prevent the infant democracy exploding. Your question about the transition to democracy would take us beyond our remit, but we must consider it in outline. It occurred during the 18th and 19th centuries when many European countries were tearing themselves apart. Aristotle gave a clear description of democracy, but the Greeks could not make it work[80]. Plato tried but ended with a description in The Republic of an idealised form of communism.

The ever present threat of riot and revolution in Britain, following the events of 1789, were avoided by measures that included the relative tolerance of dissenting voices in the community, a policy to remove rotten boroughs, the increase of Catholic emancipation, repeal of the Corn Laws and extension of the franchise when the political pressures became dangerously high. These were some of the measures taken to maintain the stability of the state and allow peaceful evolution to proceed towards what is now recognised as democratic government.

The revolution of 1688 had diminished the power of the king. The power of the Commons gradually increased as the

---

[80] "In those democracies that are supposed to be the most favourable to the people, a wrong notion of liberty prevails. There are two things that are thought to be the marks of democracy: liberty and sovereignty of the majority, for the democratic notion of justice is equality and equality means that what the masses decide is final, while liberty means that anyone can do what he likes. Consequently, in democracies of this kind, everyone lives as he pleases – following his fancy, as Euripides puts it. This is frivolous: to live in harmony with the system should give one a sense of security, not of servitude" Aristotle, Politics 5.9 (Oxford Univ Press 1952)

proportion of its members were the bourgeoisies who had become rich following the Industrial Revolution, but the landed aristocrats in the Lords still remained powerful. **Robert Blake** explains that an important reason why this apparently rigid, hierarchical, multi-storied structure extending from the king and an aristocratic oligarchy down to the people was stable was due to the fact that the system was fluid[81]. Blake points out that anyone with enterprise who acquired enough wealth could ascend from the bottom to become a landed aristocrat. In this it differed from the inflexible continental systems that had to explode to undergo change. Hence the revolutions in the middle of the century among the Principalities of what was to become Germany. In Britain, regular elections ensured that all government decisions were subject to policy reviews and a possible change of government.

But even after the Reform Act of 1832 the franchise remained narrow and governments were essentially aristocratic and aimed to 'represent' the people. By 1830, the Industrial Revolution had reduced the workers to poverty, starvation, long hours of factory life and a prey to disease, especially cholera and tuberculosis,– conditions portrayed by Dickens.

The idea of democracy was an untried possibility and not an obvious solution. **Carlyle** (1795-1881) looked for a strong, dynamic figure to produce a solution through radical change in a search for dignity and individualism. He, like many Victorians, believed that the British had been thrown off course by the Industrial Revolution. The Chartist movement of the 1830s commenced among the people and aimed to produce immediate solutions. It was a harbinger of the socialist and communist movements that emerged in the 20th century. But some were not bellicose: Lovett, a shopkeeper who founded the *London Working Men's Association,* favoured a peaceful solution and claimed that if there were universal suffrage, the Parliamentary system would deliver justice and equality.

This principle of universal suffrage, together with other political demands, were published in the Charter of 1838 and

---

[81] *The Conservative Party from Peel to Thatcher* Robert Blake, Published by Fontana Press 1985

presented to Parliament, where it was voted down. A concise review of Chartism is presented in chapter 3 of **A. N. Wilson's** '*The Victorians*'[82]. Various political elements from the old Whig and Tory parties of the 18th century were extracted and modified to form the Liberal and Conservative parties by the end of the 19th century.

You asked how the two principles you described above (tentative beliefs and innumerable, disparate 'truths' enunciated by the romanticists) came to find places in the democracy of today. These became converted into the building blocks of modern democracy in the form of pressure groups and political parties in society that try to mobilize sufficient strength to change the government, or government policies. These groups may display diversities of opinion as broad as those found in the Romantic Age and may include those of religious, atheist or humanist persuasions. But the *tentative* nature of this knowledge refers to what is acceptable to the *community as a whole* at any given time."

"You, or rather Rorty (26), said that Aristotelian, Thomist, Kantian and other metaphysical systems are no longer relevant in order for societies to discover how to exist in peace. I take it that you agree?"

"Yes, but that does not take matters very far. Let us consider another approach to the problem of peace in societies. Many thinkers have explored this topic from the point of view of the liberty, or freedom of individuals. Isaiah Berlin summarised much of this work in a series of essays called 'Liberty' in which he searches for a solution to this problem[83]. In the essay entitled, 'Two Concepts of Liberty', 'negative' and 'positive' freedoms are described. In the first, *negative freedom* is the private 'space' the subject requires in order to thrive and into which society must not intrude – what might be called an introvert requirement to compose music or write poetry. For others, individuals actively participating in the beliefs, customs and objectives of society find *positive freedom* in this process of participation– what might be called an extrovert approach necessary to give such individuals a sense of freedom.

---

[82] *The Victorians'* A N Wilson, Published by Arrow Books, 2003.

[83] *'Liberty'*, edited by Henry Hardy, Ox Univ Press 2005

Beliefs And Human Values R Sheriff Jones

Berlin's descriptions are a brilliant and detailed account of the psychology of this subject. But one is left asking what does 'liberty' mean; to what does it refer? In philosophical terms, the idea of liberty has got to refer to something and that something must be the 'self' as defined in the way already described (16).

'Negative' freedom would then be better called 'subjective' since it refers to the *self* and all its characteristics. 'Positive' freedom would be better called 'objective' since it refers to the *environment* with its physical and human characteristics. The components of the 'self' are the same in each case; the differences are in its objective requirements. In practice, individuals respond to the constraints imposed by society in positive ways and to variable degrees. 'Freedom' in this context is to seek subjective and objective expression of the abilities in whatever ways the community will allow."

"Doubtless that is so, but there can be no doubt that over the centuries the central issue has changed. The objectives were once primarily based on the need to survive, whereas now with universal education, the ease of communication and the ready provision of goods and services in the West, the demands of the individual are much broader and more demanding. Also, the age of romanticism and the wars of the 19th and 20th centuries must surely have destroyed all faith in an all-embracing ideal arrived at by reason?"

"Berlin's response is to conclude that the solution must lie in

1. The pluralism of human values: the idea that there must be acceptance of the fact that individuals have many and varied needs and desires. And only governments are able to provide an environment that allows for these.

2. Also, there are certain principles that are held widely among members of a community and today these are often called 'human rights'. These, he thought were common to most or all 'normal' humans in a democracy and could be used to enhance social cohesion.

These together, he thought, were the nearest one could get to a workable solution, and they do not depend upon any over-riding metaphysical principle.

I think his case for Pluralism is correct. But I would add that the subjective values, (Berlin's negative freedoms), must be allowed room to evolve. Also, the objective principles held by society, (Berlin's positive freedoms), must be allowed to change continuously. There is no final goal or objective. Also, human rights do not come from some inviolable superior authority, or from individuals (nobody can arrogate to him or herself a 'human right'), but from the authority of the community as a whole."

"But democracies today seem to be facing considerable problems. And in many respects they are the same old problems revealed so vividly and forcefully during the Romantic response to the Age of Reason."

"Democracy is still an unrefined tool and the problem today is to find a balance between the aspirations of individuals and the power of the state to impose solutions, ostensibly aimed at the welfare of those same individuals. Always there is the fear, as described by Rousseau, Mill and others that individual enterprise will be diminished, for without individualism there can be no progress and no democracy.

Karl Popper (1902-94)[84] helped to clarify some of these issues. He asserted that the tentative beliefs of science could be extended, using suitable criteria, to include tentative beliefs about social and political questions. Bur our analysis has made it clear that science is about the physical characteristics of the universe (including human appearance and behaviour), whereas the second is quite different, for it is about the normative beliefs, natural and supernatural, that are the *responses* of the Sensibilities to the first category.

Popper did not make this crucial distinction, but we are concerned with the implications of it. Where does it lead? Is there an end-point? It is becoming clear that normative conclusions are arrived at by trial and error and are always subject to revision. This is alluded to later when discussing the management of beliefs (Part 6). It is difficult territory in which one should always be suspicious of the significance of normative assertions, for example, about 'political correctness', 'human values', or the ambitions of a political party to

---

[84] *The Open Society and its Enemies* Karl Popper Routledge, London 1945

'change everything'.

Democracy is a secular instrument and at any moment it only satisfies a proportion of its citizens but works because all accept the principle of tolerance. That is why Christianity became tolerant as it became embedded in democratic secularism. But there are other problems about the current democratic model that are being uncovered now that technology has made communication between all levels in society virtually instantaneous. The 19/20th century model assumed that all members of society were equal in understanding and knowledge, but it has become clear that a relatively small proportion have significantly higher levels of ability and knowledge and these are the ones that produce progressive ideas. Mill feared the 'tyranny of the masses', for the majority would come to control decision-making. Is the current democratic structure leading to a form of social, as distinct from physical entropy? And is this why the democratic West is showing signs of decline, or malfunction?"

Part 6
A Minimalist Philosophy of Human Values
(Discussions 32–36)

Discussion 32

"We found earlier that the welfare of individuals cannot be considered separately from the environment in which they live. In primitive societies there were powerful motivating beliefs derived from supernatural powers, and the beliefs associated with tribalism, which produced the motives to protect the tribe from its enemies. Today there are still tribal societies motivated by similar beliefs and controlled by their warlords. But over time, these primitive tribal responses are changing. Motivating beliefs from the sensibilities, for example, caused Christians at the time of the Crusades to speak of holy war against the infidel. But these attitudes have now changed radically, yet some Muslims, for example, still speak of holy war, jihad, when their religion is thought to be under threat.

These changes over time are caused, as was found earlier, by the environment acting in some respects to permit and in others to restrict the abilities of individuals to develop and explore new possibilities. But the authority of warlords and kings greatly determined the course of events until the Enlightenment.

From the 17th century, and perhaps for the first time in history, the lowly and formerly powerless members of society exerted sufficient, sustained pressure on the authority of church and state to bring about radical changes in the way humans lived – the politico-social world had turned upside down. Hence our digression to discover these new motivating beliefs during the Enlightenment, the Romantic Age and the birth of Democracy that followed. Throughout these epochs, three motivating beliefs impinged on the various strata of society in different, but highly significant ways. These were,

> 1. Belief in the *supernatural*. The Catholic Church was convulsed by schism and religious wars. But the upshot was that the Enlightenment and the aftermath of the French

Revolution increased the power of the people at the expense of religious authority over the people.

2. Beliefs in *nationalism* as a motivating force had been powerful throughout history. This is what had held states together, built empires and protected society from its enemies. In practice, it probably had more to do with increasing royal power than protecting the peasant. These beliefs declined under pressure from the people, but not without the devastating wars of the 19th and 20th centuries before the democratic ideal took hold.

3. *Racially* motivated beliefs. It had never been difficult for leaders to convince society that people of a different race must be dangerous and therefore had to be defeated in war. But by the end of the 20th century this category of motivation also decreased as the idea of value status extended from societies to have global reach.

These three, religion, nationalism and racism were also the motivating beliefs of primitive man and were based on the model of the primitive sensory-motor axis and aimed at preserving humans in this life and a life hereafter. You can appreciate now that the painful transition from the Enlightenment and Romantic Age to democracy was the struggle by humans to progress beyond primitivism and autocratic rule. The objective remained the same – protection in a dangerous world – but the methods changed. The pressures for change came from many levels in society. The masses revolt when they are aware that the elite are weak or are uncertain and this was the case when Voltaire and his friends were screaming for change in the 18th century. But these new elitist pressures derived their strength in part from the British empiricists and Kant's idealism, which is why I spent some time reviewing their ideas.

But what was not realised at the time was that when you invoke an ideal to achieve an objective, you are simply *imposing* a new form of authoritative beliefs and, for example, that came to fruition with the French Revolution. It was not what Voltaire would have wished.

The romanticists who followed were saying: we don't want *any* authority imposing beliefs; the individual is paramount. The consequences of that view we considered in our last two discussions

(30, 31)."

"So I take it that the sequence of social change from the Enlightenment, through romanticism to democracy was all part of the attempt by humans to advance beyond primitivism. These were profound changes yet they appear to have produced relatively stable societies throughout most of Europe and North America. But they are by no means perfect. And what about the rest of the world where the main motivating beliefs systems have primitive features?"

"We must hope for changes in these societies comparable with those that were painfully acquired in Western Europe over the last 500 years. Democracies display the elements of progress in a form that is still embryonic and imperfect: They still contain primitive elements to be overcome and these include,

1. Religious differences that will have to diminish in favour of 'common values' if strife is to be minimised.'
2. Extension of the principle of tolerance to have a global reach.
3. The removal of unnecessary laws in order to extend freedom.
4. Global objectives to replace purely national objectives.
5. Acceptance of inequality, (no two individuals *are* alike), but with some way of avoiding gross financial inequalities.
6. The extension and support, as far as possible, of individual initiatives and enterprise. Without individualism, humans would cease to progress towards a better life and a diminution of the evils that plagued primitive man."

"How do you suggest that progress is to be made?"

"It is now evident that if progress towards democratic maturity is to be achieved, the series of topics just mentioned will have to be examined to see where progress is possible. Third Age Philosophy begins with an accurate description of the applications of the minome to give valid accounts of all relations between sensory experiences and the subjective. This must include acceptance of the kinds of beliefs there are; their widely differing roles and their significance for motivation. Also recognition of the crucial role of the unknowable in all objective and subjective events."

Discussion 33

"Science based knowledge and philosophy were pursued with great vigour after the Renaissance and as a consequence, beliefs declined as a social force in Western Europe during the Enlightenment. Beliefs based on scientific knowledge replaced beliefs in supernatural powers invented to explain the weather, crops, fertility and disease, etc. There has since been increasing acceptance of science-based knowledge of genetic and microbiological phenomena. Yet, as mentioned earlier, it is still amazing how many readily turn to esoteric beliefs and the hope of 'cures' when science-based medicine does not meet their expectations."

"These confusions are well described by the philosopher, Daniel **Dennett** (1942-)[85]. Many sects claim supernatural influences over natural events, which produce effects that are not explicable by science. The Catholic Church agrees and sends people to Lourdes. They do not distinguish between the two kinds of knowledge that we have discussed. Newton clearly made this distinction (15): the natural world is as described by science, but he accepted that it could have been made differently by an almighty power in which he believed.

Confusions will not cease until religions accept that the role of supernatural beliefs is to seek ways of *utilising* scientific knowledge instead of seeking ways to over-rule it. The historical record shows that when religion is on top, that is, supported by the state, supernatural beliefs lead to the persecution of non-believers, including scientists. In the Middle Ages when heretics were burnt at the stake, the Inquisition practised torture and witch hunting was encouraged. One factor that brought these excesses about was that St Augustine (4) thought that earthly cities were doomed and existence would become utterly wretched and sinful. Therefore, he had to construct an earthly church so strong that its theology would ensure

---

[85] Breaking the Spell – Daniel C Dennett   (Penguin Books Ltd, London. 2006)

for believers peace and happiness in heaven. Therefore heresy could not be tolerated, no matter what the cost.

Beliefs in the supernatural that led to these actions diminished greatly when the church was no longer 'on top'. With the advent of a democracy in Britain largely supported by beliefs in human welfare, these practises disappeared. But Islam has not yet completed the transition to objectives based on human welfare. It is not a question of abandoning belief in the supernatural, but of modifying the practices to meet the beliefs of a largely secular society with a different culture.

You also have to remember that to progress beyond primitivism it is necessary to overcome nationalism and racism. This requires the acceptance by each individual of the value status of others (12) and thus includes these dimensions. But that is a slow process."

"It has become apparent that science and philosophy have been unable to answer questions about the supernatural. Therefore many think there is a vacuum left following the decline of traditional beliefs."

"Our discussions make it possible to identify three categories of belief.

Categories of Belief

1. Absolute or faith based beliefs validated by faith in the certainty of the existence of a supernatural realm
2. Tentative beliefs about the sensory world validated by the scientific method and by lay experience.
3. Tentative, normative beliefs from the Sensibilities, which includes all ethical knowledge. Validation is from individuals and draws on the Sensibilities plus beliefs of the first and second categories.

But note the effect of minimalist beliefs which we arrive at later in this discussion. We must take into account, when arriving at this new position, the unknowable origins of all sensory and Sensibility experiences for from these come all knowledge and understanding."

"We truly live in a mysterious universe!"

"And our conclusions must reflect that. For communities, progress will be a matter of gradually shifting the grounds on which beliefs are established. I do not differ from Plato's conclusion in the Theatetus that all knowledge implies belief. In the opening sentence of these discussions it was stated that every idea expresses a belief, for that is the way the mind works. But we have since discovered that there are categories of beliefs: some unavoidable, some harmless and others harmful, unverifiable and avoidable (31). It is a question of learning to manage beliefs; some do this well and others not at all. The management of beliefs however, is not purely a matter for the individual. Everyone lives in a society and each individual is strongly influenced by others who reflect the beliefs of the society as a whole.

It is obvious that belief systems about human welfare have changed dramatically since the Middle Ages. Now I want to make a suggestion that should help to answer your question about that vacuum! Since civilisation began, there have been two intellectual epochs of immense power and influence that have already been described. I believe, however, that we are now entering a third period of great significance.

The first two epochs were,

1. The unprecedented importance of the appearance of Greek science and philosophy.

2. The reappearance of these following the Renaissance in an even more powerful, decisive and apparently unstoppable form (17). During each period, there was a marked effect on existing beliefs. We have seen during the latter period how it led to the Enlightenment, which was in effect, a re-appraisal of man's place in the universe and his belief systems.

A Third Epoch in the History of Ideas

I suggest that we are now entering *a third and perhaps more decisive period of re-appraisal*. And the reason for this is that, during the 19th and 20th centuries, science reached a new and revealing phase in our understanding of the universe. Quantum physics points decisively to the relations between the human body and mind. Sub-atomic particles are vast in number and variety. They are in perpetual motion, driven by a force that the scientists call 'energy', the unknowable 'causation' for which Hume searched. The bridge between mind and matter has become much clearer. I include in this third major advance of civilisation *learning how to manage beliefs*, which humans have not yet been able to do successfully. One reason is the failure to identify the unknowable dimensions clearly and develop a rational attitude to them.

The first two epochs may be described as the *Mythology of the Western World* and lasted from the appearance of Classical Greece until about the end of the 19th century. Every culture has its mythology, knowledge of which is fragmentary because it existed thousands of years ago and extended over many millennia. Western mythology is about 3 millennia in duration and is coming to an end. We can be sure of that because our vision of the universe has completely changed and now extends from the infinitely small to the infinitely large or distant and is bounded by unknowable components. All this was shrouded in beliefs during the Age of Western Mythology just ended.

Boethius, as we have seen (4), pointed to the fact that from the awareness of events unfolding in consciousness and the short duration for which they stay there, it is evident that sensory events extend to infinity and science is now exploring the implications of infinity in time and space. Particles in motion are the stuff from which all life is made. Certain particles form atoms and atoms unite to form molecules. From these, proteins, genes and all the larger structures of living organisms form, including the brain and all its intellectual powers."

"Why did you include intellectual powers in this third epoch?"

"One cannot separate off intellect, or mind, without indulging in gratuitous beliefs, and that would take us back to the age old habit from which we are trying to escape. Therefore, I conclude that rationality, logical reasoning and the Sensibilities are products of brain function, the minome, and in essence are from these mysterious particles in motion. The physicists will undoubtedly discover vastly more about them in time, but that won't alter where the origin of life lies. Clearly, it is not in the stars above, which are no longer regarded as divine, nor from the dust at our feet. Therefore all that we are is from particles and the energy that drives the universe.

It is hardly surprising that we are products of matter and

motion, but it does make our origins completely mysterious. We are a part of the secrets of the universe; which I call *the riches of the universe*. I use this description to refer to 'the unknowable'. All intellectual achievement, all human values reside there. One could imagine a god manipulating all the powers in the universe, but many would ask: does such a belief add anything useful to what we know, or the way we live?"

"Is this cycle of the creation and destruction of systems of ideas by individuals about the universe endless and inevitable, or is it possible to get beyond it?"

"I would not like to hazard a guess. But once the current position is fully appreciated, the result can be seen as satisfactory in the following sense. The achievements and values that become manifest in each individual's life do not 'return to dust' in the sense that they are destroyed or lost, but remain as what they always were, a part of the universe. One can think of individuals as channels of communication open to the limits of the abilities of each, and making manifest riches of the universe that would otherwise remain hidden. In other words, if we accept that we are a part of these riches, then the question of immortality does not arise because it is no longer relevant, for there is no 'destiny' to pursue; such questions become part of a redundant belief system."

"But is the view you have just suggested not a belief?"

"Beliefs in the existence of 'objects' and 'causation' that Hume abolished in the 17th century have now been replaced with the tentative beliefs of science that include the existence of sub-atomic particles and energy, but it remains true that we do not know what these are, and what they mean. Also, beliefs in the existence of gods and hidden powers I have now replaced simply with awareness of the Value and Aesthetic Sensibilities and the motivating energy that makes them manifest as an integral part of living. As Keats said, and I quote him again below: this is all we know and all we need to know. It describes the position of humans as accurately as possible.

The riches are not to be found in the dust at your feet. The gods are hidden in the mysterious energy that created and drives the universe. Built into Western Mythology, especially in medieval times were the ideas of a body that perishes and a soul that is immortal. Latin philosophy never managed, no matter how hard philosophers tried, to extricate itself from body and soul dualism.

But souls could not exist in isolation, so there had to be a god with whom the soul could communicate, which necessitated a personal god. This led to the highly complex metaphysical theology of the Middle Ages and to endless modifications after the reformation.

When one compares a minimalist philosophy with the appalling intellectual climate of faith based beliefs in most of the world's communities, you can appreciate the dangers we face and how far humans have yet to travel. Now to my mind, this new way of regarding the universe and the human situation minimizes, or abolishes the beliefs that serve only to generate dangers for individuals and societies from false hopes and fears."

"And so, as I understand the position now, everything that is most valuable we become aware of by virtue of the Aesthetic and Value Sensibilities. They are not to be 'discovered' in the tentative beliefs of science, or in the beliefs of religion."

"Correct. We are simply aware of them, as we concluded earlier, as unknowable components of the universe (13)."

"But do we not have to believe in something in order to make use of them in daily life?"

"The interplay between the three Sensibilities that I have described (9-13) gives rise, when the freedoms of a democratic state exist, to what have now come to be called 'human values'. People feel strongly about these because they motivate; they are the engines that drive societies."

"I can see now that these are the minimalist beliefs that appear in the title of these discussions."

"Exactly! That position is our objective."

"I am not convinced yet. All those with permanent beliefs hang on to the existence of something like the soul?"

"The soul may be regarded as an inherent part of what is now history and I call 'The Mythology of the Western World'. It differs from other mythologies of history in that it belonged to the first and second Epochs that were of relatively short duration and there was an abrupt termination at the end of the 19th century. But this was due to the pace at which new ideas were forming and evolving.

'To live', in computer terminology for example, is to describe a file that is the memory, or permanent record of something that exists. During life this is updated from moment to moment and resides in the memory. At death the updates cease, but the file, the 'soul', lives on. It is a record of the riches gleaned by that individual, but I must add, it contains evils as well as goods *as these are so judged* by contemporaries. This was the soul in first and second age terminology. The full record and significance of encounters between individuals of the same or opposite sexes may take years to discover, as for example in a long marriage. I consider the permanence of these riches in the discussions to follow."

"All this suggests that death need not be regarded as 'closure', nor the moment to say 'good-by' for example, at a funeral ceremony. The record, the 'soul-content', lives on to be cherished, or sometimes reviled."

"Everyone as they grow older carries a vision of death. For primitive humans struggling to survive, it appeared frightful. The gods of Homer were relatively humane. For Plato the supernatural was a shadowy world. The philosopher. Protagoras (4) was uncertain whether the gods exist, but the scholastics of the Middle Ages were quite sure and caused terror in their search for heretics. These ideas gain their validity and sense of being eternal values from the fixity of the beliefs. Yet history shows that they do change over time. The intention of a minimalist philosophy is to remove false hopes and fears, and the terrorism of the modern age. But their content does change for it is from the values experienced by each individual."

<u>Towards a solution</u>

"Clearly, logical reasoning does not solve the problems of ethics. Logic seemed to lead to a Humean sceptical desert, or a Kantian metaphysical jungle. It must be possible to improve on these?"

"When one reviews the history of ideas from primitive times to the present day, one is confronted with an extraordinary variety of beliefs and philosophical systems. They are all systems of ideas that attempt to explain the world, and the faculty that has been used to fashion them is reason, or logic, applied to sensory experience and also, mistakenly, through systems of beliefs applied to the Sensibilities.

As you know, my contention is that far too little attention has been paid to accurate introspective observation and logic has been applied there inappropriately. There is no single road to understanding. Only when we utilise *all our faculties* correctly are we likely to reach a conclusion that is as accurate as it is possible to be and, above all, does more good than harm. Let us take another step forward.

You may argue that the values derived from the sensibilities do not contain any sense of true meaning hidden in the unknowable. That is so. Any expression of true meaning inevitably can be only in terms of beliefs about the supernatural that are shot through with all the sensory experiences of *this* world. These include personal experiences, the Bible, the Koran and other holy writings together with the doctrines derived from them. Meanings emerge from belief in the supernatural components of these experiences. They invariably include expressions of hope. But anything short of certainty brings fear. And so they serve to generate hopes and fears."

"Yes, I agree. When we consider more recent times, for example, beliefs still seem to torment people. **Samuel Johnson** (1709-1784), the English poet and critic was deeply religious but, despite this, was very fearful of death. **John Betjeman** (1906-1984) was another example. **Cardinal Newman** (1801-1891) in his poem, the *Dream of Gerontius,* depicts a dying man burdened with beliefs that caused him, on the one hand to be fearful of purgatory and hell, and on the other to be buoyed up by hopes of being saved."

"And to those high profile examples could be added superstitions, such as witchcraft, magic and 'honour killings' following the break down of arranged marriages. These beliefs cause enormous stresses and loss of life. When one considers the sum total of misery with which humans have been burdened, any attempt to minimize evils can only be laudable. But there can be no doubt that many fears and hopes remain locked within the subjective of countless individuals.

Fortunately, history does show that specific belief systems, including those due to nationalism and racism, fade over time. That is what happened to the Greek pantheon. **Lecky** says, the religion of one age often becomes the poetry of the next[86]. '*The grotesque legends and the harsh doctrines of a superstitious age are so explained away, that they appear graceful myths foreshadowing and illustrating the conceptions of a brighter day. For a time they flicker upon the horizon with a softly beautiful light that enchants the poet.*' The pressures of the Enlightenment played no small part in bringing this about and the democracies of today exhibit many of the consequent benefits."

"When beliefs that bring about unfortunate consequences are removed, I am sure that deep within the minomes of most people there is simply the idea of some 'spiritual power' somewhere that explains all that seems unknowable, or mysterious. I take this change from the rigours of violence and heresy to muted spirituality to be evidence of the evolution of civilisation from the gods of Homer to Greek philosophy and onwards to a modern civilised democracy."

"Beliefs have been so universal since the dawn of history that for many it is impossible to contemplate a world in which they are absent. There is an inability to separate freestanding human values from values accompanied by beliefs in the supernatural. Yet as we found, values and beliefs based on the supernatural are not necessarily interdependent. That distinction is what people find difficult. But this need not be, for the idea of the spiritual preserves

---

[86] *Rise of Rationalism in Europe* W. E. H Lecky

belief in a future life, yet without heaven, hell and a personal god so that ethics are then based on the welfare of the individual in society.

Hope and associated beliefs are from the value sensibilities. They promote any action that will sustain and preserve faith. Fears are from the feeling sensibilities and generate defensive, aggressive reactions, and together these sensibilities powerfully motivate the subject to defend beliefs against persons, tribes, or communities that constitute a threat. And so together, fear and hope bring the inevitable dangers of strife that are derived from the doctrines of individual religions."

"Are such belief systems necessary?"

"Consider this thought. Fear of death is the product of one belief or another. I think it would be true to say that all relevant beliefs contain the idea of fear and the counterpoise of hope or expectation. Now in the context of all the ground we have covered, all ideas of this kind are meaningless without faith, which is the additional belief that what is believed is true. But when these beliefs are scaled down, hopes and fears become minimised as they are for many people today and the result may approach indifference."

"How is the 'scaling down' achieved?"

"By adopting the countervailing idea that was discussed under the third epoch. This was the fact that all that has proved most valuable in human experience comes from the stuff of the universe and so remains there as what I have called the 'riches of the universe'. And by that I mean that we do not know where the riches come from, or what they mean. To attach labels such as pantheism or spiritualism merely adds confusion because such labels carry their own collections of irrelevant beliefs. We do not need specific beliefs.

Apart from these otherworldly hopes and fears, all others relate to events and possibilities in the world of sensory experience. These, as we have said, can be frightful, from poverty to various forms of violence, including slavery and torture that are widely practised today. But fortunately hopes and fears of this kind greatly diminish when ethical objectives are focussed on the welfare of individuals in society."

"All that applies to the other end of life, but when one is young, hopes and fears relate to jobs and a roof over ones head: they are very much worldly."

"But as one grows older, those concerns diminish when one doesn't have to work, and if one is lucky, they may largely disappear. However, there is the concern of individuals of all ages: how to arrange that society delivers what its individuals want, as distinct from what a remote, autocratic government or god thinks they want. And here otherworldly beliefs as well as beliefs about how to manage societies may help or hinder."

"Are you suggesting that a minimalist belief could give a sense of meaning from the sensibilities?"

"Consider the position if the universe contained no secrets, if there were no unknowable aspects to it, then that would create a paradox and a problem. Values and aesthetic appreciation would be reduced to something equivalent to feelings: you would be restricted to seeking happiness and loving or hating your neighbour. Feelings do not require 'explanation', or 'meaning'. They are simply unique experiences and perhaps that is how they appear in the consciousness of animals. This would be a matter for concern because for many, life is nasty, brutish and short, as Hobbes said; and it certainly was for Keats. And there would be no remedy. But as things are, there is a choice. We can choose the beliefs of old that often conflict and thereby present problems, or we can be content with the tentative beliefs from sensory experience and the sensibilities that give awareness of values free from false hopes and fears. These beliefs have also done much to relieve the nastiness of life."

A Minimalist Philosophy
Discussion 35

"The attempt to reduce the risk of strife has led to the search for common ground between religions. But in the extreme, this policy emasculates doctrine and ends with common values that entail a minimalist belief – virtually the position at which we have arrived. Can you give some examples to illustrate the position at which we have arrived?"

"In literature, the effect of science and faith based knowledge on individual writers is often ambivalent. But there are exceptions. For example, consider **John Keats** (1795–1821)[87]. He was born at the Swan and Hoop tavern, Finsbury, north London, where his father was the proprietor. His parents died when he was still at school so that he and his two brothers and younger sister were denied a family life. He lived a lonely life in lodging houses and was nearly always short of money. One brother, Tom, died young and the other emigrated to the States. He saw little of his sister.

The first volume of his poems was received in silence and the second volume, Endymion, the critics "pelted with savage ridicule." At 24 he fell in love, but at 25 he died in Rome of tuberculosis after a long, stressful illness. Yet despite a short, wretched and tragic life, he managed to achieve a unique place in literature and expressed the most profound ideas with great force and clarity. Despite the fate that was soon to overtake him, he does not seem to have resorted to the comfort of beliefs.

He showed little of his achievement at school until his 'teens, when the full force of the mental turmoil of adolescence burst upon him. From this time onwards, he composed in feverish haste and, realising by the age of 22 that fate was against him, in January 1818 he wrote the sonnet, 'When I have fears that I may cease to be'.[88] What riches he would have bestowed if he could have lived

---

[87] A concise summary of his life and work is contained in the Introduction by Gerald Bullett to the Everyman edition 1944, J.M. Dent and Sons Ltd

[88] 'When I have fears that I may cease to be

longer! He died not knowing the value of his achievement, and hence at the end, he wrote his own epitaph: *"here lies one whose name is writ in water."*

"Why do you single him out?"

"Because, and I quote, '....as a poet he was concerned not with doctrine as Shelly was, not with finding moral lessons in the natural scene as Wordsworth was, but with what he himself termed....the truth of imagination', a truth of which 'beauty was the assurance and the sign' (*from the Introduction to the Everyman edition*[89]). He found truth in the intense awareness of the Value and Aesthetic Sensibilities. And when he uses value sensibilities to express human relationships in thought and action, which is the ethical dimension, Keats frequently resorts for their expression to the language of Greek mythology, as in Endymion, Hyperion and elsewhere.

Before my pen has glean'd my teeming brain,

Before high piled books, in charact'ry,

Hold like full garners the full ripen'd grain;

When I behold, upon the night's starr'd face,

Huge cloudy symbols of a high romance,

And feel that I may never live to trace

Their shadows, with the magic hand of chance;

And when I feel, fair creature of an hour!

That I shall never look upon thee more,

Never have relish in the faery power

Of unreflecting love! – then on the shore

Of the wide world I stand alone, and think,

Till Love and Fame to nothingness do sink.'

---

[89] Introduction to *The Poems of John Keats* by Gerald Bullett. Everyman Edition. J M Dent and Sons Ltd Vol 101, 1944

Keats uses ideas in poetic form to express this in many places in his works. While beliefs are minimal, he uses his newfound awareness of the sensibilities to express the unknowable. He accepts that all the sensibilities of which we are aware, as well as the dust beneath our feet, are equally a part of the universe.

In the Ode to a Grecian Urn, he asserts that the nearest that we can get to truth, is the appreciation of beauty[90]." The aesthetic sensibilities were for Keats a part of our experience of what is essentially unknowable."

"But surely that is aesthetics, not human values?"

"He does not make distinctions, as we did not in our descriptions. The aesthetic sensibilities were for Keats a part of our experience of what is essentially unknowable. Much of his writing was about human values. Among many other examples, take Sonnet 14 (1817)[91]. Moreover, as we have seen, the sensibilities operate as a unit: one cannot be aware of Aesthetics without being aware of Values in other humans.

---

[90] *Ode to a Grecian Urn*

'When old age shall this generation waste,

Thou shalt remain, in midst of other woe

Than ours, a friend to man to whom thou say'st,

'Beauty is truth, truth beauty, - that is all

Ye know on earth and all ye need to know.'

[91] 'Great spirits now on earth are sojourning ...

(and the final lines,)

And other spirits there are standing apart

Upon the forehead of the age to come;

These, these will give the world another heart,

And other pulses. Here ye not the hum

Of mighty workings?.....

Listen awhile, ye nations, and be dumb'.

Despite the fact that he knew his life would be short, he did not stoop to the age old temptations of imagined solutions to what the future may hold in store. He stated his position decisively at the age of twenty-one in the sonnet, '*Written in Disgust of Vulgar Superstition*'. He reveals and expresses a range and intensity of sensibilities, which is such that to introduce overt beliefs would break the spell by substituting an imaginative world of ideas that, by comparison with his own thoughts, would be unreal and false.

We each have the potential to explore these riches of the universe, but the genius of individuals such as Keats extends these possibilities immeasurably for all. These are the benefits that great scientists, artists, musicians, and literary figures bestow. They introduce everyone to the essence of human values and thereby to the meaning of life and culture."

"Yet today, if I understand you correctly, we treat this rich heritage more as entertainment than as a conduit illuminating all we need to know. Surely, it misconceives our true objectives, which are not primarily to be entertained, but more importantly, to understand?"

"That is true. The Greeks, of course, made an immense contribution to these cultural riches but, since the Middle Ages progress has been mainly in Europe and N America. Compare this with other parts of the world where cultural deserts still exist because humanity has been prevented from achieving its potentials by beliefs in primitivism, communism and some religions. The people who inhabit these deserts sometimes have such strong beliefs, religious, racist and tribal, or nationalistic, that they breed fanaticism, strife and wars. But, governments that have been in the habit of impoverishing their people by these means now have the possibility of serving mankind by providing the conditions that will foster culture, for only governments can do this. I repeat again, the essence of progress resides in the management of beliefs."

"We mentioned the physicist, Paul Dirac earlier (11). I have two quotations from him that appear confusing,

'*In science one tries to tell people, in such a way as to be understood by everyone, something that no one ever knew before.*

But in poetry, it's the exact opposite',[92] and

    'This result is too beautiful to be false; it is more important to have beauty in one's equations than to have them fit experiments'.[93]"

    "Dirac and Keats rely on sensory experiences, (of sub-atomic particles in the case of Dirac and the Grecian urn in the example from Keats). Each makes use of minomic functions (mathematics and the aesthetic sensibility in the case of Dirac and poetic language and the aesthetic sensibility in the case of Keats). But the truth or falsity of their conclusions resides for Dirac in the sensory experience and for Keats it is in the opposite, the aesthetic experience. And in each case, the truth or falsity of their claim is judged by their peers.

    The responses to the sensibilities are always complex. Even from the Value Sensibility, there may be more than one identifiable motivation and belief system operating. Take the example of **Florence Nightingale**, (1820-1910). She was born into a wealthy family, but like many in her position at that time wished to help the poor. She differed in that she was very highly motivated, highly intelligent and, like most in her position, was an Anglican. Nevertheless, her work was not motivated solely or even primarily by religion. When nursing in the Crimea, she was primarily and strongly motivated by the courage and devotion to duty of the common soldier. She focussed on the human values evoked by the fact that they died mainly of disease, privation and starvation; essentially the lack of proper nursing care.

    Before working abroad, she had established and then applied in England the principles of nursing care that form the basis for the nursing profession today. Her biographer, Woodham-Smith, describes some of the problems she had to overcome by quoting from her reports as follows[94]:

    'But religious differences were not the only difficulty.

---

[92] *Mathematical Circles Adieu* H Eves, Boston 1997

[93] Scientific American 208 (5) 1963

[94] *'Florence Nightingale'*, Woodham-Smith The reprint society, 1950

Amongst women who were prepared to devote themselves to the sick, there were two totally different conceptions of the functions of a nurse. The hospital nurse, drunken, promiscuous and troublesome, considered that her function was to tend her patient's sick body and restore him to physical health by carrying out the doctor's orders. [On the other hand] *The religious orders, sisters and nuns, were neither drunken nor promiscuous, but were apt to be more concerned with the souls of their patients than with their bodies. Since the middle of the 18th century, the great medieval tradition of nursing among religious orders had decayed. Physical and spiritual were thought incompatible. Lofty sentiments were encouraged but cleanliness was ignored.'*

'*Excellent self devoted women,*' wrote Miss Nightingale of certain nuns, '*fit more for heaven than a hospital, flit about like angels without hands among the patients and soothe their souls while they leave their bodies dirty and neglected.*'

An important aspect of our discussions has been to describe the minome and the role of the Sensibilities in the lives of individuals as illustrated by lives such as Keats and Nightingale. But we need to know much more about the content of minome functions across societies, as discussed in 13.

This is where the scope of philosophy extends to meet with psychology. The Feeling Sensibility is highly complex, for example, especially when you consider the many variations of sexuality. Attention focuses on specific problems for the psychologist, but we know remarkably little about the details of minomic function in societies."

Riches Of The Universe
Conclusion to the Dialogues

The Dialogues investigate human understanding, its history and why all understanding of science and religion, depends upon beliefs. Beliefs are an inevitable part of consciousness and have changed dramatically during the course of civilisation. In essence they are of three kinds,

1. *Necessary Beliefs.* There are two categories that become manifest through objective, sensory experience and subjective awareness of what are called here the Sensibilities. These beliefs cannot be avoided because all objective and all subjective experiences contain unknowable components: we do not know what objects in space really are and we do not know the origin of human values, for example. Care has been taken to allow for these facts, for this is where much confusion has occurred and still does.

2. *Tentative Beliefs*, or hypotheses, which are the foundations of scientific knowledge and the lay knowledge of everyday life. The Greeks first discovered the scientific and philosophical methods of understanding the universe. This was the *first epoch* in human understanding since it was a decisive departure from the primitivism that had characterised the whole of previous human history. A *second epoch* commenced at the Renaissance and from then until the end of the 19th century dramatic further advances were made in science and philosophy. In particular, methods of experimentation and techniques for validating beliefs with great accuracy were developed. Since then, a *third epoch* appeared and is dramatically changing our understanding of the universe. But it has also focussed attention on the management of beliefs for the persistence of primitivism is now increasingly disrupting life in Western societies. .

3. *Normative Beliefs* are the ways in which humans *respond* to the sensory knowledge from everyday life and from the sciences. They take the form of strongly held beliefs, yet their truth or falsity is unknowable. In other words, they cannot be validated by methods comparable with those of science. They are the ethical norms of individuals including

any beliefs in a supernatural dimension. Strongly motivating beliefs of this third category are now often called memes by Richard Dawkins[95] and other authors.

The point was made in the Introduction to these Dialogues and elsewhere that science and technology have now developed to the point at which the human struggle for survival, out of which the Darwinian principle of survival of the fittest evolved for all species, is now largely from mimetic objectives. These objectives always have their own beliefs of the third category built into them. But the memes, of which all are aware, have functions that are quite separate and distinct from those of genes. The position is that the hidden functions of the minome are *expressed* as 'memes' (page 97).

Dawkins and others believe that the method of science is now so powerful that responsive, normative beliefs in say, a creator god, or Augustinian Divine Illumination are now redundant and meaningless. He believes that questions of this nature could be answered using the scientific method if not now, then at some future time when sufficient further progress has been made.

But this is incorrect. The tentative beliefs of science cannot be used to make assertions about the truth or falsity of normative beliefs of any kind. A scientist may express an *opinion* about a supernatural realm but will never be in a position to deny the existence of such a realm now, or in the future. Similarly atheism is a normative belief and logically not supportable by scientific evidence.

The growth and refinement of scientific method during the first two epochs of its existence were dramatic, so that it has now become a very powerful method of obtaining knowledge from sensory experience. There is only one circumstance in which a clash could occur between science and theology, two logically different categories of belief. It may be claimed that a god exists with the power to perform miracles that contravene laws governing the universe known to scientists. One thinks of the position in say the

---

[95] *A Devil's Chaplain,* Richard Dawkins, Published by Weidenfeld and Nicholson 2003   ISBN 0-297-82973-4 Also,

The Selfish Gene, , Paladin Books, ISBN 0 586 08316 2

12th century when theology was claimed to be the 'Queen of the sciences'. At this level of primitivism, theology was the primary agent of understanding and gave knowledge that was thought to be incontrovertibly true, whereas scientific knowledge was secondary and normative since it had to conform to the 'laws' of theology. That would have caused Dawkins to die of a brainstorm! But fortunately today, scientists are correct to deny the validity of any such claim. The claims of many paramedical 'sciences' using methods that have not been validated are equally at fault and are rightly criticised by Dawkins.

To allow such claims would be to deny the validity of all that the Western World has fought for since the Renaissance. As pointed out in the Dialogues, religion should aim to use the powers of science to further humanitarian ends and should not meddle with or contravene its methodology.

It should be emphasised that science could not have developed in isolation. It evolved in a complex environment. The world of today is the product of advances in science, philosophy and religion against a background environment of evolving political, social events. Europe came through social upheavals and wars during the Enlightenment and the Romantic Age to arrive at democracy and rising standards of living due to scientific advances.

It is not possible therefore to understand the world of today with its knowledge from sensory experience and the normative responses to this without the necessary historical background. An outline is given therefore in the Dialogues of how this phenomenal transition from the medieval to the modern world came about.

These historical considerations made it possible to contemplate an outline of the third Epoch in which we now live and to offer glimpses of where it may take us. In this last part of the investigation, it was necessary to examine what 'understanding' means and to do this it was necessary to describe the minome, which is a description of these hidden functions, as distinct from the knowledge from tentative and normative beliefs that it produces.

Here are some of the practical difficulties that lie on the path to a better future. It became evident during the course of the investigation that there is an inherent problem for religions with strong supernatural beliefs because faith inevitably generates high degrees of hope and fear concerning a possible future life. But in addition, the consequence is that ethical inflexibility often accompanies these beliefs and this has had serious disruptive effects on society in the past, and that remains true today when there is a mixing of cultures.

There can be no doubt, however, that this is not inevitable. It was found that Christianity over the last few hundred years has become much more tolerant of other ethical positions in society. So it seems possible to preserve strong supernatural beliefs in a mixed society and yet achieve tolerance. And tolerance was taken to mean acceptance in a society of people with other ethical beliefs or minimal beliefs. That is a position that was not tolerated in the Middle Ages.

It took Christianity 500 years to make the journey to the present day, moulded by pressures from the Enlightenment period onwards. But for other religions, such as Islam, that period should be much shorter for the social pressures to evolve are much greater, as in Britain today. The questions investigated in Parts 5 and 6 are how to proceed from the position reached today.

An important reason for intolerance is often not primarily the basic, indispensable doctrines of a religion, but the added beliefs in the formal traditions of dress, food, habits and customs, including for some, belief in the merits of martyrdom. All these have often come to characterize a culture and, by default, to stand for the religion itself. It would appear possible to lose some or all of these, yet retain the essential beliefs, but for many this only happens with great reluctance. One approach to the objective of peace in societies is to investigate how to reduce, or remove these ethical walls due to subsidiary cultural beliefs.

A possible end-point is the 'minimalist philosophy of human values' developed in Part 6 because it avoids or minimises these ethical and cultural problems. This approach is not new, for many in Western societies already accept these ideas. Belief in the supernatural has existed since primitive humans first walked the earth, but it was found that such beliefs are not inevitable and, when abandoned, what is left is awareness of the responses to sensory experiences from the Sensibilities. These were called collectively, the 'riches of the universe'. This does not imply that something supernatural exists but, since this awareness from the Sensibilities (9-12 and 33) is very clear and powerful, these riches are simply markers of our experience of the universe.

The choice was to accept one of these positions or return to the primitivism that humans have been struggling for two and a half millennia to escape from. In summary, agonising over future hopes and fears, which are necessary parts of beliefs in the supernatural, disappears. And since the ethical norms of a minimalist system do not have a supernatural origin, they are focussed instead on the welfare of individuals in society.

It has to be said, however, that today the majority in civilised communities believe in something supernatural because it appears to reduce fear and give satisfaction. But for some the threat of eternal damnation may *increase* fear and may also *cause* communal strife and war. Alternatively, a minimalist belief system avoids these problems and minimises the hurdle of fear. So there is much scope for managing beliefs.

It remains true, however, that much of the wisdom of mankind has been the by-product of the traditional belief systems. But it came with a price. Today, in the interests of diminishing the risk of conflicts, the tendency is to say that the various beliefs are different ways of expressing truth, which is a step towards a minimalist philosophy; but one that may still engender false hopes and fears.

In order to progress beyond the grievous state that exists in many parts of the world today, the solution must surely be to approach as nearly as possible to a minimalist belief system. All the richness of human values accumulated down the centuries is still there, but not dressed in the imaginative ideas that have been so destructive. That is what is required in order to address directly the task of managing ideas about the unknowable in this third age.

The 'riches of the universe' does not imply that something exists. The term could be regarded by some as asserting either,

-That nothing exists, a position that is commonly called atheism

-That something exists, which is commonly called theism, or pantheism, or humanism.

But each of these ideas takes the form of a belief, the truth or falsity of which we cannot know. I reserve judgement on this and simply *describe* values as they appear. This takes matters as far as it is possible to go, because it is not possible to turn something unknowable into something knowable without becoming bewitched by the power of language to cause us to succumb to the supposed clarity of a belief.

We live in an age when, in theory, the full potentials of individuals are beginning to be realised, now that the way is known, beliefs need not obstruct and the means are available. At least the third major revolution is in motion! How could beliefs add to these objectives except by instilling fear and hope again that have no place in a future now possible? Perhaps the third age, when it has run its course, will have solved this problem and made it possible for all to die contented!

Index